American Presidential Elections

MICHAEL NELSON

JOHN M. MCCARDELL, JR.

MINORITY VICTORY

MINORITY VICTORY

GILDED AGE POLITICS AND THE FRONT PORCH CAMPAIGN OF 1888

CHARLES W. CALHOUN

UNIVERSITY PRESS OF KANSAS

Published
by the
University
Press of Kansas
(Lawrence,
Kansas 66045),
which was
organized by the
Kansas Board of
Regents and is
operated and
funded by
Emporia State
University,
Fort Hays State
University,
Kansas State
University,
Pittsburg State
University,
the University
of Kansas, and
Wichita State
University

Library of Congress Cataloging-in-Publication Data

Calhoun, Charles W. (Charles William), 1948–
   Minority victory : gilded age politics and the front porch
campaign of 1888 / Charles W. Calhoun.
      p.   cm. — (American presidential elections)
   Includes bibliographical references and index.
   ISBN 978-0-7006-1596-4 (cloth : alk. paper)
   1. Presidents—United States—Election—1888. 2. Political
campaigns—United States—History—19th century. 3. United
States—Politics and government—1885–1889. 4. Harrison,
Benjamin, 1833–1901. 5. Cleveland, Grover, 1837–1908.
6. Rhetoric—Political aspects—United States—History—19th
century. 7. Tariff—United States—History—19th century.
8. United States—Commercial policy—History—19th century.
9. Protectionism—United States—History—19th century.
I. Title.
   E700.C35 2008
   973.8′5—dc22   2008022801

British Library Cataloguing-in-Publication Data is available.

Printed in the United States of America

10 9 8 7 6 5 4 3 2 1

The paper used in this publication meets the minimum
requirements of the American National Standard for
Permanence of Paper for Printed Library Materials z39.48-1984.

CONTENTS

Editors make choices. Sometimes those choices, at first glance, seem curious. Asked to identify the most important presidential elections in our history, few Americans, one suspects, would include 1888. The major party candidates—Grover Cleveland, the Democratic incumbent, and Benjamin Harrison, the Republican challenger—did not ooze charisma. For most of the period since the end of Reconstruction in 1877, neither party controlled both the presidency and both houses of Congress, and no presidential candidate received a majority of the popular vote.

Moreover, it may be difficult for Americans in the twenty-first century to understand why issues like the tariff or civil service reform or veterans' pensions might send the blood pulsating through the body politic. Or what it meant to be a "stalwart," a "half-breed," or a "mugwump." As a result, too many Americans might endorse the observation of one wag that the only difference among the presidents during the Gilded Age was that some had beards and some didn't.

But we did choose 1888, and we chose Charles W. Calhoun to tell the story of that campaign, with reason. To begin with, the politics, like the politicians, in the Gilded Age possessed energy and color. That little may actually have been accomplished in Washington during this period is testimony to just how close elections and how fragile partisan majorities in the House and Senate actually were.

Furthermore, as the pace of urbanization and industrialization quickened, old economic arrangements and understandings came under challenge. Banks, corporations, farms, trade—all experienced the stress of growth under the absence of regulation. Pressure began to build.

And so voter turnout in 1888 reached 79.3 percent, the fifth-highest turnout in American history and a figure that has not been surpassed in any election since. Clearly, this election mattered.

Its outcome continues to astonish. For the second time in a dozen years (and only the third time in American history, until the election of 2000), the Democratic winner of the popular vote, Cleveland, did not receive a majority in the electoral college. Meanwhile, the Republicans swept significant congressional majorities: the House went from

167–152 Democratic to 179–152 Republican; the Senate, from 39–37 Republican to 51–37 Republican.

This contest and its stunning outcome have awaited a historian of Charles Calhoun's stature to do it justice at long last. In the pages that follow, a compelling narrative unfolds. Readers will revisit a period of high voter involvement (hence faith in the system), very close races (even though most states were "safe"), and closely divided government, which stymied much innovation and created a politics of stalemate. They will understand how Cleveland tried, in his 1887 annual message, to break the stalemate, and why he failed. And they will experience the color and excitement and uncertainty of a lively campaign.

In the end, Harrison as president would actively use his working majorities and overreach. The incredible congressional volatility that followed would indeed, as Calhoun notes in conclusion, presage the critical election of 1896. The consequences of this election would be profound.

Those who would attempt to comprehend the contemporary political environment, then, might profitably study the presidential election of 1888. Different readers may draw different lessons. But we anticipate that they will affirm the editors' judgments that this election did indeed matter greatly and that, in the capable hands of Charles Calhoun, its significance is now made clear.

AUTHOR'S PREFACE

My interest in the presidential election of 1888 extends back for nearly four decades, when, as an undergraduate and graduate student, I first studied the contest in some depth. Since those days, I have spent most of my professional career trying to make sense of the political life of the late nineteenth century. The more I explore that period and the more I endure the conduct of national politics in the twenty-first century, the more I find to admire in the earlier time in comparison with our contemporary political game. The nation is thankful that the electorate now includes women and African Americans as well as white males, but the political engagement of modern citizens seems anemic indeed when compared with the intense interest in politics and governance exhibited by our Gilded Age counterparts. Scarcely half of Americans today bother to vote in presidential elections, whereas participation by eligible voters in the late nineteenth century was extraordinarily high, in some states exceeding 90 percent. Party loyalty bore much more strongly on voters in the earlier period, but the supposedly more independent voters of today often bend like reeds before the political winds driven by the mass media's punditry and prognostication. In the late nineteenth century, the flow of political information to citizens was not as voluminous as today, but its quality was as high or higher. Masses of people listened to speeches that could go on for hours, and they gathered political news and opinions in depth and detail from newspapers and pamphlets. In the absence of opinion polls of the kind that track Americans' attitudes on public questions today, Gilded Age politicians paid close attention to the numerous letters they received from constituents and others. Their surviving correspondence demonstrates a broad citizen interest in national issues and a meaningful dialogue between leaders and voters. The potential for thoroughly informing citizens is much greater now, particularly with the availability of the Internet, yet we still seem mired in a political culture dominated by the thirty-second attack ad and the sound bite. In arriving at their political judgments, Americans have always responded to the sometimes contradictory promptings of the head, the heart, and the gut. In retrospect, the balancing of those varied influences in 1888 seems as good as, if not better than, today.

In researching and writing this book, I have incurred numerous obligations, only a small portion of which I can begin to repay through acknowledgment here. Many librarians and archivists have gone the extra mile in helping me in my quest for source material. At the top of the list, as usual, is Jeff Flannery of the Manuscript Division of the Library of Congress, whose encyclopedic knowledge of the division's collections helped me solve many a riddle. I also thank Bonnie Coles of the Library's Photoduplication Service for her speedy and efficient help with illustrations. I am grateful to Jennifer Capps of the Benjamin Harrison Home in Indianapolis for her tireless and patient assistance. Dr. Benjamin Harrison Walker generously allowed me unlimited access to his family's rich trove of his great-grandfather's papers, which are now housed in the Harrison Home.

I am also grateful for the valuable assistance provided by the librarians and archivists at several other repositories, especially the Historical Society of Pennsylvania, the Indiana Historical Society, the Indiana State Library, the Library of Congress, the Lilly Library of Indiana University, the Massachusetts Historical Society, the Nevada Historical Society, the New York Public Library, the New York State Library, the State Historical Society of Iowa, the U.S. Senate Library, the West Virginia University Library, and the Yale University Library. I thank also the capable and efficient staff of the Inter-Library Loan Office of Joyner Library at East Carolina University.

I express my gratitude to Fred Woodward of the University Press of Kansas for inviting me to prepare this volume in the press's series on presidential elections. Michael Nelson and John M. McCardell Jr. read the manuscript and provided many valuable suggestions, although I alone bear responsibility for what I have written. Professors R. Hal Williams and Lewis L. Gould shared their insights on Gilded Age politics, and Lew generously provided source materials from the Gould Collection in the Center for American History at the University of Texas.

A substantial portion of the material presented here derived from research I conducted under the auspices of a fellowship from the National Endowment for the Humanities. I am also grateful for support from East Carolina University, especially a College of Arts and Sciences Research Award. I wish also to thank my department chairs, Michael A. Palmer and Gerald J. Prokopowicz, for their encouragement and support, particularly for their arranging my teaching schedule in ways conducive to this project. I very much appreciate the interest, encouragement, and support of my department colleagues, especially Tony Papalas and Michael Gross. For years, Rebecca Futrell, the chief administrative associate in the History Department at East Carolina, has smoothed the path for my work in countless ways.

Once again, I owe my greatest debt to my family—to my loving wife Bonnie, who patiently puts up with a man hopelessly embedded in the nineteenth century, and to my dear daughter Elizabeth, whose growth as a fine writer and editor I greatly admire. I deeply appreciate the encouragement that my sisters, Judy Blakely and Mary Howard, provide from afar.

Finally, I dedicate this book to Vincent P. De Santis, Lewis L. Gould, Ari Hoogenboom, H. Wayne Morgan, and R. Hal Williams, all master interpreters of American politics in the Gilded Age.

Charles W. Calhoun
Washington, D.C.
February 2008

INTRODUCTION

For Americans in the presidential election year of 1888, politics was both fun and fundamental. They flocked to party rallies, ate mountains of picnic food, imbibed more than a little party cheer, marched in endless parades, shouted lustily at rallies, sang campaign songs at the top of their lungs, blew horns and banged drums, put pictures of their favorite candidates in their windows, wore buttons and ribbons proclaiming their fealty, argued with their neighbors, loved their party with deep devotion, and hated the enemy with equal passion. "Men, women and children, boys and girls, have all gone crazy on the subject of politics," a party worker reported two weeks before the election.[1]

But it was also serious business. Although most Americans' contact with their government was with officials at the local level, they nonetheless saw the quadrennial contests for the White House as supreme moments of self-definition for the nation and for themselves. Citizens in the late nineteenth century felt their party loyalty with great intensity, but their deep commitment was not a blind adherence to a mere Potemkin organization. They believed that their parties stood for something, and they believed what their parties stood for. For decades, party feeling had been inextricably mixed up with matters of race and section: slavery, abolitionism, the Civil War, and Reconstruction. Those feelings lingered in 1888, but they were giving way to a different set of partisan understandings.

In the late nineteenth century—the Gilded Age—industrialization, urbanization, the development of a wage-earning working class, the growing disparity between rich and poor, and other momentous changes led Americans to give increasing attention to the relationship between their government and the economy and society. Neither major party could be said to endorse class warfare in 1888, but both the Republicans and the Democrats constructed their appeals in the election year primarily around economic questions of deep concern to the masses of the country. Grover Cleveland urged Americans to join him in a grand crusade to change the nation's tax structure, particularly to reduce the tariff on imported goods. Such a reduction, he insisted, would alleviate a growing federal surplus, leave more money in the private economy, and relieve working people from the burden of high taxes and high prices. Republicans responded with a call to revise the revenue structure in a way to reduce the federal government's burgeoning surplus but also protect American producers and workers from competition from cheap foreign goods. What ensued was a nearly year-long conversation (if not a shouting match) that played out on the political stump, in the halls of Congress, in newspaper editorials, in hundreds of thousands of pamphlets, in countless street-corner dialogues and country-store disputations. In some ways it was an exquisite moment in the evolution of American politics. Huge numbers of Americans took part (turnout in the election was 79.3 percent of the eligible electorate, one of the highest in history), and they argued over something that they all considered important.[2]

The contest of 1888 featured two candidates who, by modern criteria, seem unlikely to lead a major party to victory. Neither Democrat Grover Cleveland nor Republican Benjamin Harrison was charismatic, physically attractive, or personally charming. Each bore a deep streak of self-righteousness. Cleveland had risen rapidly from obscurity, virtually unknown beyond the confines of Buffalo, New York, just three years before his election to the presidency in 1884. Harrison's honored political lineage as the grandson of a president had opened a few doors for him in his early years, but he was essentially a self-made man. In his march to political prominence, Cleveland had traded on his vaunted commitment to duty and on his essentially negative notion that the central purpose of a leader was to protect the people from being cheated or otherwise harmed by the government. Harrison took a more positive approach, believing that in an industrializing and modernizing society the federal government had a role to play in securing the nation's orderly economic development. In 1888 those contrasting notions found expression in the great debate over the tariff.

In 1888 the two major parties were almost equal in strength, but what seemed like a level playing field was instead a field strewn with mines. Any misstep by a candidate or his campaign could offend an indispensable constituency and throw the victory to the other side. Cleveland avoided gaffes by making no speeches and limiting his overt campaign participation to a single written statement of his beliefs. The challenger Harrison proved bolder. At his home in Indianapolis he conducted a brilliant and flawless front porch campaign that garnered national attention for him and his views day after day.

The delicate balance of the national political equilibrium required each party to be both intense and circumspect in its quest for votes. For most of their support, Democrats depended on the Solid South, where in many states they routinely disfranchised African American Republicans. For their part, Republicans had a near lock on an even greater number of electoral votes from northern and western states. As in other elections in this period, the outcome turned on a handful of key swing states in the North, principally New York and Indiana. It was no coincidence that the Democrats' candidate hailed from the Empire State and that the Republican nominee was a Hoosier. In these doubtful states, the parties scheduled their best speakers, distributed most of their literature, and expended the lion's share of their party funds. In these states, too, the parties felt great temptation to supplement argument and persuasion with methods less honorable.

In the end, Harrison edged out Cleveland in a victory so narrow that any number of factors could have made the difference. Harrison trailed Cleveland in the popular vote, but he nonetheless believed that the American people had given him and his party a mandate to carry out their stated intentions. Harrison carried a Republican Congress with him to Washington, and together they set a record of achievement that belies the image of do-nothing governance in the Gilded Age. In a host of ways the victor of the presidential election of 1888 set important precedents for campaigning in an evolving political universe and fashioned new techniques for governing in a modernizing nation. Harrison lost his bid for reelection in 1892, but after Cleveland's second term, his Republican successors built on the transformations begun by Harrison, making the GOP the majority party for a generation and putting the presidency at the center of American governance, where it has remained ever since.

1

THE POLITICAL UNIVERSE OF THE 1880S

The centennial campaign for the presidency in 1888 marked the close of the nation's first hundred years under the Constitution. During the previous century the country had experienced profound changes. The original fledgling Republic of fewer than 4 million people huddled in thirteen states along the Atlantic seaboard had burgeoned into a republican empire of more than 60 million residing in thirty-eight states spread across the continent. And the populace had grown more diverse. In George Washington's day, some indigenous peoples still inhabited the states, but the first president's countrymen traced their origins primarily to the British Isles and, to a lesser degree, elsewhere in Europe, and to Africa. By 1888 immigration had stirred new elements into the mix; large numbers had come from Ireland, Germany, and Scandinavia and increasingly from eastern and southern Europe, as well as a moderate number from east Asia. In the decade of the 1880s, more than 5 million immigrants entered the United States, more than a half million in 1888 alone. These newcomers both enriched and complicated the nation's political life.

When Washington took the oath of office, the vast majority of Americans, both free and enslaved, labored in agriculture. By 1890 the farming portion of the workforce had fallen to 43 percent. Nineteen percent earned their living in manufacturing, and another 16 percent worked in trade or transportation. The total of capital invested in manufacturing amounted to $5.7 billion, having more than doubled in the previous ten years. Textile manufacturing still led industrial production and was capitalized at $1 billion. But rapidly catching up was steel output, which had quadrupled in a decade and had reached 3.2 million tons. By 1888 the question of what role the government should play in securing and managing this immense economic development had emerged as a central issue in the nation's politics.

Much of the new American steel wound up as locomotives, cars, and rails in the rapidly expanding railway system, whose total trackage reached 191,000 miles in 1888. In Washington's day, the difficulty and slowness of transportation and communication had rendered the country's towns and regions detached if not autonomous entities. But by 1888 railroads linked not merely the major metropolises but also hundreds of small cities and towns and fostered the emergence of a national market and a national culture. Along with the railroads, the Western Union system, comprising 616,000 miles of wire stretched between 17,000 telegraph offices, permitted the instantaneous transmission of information—personal, commercial, and political—to virtually any point in the country. These developments went far to diminish Americans' isolation, but by 1888 they had not yet lost their sense of sectional identification. Sectionalism had taken root far back in the nation's past and had become deeply embedded in the psyche of many during the Civil War and its aftermath. It remained a puissant force in American politics in the centennial year.[1]

Americans witnessed an extraordinary transformation in their country during the nineteenth century, but in 1888 the inherited constitutional framework of president, Congress, and the judiciary had changed relatively little since the days of the founders. In the early days of the Republic, contests over power and principles led almost immediately to the development of political parties, and the dichotomized nature of political discourse soon resulted in the emergence of two principal organizations. This two-party pattern was, moreover, buttressed by the constitutional structure itself, especially the stipulation that victory in presidential elections required a majority rather than a plurality in the electoral college, thereby necessitating the building of broad coalitions before rather than after elections. Although Americans initially disdained the idea of party contention as somehow improper, the development of party organizations and their spirited competition proceeded inexorably. The widespread adoption of universal white male suffrage during the first half of the nineteenth century dictated that these parties would be mass institutions requiring broad-based organizations and popular appeals to achieve election victories.

Thus, by the 1880s, intense commitment to party had long been a defining feature of the civic life of the American people, who had come to view parties as integral to republican institutions. "Unless free government is discreditable," said Benjamin Harrison, "it is the duty of every American citizen to support that party to which he gives the allegiance of his heart and mind."[2] Party organizations formed a vital connection between leaders, who devised policy and governed, and voters, who had their own ideas and values but also sought instruction and inspiration. In the absence of independent means for reaching masses of voters (such as television in the twentieth century and the Internet in the twenty-first), leaders looked to the party as the indispensable agent for informing and mobilizing the electorate.

In organizational structure, both parties resembled a pyramid. At the broad base was an array of precinct and ward committees and organizations that fed upward through town, city, county, legislative and congressional districts, state, and nation. At each level, the basic governing unit was the periodic convention, where leaders and activists chose nominees for public office, issued platforms, selected delegates to attend subsequent conventions up the pyramid, and created committees to manage campaigns and conduct the party's business until the next convention. Within this framework, the national party appeared to be little more than a confederation of state and local parties, held together between presidential elections by a weak national committee. Nonetheless, the quadrennial national convention stood in many ways as the crowning event in the party's cycle. Here delegates on the platform committee from around the country forged a declaration of shared ideals, and here delegates sought to choose a presidential ticket that would win the confidence and votes of party members everywhere. Although local issues and contests held great significance for voters, the national convention and campaign powerfully reinforced their sense of party identification.

Much more than their modern counterparts, national conventions in the late nineteenth century actually chose the parties' presidential nominees. Hotly contested races usually required multiple ballots before the delegates settled on a choice. Except in the cases of renominations, rarely did a clear front-runner emerge before the convention or coast to an easy nomination. In the Democratic Party, the rules required a two-thirds vote to win, thus making a choice all the more difficult. Neither party held primary elections in the modern sense, although conventions at the most basic local level were sometimes called "primaries." Instead, the selection of national convention delegates followed the sequence of local through state conventions in each state. Typically, local conventions chose delegates to conventions in each congressional district, which chose the bulk of the state's national convention delegation. County or other local political units selected delegates to attend a state convention, which selected a small number of delegates at large for the national conclave. In 1888, in both major parties, each state delegation was twice the number of the state's congressional delegation; each district convention selected two delegates, and the state convention selected four. Neither party had yet adopted a scheme of assigning additional delegates to a state party as a reward for its performance in previous elections.

In the absence of primaries, preconvention campaigns in the first half of a presidential election year tried to win support among party cadres who would take part in the selection of national convention delegates. Rarely did a putative candidate formally announce his intention to run, although he might give an occasional speech to signal his capacity to articulate the party's views. The candidate mapped strategy from behind the scenes, but to a significant degree, his hunt for delegates was, in the parlance of the day, "in the hands of his friends." Favorable newspapers labored to capture public opinion by "booming" a candidate both in laudatory editorials and in flattering coverage on the front page. Allies of the candidate, traveling widely and engaging in extensive correspondence, worked to convince local and state party leaders not only of the candidate's ability to lead but also of his "availability," his ability to win in November. Week after week through the winter and spring, state after state selected national delegates, sometimes instructed to vote for a particular candidate or clearly leaning toward one. In this era, because convention delegates were often less securely tethered to particular candidates and retained more autonomy than is the case today, determining the delegates' preferences and the overall standings in the delegate count remained imprecise. Seldom did one candidate amass a majority in advance of the national convention. Once states had chosen delegates, they found themselves inundated with information about the candidates, and even if their preference was known, they came under pressure to consider other men as viable second choices.

After the national convention, the practice through most of the nineteenth century was for the presidential nominee to stay at home and take no extended speaking tour. He made his principal campaign statement in his formal letter of acceptance in response to his nomination. Here, in a document of several thousand words, the nominee presented his ideas on the issues. Breaking this pattern, Horace Greeley, the Liberal Republican and Democratic candidate in 1872, and Republican James G. Blaine in 1884 both took speaking tours, but neither managed to parlay the tactic into a November victory. In 1888 incumbent Grover Cleveland, never a happy campaigner, gladly invoked the dignity of his office to avoid the stump. His opponent, Republican Benjamin Harrison, also stayed home but, as a veteran campaigner, made scores of short speeches in a highly effective front porch campaign.

Whatever the nominee's speaking role, he kept close tabs on the conduct of the campaign, albeit usually from afar. Primary responsibility for managing the campaign lay with the party's national committee. In 1888 both parties established their national headquarters not in Washington but in New York, the nation's financial and communications hub. The committee included one member from each state, but the close direction of the campaign lay with the party's executive committee or campaign committee and officers: chairman, vice chairman, and treasurer. The officers, committee, and staff performed a variety of tasks: fundraising, distribution of money to state and local committees, organizing of events, recruitment and assignment of campaign speakers, and preparation, publication, and distribution of party literature.

National party officials had no power to dictate to state and local committees but tried to coordinate their activities as best they could. Perforce, they relied on these local entities to manage the "organizational" side of the campaign effort through such techniques as advance polling schemes and get-out-the-vote mechanisms. Late-nineteenth-century electioneering still included parades, picnics, bonfires, rallies, and similar devices to ignite the emotions of the party faithful, but the impact of mere hoopla was waning. Party managers considered the most successful events those that featured big-name party speakers who forcefully expounded party doctrine to rally the faithful and attract converts. More and more, party managers turned to what they termed the "campaign of education," appealing to voters on questions of governmental policy, especially as it affected citizens' economic well-being in an emerging industrial society.

Because communications technology had advanced little beyond the telegraph, politicians could reach voters only through public speeches or in print. With the presidential nominees on the sidelines, most of the speaking fell to surrogates, hundreds of national and state party leaders who took to the hustings, speaking to audiences day after day, laying out the party's doctrines and appealing for support. An effective orator might convey his message to several thousand listeners, but a printed version of his address could expand his audience many times over. The production and distribution of such speeches and other printed matter played a pivotal role in the campaigns. Typically, the parties distributed millions of campaign "documents," which included congressional speeches, other addresses, statistical tables, reproduced newspaper items, and other tracts and broadsides. The parties also published so-called campaign textbooks, compilations that included excerpts from congressional debates, other speeches, sketches of the national candidates plus their letters of acceptance, party platforms, political and governmental statistics, and similar material. State and local speakers and editors borrowed heavily from these textbooks when they composed their appeals to local voters. Hastily prepared campaign biographies offered fuller, sometimes fanciful, details about the candidates' lives, as well as material similar to that in the textbooks.

The parties did not fight their battles alone. Newspapers played a key role in partisan politics. Although in the late nineteenth century the press was moving toward greater independence, most dailies and weeklies remained intensely loyal to one party or the other, in both their editorial columns and their "news" pages. They gladly inserted boilerplate provided by party committees. Leaders often furnished advance copies of their speeches so that they could be set in type and thus appear in a paper's columns the morning after delivery. Some politicians ghostwrote editorials, and it was not unusual for prominent figures to give papers canned "interviews" that they composed entirely themselves, questions as well as answers. In election seasons, the parties not only supported increased circulation of influential papers such as the *New York Tribune* but also helped fund hundreds if not thousands of country weeklies and dailies. Party leaders much appreciated the newspapers' help, and many editors received government appointments, especially diplomatic posts, in recognition of their party service.

In waging the "campaign of education," the parties also benefited from the distribution of literature by special-interest groups, especially economic interests affected by governmental policies. Thousands upon thousands of pamphlets flowed from the Honest Money League, the American Tariff Reform League, the Boston Home Market Club, and similar organizations. During the 1880s, for instance, the American Iron and Steel Association published a series of *Tariff Tracts* with individual titles such as *How Protection Benefits Farmers and Mechanics* and *The Western View of the Tariff.* In 1888 the association distributed well over a million of these tracts in service of the Republican Party.

Besides this work, in 1888 the Iron and Steel Association made substantial financial contributions to the Republicans. Campaigns were costly. The parties faced a consistent and pervasive drain on their resources to meet expenses such as the salaries of paid party officials and workers, travel for campaigners, polling, outfitting headquarter rooms and lecture halls, advertising, office supplies, postage, printing and distributing documents and textbooks, financial support for newspapers, and on and on. Party committees often found fund-raising difficult. Traditionally, they expected state and federal officeholders to contribute a portion of their government salaries to the party cause. Of course, this source was not available to the party out of power, and the Pendleton Civil Service Act of 1883 made federal officials less vulnerable to this kind of political assessment. As a result, parties looked increasingly to other sources of revenue. But despite the conventional image of Gilded Age politicians "frying the fat" out of businessmen, they could not be certain that such contributions would be forthcoming. After narrowly losing his race for the presidency in 1884, Republican James G. Blaine complained, "I was beaten in New York simply for the lack of $25,000 which I tried in vain to raise in New York in the last week of the campaign. With all the immense interests of the tariff at stake, I don't think a single manufacturer gave $20,000. I doubt if one gave $10,000." Blaine had tried to emphasize the tariff issue, but four years later, when the tariff issue clearly dominated the 1888 campaign, the national committee amassed a war chest in excess of $1.2 million.[3]

In addition to covering legitimate campaign expenses, some funds occasionally went directly into voters' hands. Rarely did an election pass without a barrage of allegations of fraud hurled by the parties against each other. Scant hard evidence makes it difficult to gauge the impact or even the existence of the corruption of voters. The vast majority of voters trooped to the polls out of long-standing party loyalty and a sense of how the parties' policies could affect them. Voter interest and turnout in the late nineteenth century were extraordinarily high, and nearly all voters cast their votes eagerly and without a cash inducement. But in those states where the parties stood evenly matched, a small number of votes could spell the difference between victory and defeat. The targeted application of funds on election day could affect the results in these so-called doubtful states.

Swing states in this era were relatively few. From the mid-1870s to the mid-1890s, the two major parties enjoyed nearly equal support nationwide, and in presidential elections each could expect to win a large bloc of reliable states. The division was substantially sectional. For the Democrats, the great bastion of strength was the Solid South. Memories of northern abolitionism, the Civil War, emancipation, and Reconstruction remained deeply etched in the minds of the white southerners who dominated the region's political life. Although in the 1880s the Republican Party remained viable in some upper South states, after 1876 not a single state of the old Confederacy cast an electoral vote for a Republican until 1920. The Republicans' bloc of states, only slightly less dependable than the Democrats', lay in the Northeast, the upper Midwest, and the West. States such as Vermont, Massachusetts, and Minnesota returned comfortable Republican margins as regularly as Mississippi, Louisiana, and South Carolina fell in line for the Democrats.

But neither the Republican nor the Democratic bloc held enough electoral votes to ensure victory in presidential elections. The outcome usually turned on the results in a handful of doubtful states, principally New York and Indiana and, to a lesser degree, New Jersey and Connecticut. Each election year, party leaders studied the numbers and mapped campaign strategy accordingly. In the 1880s, out of a total of 401 electoral votes, a majority of 201 was necessary for victory. The electoral vote of the Democratic bloc totaled 153, while the Republicans' bloc amounted to 182. The biggest prize among the doubtful states was New York, with 36 votes, while Indiana had 15, New Jersey 9, and Connecticut 6. The Republicans could win by taking New York alone among the swing states, and if they lost New York, they could still win with a combination of Indiana plus either New Jersey or Connecticut. For the Democrats, however, New York alone would not bring victory; they must also win either Indiana or both New Jersey and Connecticut or assemble some combination that included states that were normally Republican. Needless to say, this configuration of strength impelled both parties to concentrate heavily on the swing states, often selecting nominees from

Table 1. Partisan Blocs in Presidential Elections in the 1880s

Republican States (182)	Democratic States (153)	Doubtful or Swing States (66)
Northeast	South	Connecticut (6)
Maine (6)	Alabama (10)	Indiana (15)
Massachusetts (14)	Arkansas (7)	New Jersey (9)
New Hampshire (4)	Florida (4)	New York (36)
Pennsylvania (30)	Georgia (12)	
Rhode Island (4)	Louisiana (8)	
Vermont (4)	Mississippi (9)	
Midwest/Plains	North Carolina (11)	
Illinois (22)	South Carolina (9)	
Iowa (13)	Tennessee (12)	
Kansas (9)	Texas (13)	
Michigan (13)	Virginia (12)	
Minnesota (7)	Border	
Nebraska (5)	Delaware (3)	
Ohio (23)	Kentucky (13)	
Wisconsin (11)	Maryland (8)	
West	Missouri (16)	
California (8)	West Virginia (6)	
Colorado (3)		
Nevada (3)		
Oregon (3)		

Figures in parentheses are electoral votes in 1884 and 1888. Total electoral votes, 401. Number necessary to win, 201.

them, focusing their advertising and speaking campaigns in them, and spending the bulk of campaign funds there. Because of the unpredictability of the doubtful states, each party's leaders also gave some attention to wooing possibly soft states in the other camp: upper South states such as the Virginias, Maryland, Tennessee, and North Carolina for the Republicans, and big industrializing northern states such as Illinois and Ohio for the Democrats. Despite the sordid image of Gilded Age politics, neither party had enough money simply to go in and buy up enough voters in these marginally winnable states. Breaking the other party's hold on such states required other strategies, such as Cleveland's selection of a running mate from Ohio, Allen G. Thurman, in 1888.

In the 1880s third parties further bedeviled the calculations of major party leaders. The Prohibition Party appealed to temperance advocates but also proposed a broad array of reforms in its platforms. It drew most of its support from the Republicans. Early in the decade the Greenback-

Labor Party occupied a position on the left end of the political spectrum, pushing currency inflation as a cure for the nation's economic ills. Toward the end of the decade, various other labor parties emerged, although agrarian political protest had not yet achieved the visibility and strength it would momentarily enjoy in the 1890s. The third parties' "spoiler" threat proved most potent in the doubtful states. In 1885 Senator Benjamin Harrison lamented that he had "little hope of making Indiana a Republican state with 4000 Republican Prohibitionists and 8000 Republican Greenbackers voting separate tickets." The possibility of such parties achieving power themselves remained virtually nonexistent, and fringe groups, such as the Socialists, had even less chance. Nonetheless, their ability to attract even a small fraction of the electorate in swing states could influence the outcome of elections.[4]

One of the most important consequences of the national equilibrium in major party strength and the resulting unstable political environment was a tendency toward divided government at the national level. Between 1875 and 1897 each major party held the presidency and a clear majority in both houses of Congress for only a single two-year period. During most of the Gilded Age, Congress itself was divided, the Democrats usually controlling the House of Representatives and the Republicans more often than not holding a majority in the Senate. Not entirely barren, Congress during the years of divided government managed to produce some notable legislation, including the Pendleton Civil Service Act and the Interstate Commerce Act. But fractured power often led to stalemate, thus contributing to the impression that government in the period accomplished little. In 1888, however, the GOP at last took control of the White House and Congress, and the Republicans proceeded to govern with vigor.

In the long struggle to break the stalemate, both Republican and Democratic leaders understood the value of a well-oiled organization, and they placed great emphasis on the virtues of party loyalty. But they also recognized the need to make effective appeals based on the party's approach to the central issues of the day. On the one hand, the equilibrium between the parties called for caution; any position too far from the mainstream might alienate some party members, and even a small decline in a party's normal vote could sink its chances. On the other hand, party strategists also saw the need to draw sharp distinctions between their own party and the opposition to energize their base of supporters and entice defectors from the other side. Along with the politics of organization, the skillful treatment of substantive issues formed an indispensable element in presidential campaigns.

By the 1880s economic questions had come to dominate national political discourse, but sectional issues, especially concerning federal protection of the rights of African Americans in the South, continued to divide the two major parties. One of the main reasons the South had become solid for the Democrats was that, as Reconstruction waned, white conservatives had employed a variety of means to curtail voting by blacks, who supported the Republican Party overwhelmingly. With the Fifteenth Amendment and enforcement legislation in the early 1870s, the Republicans had underwritten blacks' right to vote, but after 1877 the Democrats had regained control in all the southern states, and blacks were systematically excluded from the polity. More than a decade of divided government at the national level prevented the Republicans from erecting new protections for equal suffrage, but in 1888 many party members still advocated the securing of blacks' rights as one of the party's essential goals. Democrats, both in the South and the North, disagreed, warning ominously of a return to the "bayonet rule" of Reconstruction. They dismissed the Republicans' calls for corrective action as "waving the bloody shirt," exploiting the lingering passions of the Civil War for partisan purposes. Many Republicans, as it happened, had come to view the emphasis on the issue as counterproductive. Recognizing that the party had considerable strength in the upper South, these Republicans favored using economic issues to try to wrest states in that region from the Democrats' grip.

In the 1880s the principal economic issue that separated Democrats from Republicans was the tariff. In the century since the nation's founding, customs duties had yielded a preponderance of the federal government's receipts, and in the 1880s tariff revenues typically amounted to 60 percent or more of the total. During the Civil War, federal taxation overall had risen to unprecedented heights to meet the costs of the national emergency. The Republicans in charge of the Union government had raised tariff rates not only to generate additional revenue but also to provide a financial offset in the form of protection for American producers burdened by excise taxes and other internal levies that made their goods less competitive with foreign imports. In the postwar years the government reduced most internal taxation, but protected interests resisted a wholesale lowering of duties on imports. Although tariff rates declined somewhat, revenues remained high, and in every fiscal year from 1866 to 1893, the federal budget exhibited a surplus. Such a fiscal balance sheet would delight political leaders today, but the nineteenth-century surpluses grew so large that most politicians and citizens regarded the government's buildup of funds as a threat to the country's overall economic health. From 1881 to 1887 the excess over expenditures averaged nearly 30 percent of federal revenues. Cartoonists frequently depicted the surplus, which withdrew money from the private economy, as a monster gorging on the nation's vitals.

Republicans and Democrats differed sharply over how best to slay this beast. Democrats typically (but by no means unanimously) favored a general lowering of tariff rates, arguing that this would not only cut down on revenues but also help reduce prices for consumers. In addition, Democrats insisted that cheaper imported raw materials would allow American manufacturers to produce less expensive goods that they could sell more competitively in overseas markets. A lower tariff had long borne particular appeal for the agricultural South, but it also found favor in mercantile centers such as New York, which stood to benefit from increased trade. Not all Democrats agreed, however. Many in Congress who represented districts with manufacturing or extractive industries often found themselves siding with Republicans in favor of protectionist legislation.

Although some tariff reformers among Republicans supported lower duties, most Republicans remained solidly committed to maintaining protectionist rates. They were much more willing to cut internal taxes on such items as tobacco and alcohol, if need be, to reduce the surplus rather than subvert the protective system. Republicans never tired of stressing the benefits of tariff duties high enough to sustain prosperity not only for factory owners but also for laborers, farmers, and the economy at large. Both parties sought to cast their tariff positions as defending the interests of average Americans. Republicans emphasized the tariff's impact on Americans as producers, especially the protection it afforded labor from the influx of goods made by foreign workers who were paid "pauper wages." Democrats, in contrast, appealed to Americans as consumers suffering from tariff-generated high prices and as taxpayers burdened by duties exacted from them for the benefit of special interests.

While the two parties disagreed on how to deal with the fiscal surplus on the revenue side of the equation, they also differed in their approach to expenditures. Democrats generally clung to Jeffersonian ideals of

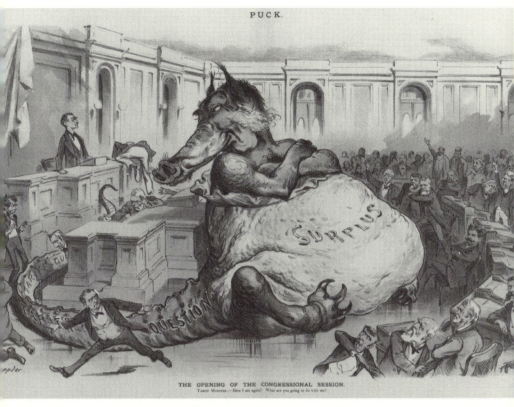

THE OPENING OF THE CONGRESSIONAL SESSION.
Tariff Monster.— Here I am again! What are you going to do with me?

Puck, *a Democratic-leaning magazine, dramatizes the central question confronting Congress in December 1887. (*Puck, *December 7, 1887)*

small, inexpensive government. One of the chief dangers they saw in the surplus was the implicit temptation to indulge in extravagance and wasteful spending of the people's money, much of which ought not to be collected in the first place. Republicans conceded the potential problems in a burgeoning surplus, but they tended to regard it more as an opportunity than a curse. Much more than the Democrats, Republicans favored spending the excess funds for a variety of worthwhile purposes. Republicans, for instance, advocated ample expenditures to improve harbors and rivers in the interest of defense and commerce. Democrats were less willing to endorse such projects, with the notable exception of the Mississippi River, the South's great waterway. Republicans, more than Democrats, embraced the idea of federal aid to education, especially to attack illiteracy among the former slaves and their descendants. Although both parties condemned the abuse of federal land grants made to railroads in the 1860s and 1870s, the Republicans were more disposed to accept the idea of subsidies, especially to revive the nation's merchant fleet crippled during the Civil War. These contrasting notions reflected the parties' general notions about the meaning of the Constitution: Republicans interpreted the document broadly to find sanction for national government action; Democrats viewed federal power as more restricted and adhered to notions of states' rights.

In addition to national fiscal policy, the era's other prominent economic issue revolved around monetary policy. Often referred to as the money question or the currency question, the issue fueled fierce internal divisions within the two major parties, much more so than the tariff. Inflationists in both parties favored an expansion of the money supply to protect debtors and the less well-off generally from the damaging impact of a secular deflationary trend. Their opponents in both parties advocated "sound money," generally backed by specie, as necessary to preserve values and secure a stable operation of the economy. The money question grew primarily out of enormous changes wrought in the nation's financial system during the Civil War. In addition to implementing a vast new tax structure, the Union government borrowed heavily and saddled the country with a huge bonded debt. Before the war, the nation's currency comprised gold and silver coin plus state or private banknotes more or less backed by coin. During the war, to supplement an inadequate volume of money, Congress created a national banking system that circulated national banknotes as currency, and the government also issued legal-tender paper money—greenbacks—unbacked by gold or silver. The great question in the immediate postwar years was when and how the government should resume specie payments. After an intense political struggle, the Treasury starting paying coin for the greenbacks in early 1879, although inflationists continued to seek repeal of the policy and to advocate an expansion in the volume of the paper currency.

The 1870s also witnessed the emergence of the silver issue. In 1873 the government had ceased coining silver dollars, but five years later intense public pressure pushed the government to resume silver coinage on a limited basis. In the view of inflationists, however, this limited coinage mandated by the Bland-Allison Act of 1878 was insufficient to meet society's needs; their ideal solution was the free and unlimited coinage of silver at a fixed ratio with gold. Their opponents, while conceding the need for an adequate currency, argued that a unilateral free silver coinage without an international agreement on the ratio with gold would soon drive the nation off the gold standard, undermine values, and wreck the economy. The national leaders of both parties tended to espouse the latter view, but they faced such substantial inflationist minorities that neither party in the 1880s could unite on an unchallenged approach to the issue. In election years, the question disturbed the planning of party strategists, especially when inflationist third parties threatened to draw strength away from the major parties.

Party leaders also wrestled with the civil service reform issue. During and after the war, the federal bureaucracy burgeoned and by 1881 comprised more than 100,000 officeholders in Washington and around the country. Increasingly, the appointing powers in the capital, from the president down, relied on a system whereby senators, congressmen, and other party officials recommended individuals to fill federal posts. Inevitably, party fealty as much as administrative competence came to dictate these recommendations, and within each party growing numbers of "reformers" alleged that the public service was falling into the hands of partisan hacks of limited fitness. In 1883 the Pendleton Act instituted the merit system for a small portion of federal offices. In subsequent years reformers pushed to extend the coverage of the system, but party leaders remained of two minds. On the one hand, the patronage process was enormously time-consuming, and those who recommended appointments bridled at being constantly hounded for endorsements, often by people they barely knew. On the other hand, leaders recognized the potential that patronage offered for securing the attachment of loyal cadres. Under counterpressures from reformers and regulars, both major parties in the 1880s treated the issue in a gingerly fashion.

In the distribution of government jobs, Republicans often gave preference to Union war veterans, many of whom were maimed and faced limited opportunities for other kinds of work. Although many veterans were Democrats, the Republican Party cast itself as the soldiers' friend, and veterans' organizations in turn frequently operated as auxiliaries to the GOP. Topping the list of veterans' concerns was the question of government pensions. Since Appomattox, hundreds of thousands of former Union soldiers and sailors who were in some measure disabled by war-related injuries or illness had received pensions. But as the veteran cohort grew older, Republicans showed an increasing willingness to grant pensions to all veterans unable to support themselves, regardless of the source of their disability. At this measure of generosity, many Democrats, most notably Grover Cleveland, drew the line, arguing that such a step would cost too much and swamp the pension system with a flood of fraudulent claims. The issue had an obvious sectional character. Republicans' liberality appealed to one of their natural constituencies in the North. Democrats' restraint appealed to ex-Confederates who bristled at being taxed to pay for federal largesse from which they were excluded.

Democrats' pension frugality reflected their general notion that government should be cheap. The one notable exception to this parsimony was defense spending, especially for the navy. In the 1880s both major parties favored an overhaul and expansion of the nation's fleet to prevent the United States from falling too far behind the other major powers of the world. Overall, to the extent the nation had a "foreign policy," it centered on defense. America occasionally tangled with foreign countries over a variety of "incidents," but in truth, thanks to the two great oceans, the nation was eminently secure; maintaining an adequate navy and coastal defenses was the key to keeping it so. Both parties had begun to tout trade expansion as an important foreign policy goal, but the issue was intertwined with the tariff question. Democrats argued that lower duties generally would help open markets overseas for American goods. Republicans favored keeping duties high and using negotiated reciprocity agreements to gain access to the markets of specific countries.

Foreign policy in the 1880s was in transition, and in politics it generally took a backseat to domestic issues. Still, certain elements in foreign affairs had the potential to spark voters' concern. Most Americans opposed further immigration of Chinese laborers, and Republicans and

Democrats regularly accused each other of being insufficiently vigorous in keeping them out. But, as for decades, Great Britain remained the nation's particular bête noire, at least in American political rhetoric. Each party accused the other of weakness and incompetence if not outright kowtowing in dealing with the British. With an eye to the volatile Irish American vote, both parties expressed sympathy for Irish home rule. On the tariff issue, Republicans accused the Democrats of favoring "British free trade," while the Democrats charged that the Republicans' high tariffs had caused Americans to lose markets around the world to the British. And in 1888 the two parties wrangled over a festering issue with Britain over American fishing rights off Canada. To a degree, these "foreign policy" questions, as political issues, related less to national security than to voters' ethnic animosities.

Ethnic and cultural divisions also colored social issues on the domestic side of politics, especially at the state and local level, in places that had experienced large increases in foreign immigration. Most notably, Republicans' tendency to favor temperance measures won support from pietistic, often native-born elements in the population, but it offended many immigrant groups. Democrats, who enjoyed strong support in many immigrant communities, denounced sumptuary legislation and governmental interference with individuals' decisions about their private conduct.

Through much of the twentieth century, the standard interpretation cast politics in the late nineteenth century as an issueless scramble for office with scant ideological difference between the parties. Modern scholars realize that this characterization was far off the mark. On several important issues, Republicans and Democrats presented contrasting positions on public issues and on the broader question of the meaning and purposes of government. Citizens attended the debate with intense concern and engaged in politics with a consuming passion. Most Americans clung tenaciously to their party as the defender of their own interests and the paladin of the nation's prospects. In 1888 the political stakes were high, and most citizens saw the nation's future direction riding on the outcome.

2

"GROVER, GROVER, FOUR MORE YEARS!"

Grover Cleveland was the first sitting president the Democratic Party renominated since Martin Van Buren had sought a second term in 1840. Unlike Van Buren, who had enjoyed a distinguished career before his first nomination, Cleveland had acquired little experience in public office before the Democrats tapped him for the nation's highest honor. He had never served in the cabinet or in Congress or any other legislature or in any federal position in Washington or elsewhere. His public service had been relatively brief and exclusively in local or state government. As late as 1881 he was practicing law in obscurity in his adopted hometown of Buffalo, New York. He served briefly as mayor there before being elected governor of New York in 1882, and after serving eighteen months in Albany, he received his party's nomination for the White House. In the fall of 1884 he won election as the country's twenty-second president.

CLEVELAND'S RISE TO POWER

Few presidents have risen to national prominence as rapidly as Cleveland. He did so less because of his ability to articulate the position of his party on the issues of the day than because of his reputation for honesty and devotion to duty. During the Gilded Age many Americans were highly sensitive to questions relating to politicians' integrity, and Cleveland cleverly and carefully projected an image of honor and probity. The roots of that vaunted good character lay deep in his personal history.

Cleveland was born in 1837, the fifth of nine children of a Yale-educated but financially pressed Presbyterian minister. In the Cleveland household, both the Reverend Richard Cleveland and his wife Ann—"a sainted mother," according to her son—laid particular emphasis on religious teaching and on the proper fulfillment of "stern labors and duties." As Grover Cleveland later recalled, these "precious precepts and examples of my early days" provided "every faculty of usefulness I possess, and every just apprehension of the duties and obligations of life."[1]

Yet when, as a young man, Cleveland left the family circle in tiny Holland Patent in western New York to study law in Buffalo, he stopped attending church and drifted away from the formal exercise of religion. More concerned with his earthly sojourn than the hereafter, he devoted his considerable energy to his legal studies and, after admission to the bar in 1859, to creating a paying practice. Under the influence of his legal preceptors, he affiliated with the Democratic Party and labored in its behalf in local Buffalo politics. In recognition of his legal skills and his work as a minor party functionary, he received an appointment as an assistant district attorney in January 1863. A few months later when he was drafted for the Union army, he paid for a substitute for the required $300, which he borrowed, and kept his office. In 1865 he lost election as district attorney, but in 1870 he narrowly won a three-year term as sheriff of Erie County.[2]

Although Buffalo was something of a "sin city," replete with saloons, brothels, and gambling dens, Cleveland had not maneuvered his way into the sheriff's job to launch a cleanup crusade. His motive was pecuniary; his substantial fees as sheriff would leave him better fixed financially than would three years' toiling at the bar. Moreover, Cleveland himself had regularly partaken of the city's lower offerings. After a hard day at the law, he would, as sympathetic biographer Allan Nevins put it, seek release in the "German beer-gardens, with their sawdust, music, pretty girls, and jovial banter," where he "led the chorus in lusty drinking songs, and prided himself on feats of conviviality." Cleveland's service as sheriff did not curtail these activities. He was unmarried and his relations with women remain hazy, but sometime around the close of his term as sheriff he had an affair, or at least a liaison, with Maria Halpin, a young widow and mother of two children. A few weeks short of nine months after Cleveland handed the keys to the Erie County Jail over to his successor, Halpin gave birth to a son on September 14, 1874.

She cited the thirty-seven-year-old Cleveland as the father. Halpin expected Cleveland to marry her, but he refused. Although he provided financial support for mother and son, Halpin's decline into drinking and erratic behavior finally moved Cleveland to arrange a suitable adoption for the nineteen-month-old boy.[3]

What Cleveland referred to as his "woman scrape" had a profound but paradoxical effect on his political career. Its revelation in the midst of his first presidential campaign in 1884 nearly derailed his chances, but ironically, the episode had helped put him on track toward nomination and election in the first place. These harrowing troubles in the mid-1870s shook Cleveland to his core, convincing him that if he harbored any hope for political advancement, he must abandon his roistering ways and minimize the blemish on his private life by cultivating an impeccable reputation in his professional and public life. In subsequent years Cleveland labored to make irreproachable probity and selfless commitment to duty the central elements of his political stock-in-trade. The strategy worked. As David Day, a fellow lawyer in Buffalo, wrote in 1884, "there is no one here, whether his friend or foe, political or personal, who will speak of his business or official character in any other than the highest terms." "He has not," Day added, "I am very sure, to any large extent the acquaintance of ladies."[4]

By 1881 Cleveland had so successfully buried his transgression that he caught the eye of Democratic reformers who urged him to run for mayor of Buffalo. The group was looking for a clean candidate to mount a campaign to rescue the city's government from a corrupt ring that involved both Republicans and Democrats. After several other men declined, Cleveland reluctantly agreed to run. He promised "better rule in municipal affairs," but he made no bones about his own Democratic partisanship, even insisting that the party refuse renomination to one city official who in the last election had put his own interest above that of other Democrats. Cleveland campaigned hard on the reform issue and attracted substantial numbers of Republicans fed up with the ring's depredations. He garnered 57 percent of the vote. Although Cleveland carried other Democrats into city offices with him, none of them matched his majority, and Democrats on the state ticket lost Buffalo to their Republican opponents. The personal nature of this victory, on top of Cleveland's perception of his nomination as a "call" to duty, easily fed his self-image as a popular tribune, unlike other politicians who merely grasped for power. He became convinced that he himself embodied the maxim he had cited in his acceptance address, that "public officials are the trustees of the people."[5]

Entering city hall January 1, 1882, Cleveland seized the opportunity to burnish his reformist image. He blocked council passage of a street-cleaning contract that included exorbitant rates, aggressively pushed for improvements in the city's noisome and unhealthful sewage system, and regularly vetoed appropriations that he thought violated the public interest. Within a few months he earned the sobriquet "veto mayor," and his executive forcefulness won notice in other parts of the state. His star was clearly on the rise.[6]

In 1882 deep divisions plagued New York Republicans, encouraging the state's Democrats to believe that in that year's elections they could regain the governorship they had lost three years earlier. But the Democrats were far from unified, and as the prenomination campaign heated up, neither of the two front-runners, Henry P. Slocum or Roswell P. Flower, could manage to move ahead. Recognizing the opportunity the situation offered to a newcomer, Cleveland shrewdly avoided aligning with any of the major party factions but instead dispatched friends from Buffalo to quietly cultivate favor among upstate party leaders.

By the time the Democratic state convention opened in late September, Cleveland had attracted enough support to be an important if not yet a leading player in its proceedings. His candidacy received an immeasurable boost when the Republicans, meeting the previous day, spurned the sitting governor, Alonzo Cornell, in favor of Secretary of the Treasury Charles J. Folger, who had been pushed by Cornell's factional foes, President Chester Arthur and former Senator Roscoe Conkling. The political bludgeoning of the capable and popular Governor Cornell incensed independent and reform Republicans, whose votes seemed eminently accessible if the Democrats should nominate an appealing candidate. No Cincinnatus at the plow, Cleveland grasped the chance and ordered his managers to meet with party leaders and "pound away" and "urge my nomination with the *utmost vehemence*." On the eve of balloting, the candidate himself sped to the convention in Syracuse to mingle with delegates and plead his cause in closed-door sessions with party bigwigs, especially state chairman Daniel Manning. Although such personal solicitation breached convention ethics, Cleveland was determined to give the gathering "a chance to look me over." In the voting, Slocum and Flower ran in a dead heat on the first two ballots, with Cleveland in third place. The next ballot brought a movement toward

Cleveland led by the County Democracy, an anti–Tammany Hall organization representing New York City. Other delegations followed, and Cleveland won the nomination.[7]

Cleveland's nomination for governor marked a signal triumph for his ambition as well as for the "reform" image he sought to project. Democrats soon realized that choosing him had made superb political sense. The *New York Tribune,* the nation's premier GOP newspaper, warned Republicans that the mayor's nomination "means hard work for the Republicans. Mr. Cleveland is young, able, and has a clean record." Confident of victory, Cleveland gave no speeches in the general campaign. In his official letter accepting the nomination, he touched lightly on pending state issues and devoted considerable space to civil service reform. Once again he declared, "Public officers are the servants and agents of the people."[8]

Cleveland's November victory was no surprise, although few had predicted the magnitude of his plurality. He garnered 535,318 votes to Folger's 341,464, for a difference of 193,854, a margin unprecedented in the state's history. Yet the outcome did not represent a shift in the equilibrium between the two major parties in "doubtful" New York. Cleveland won only 807 votes more than the Democrats' losing presidential candidate, Winfield Hancock, had received in New York two years earlier. Folger's vote, however, fell 214,080 below the victorious James A. Garfield's New York tally in 1880. Clearly, the outcome was as much, if not more, a rejection of Folger as an embrace of Cleveland. Nonetheless, Cleveland insisted that his victory was "a grand and brilliant manifestation of popular will." The result fed his and other men's notion that he was a different sort of politician, beholden only to the electorate and independent of bosses or machines. As he wrote to his brother on election day, he intended to approach his service as governor as "a business engagement between the people of the State and myself, in which the obligation on my side is to perform the duties assigned to me with an eye single to the interests of my employers."[9]

A landslide in a New York gubernatorial race immediately cast the victor into the charmed circle of "presidential possibilities." Cleveland did not discourage the speculation that turned his way. Reprising his performance as mayor, he administered the state government in a methodical, clean, and conservative fashion. Again he regularly reached for the veto stamp to arrest what he considered legislative extravagance or error. Most notable was his veto of the Five Cent Fare Bill, which aimed to decrease the fares on New York City's elevated railroads from ten cents to five cents. The financial schemer Jay Gould controlled these commuter lines, and the bill had wide support from antimonopoly forces, labor organizations, and much of the New York press. Nonetheless, Cleveland vetoed the bill on the grounds that it altered the original charters of the roads and thus represented an infringement of contract, in violation of the U.S. Constitution. Although the legislature had passed the measure handily, it failed to repass it over the governor's veto. The National Anti-Monopoly League denounced Cleveland for "observing the rights of capital" while ignoring "the rights of the public," but his action won praise from property owners and corporate interests. Reformist observers also hailed his courage in taking an unpopular stand for what he believed to be right.[10]

Among those most angered by Cleveland's veto were the Democrats of Tammany Hall, whose chief spokesman in the state senate, Thomas F. Grady, defended the Five Cent Bill as "a measure of justice," especially for the city's laborers. Tammany was a constituency that Cleveland did not mind offending, despite the Hall's work on his behalf in the 1882 campaign. Indeed, nothing could enhance his reputation for independence and rectitude more than a fight with the Tiger, and Cleveland did not shrink from the inevitable combat. Since the days of the infamous Boss William M. Tweed in the 1860s and early 1870s, many Americans regarded Tammany Hall as the epitome of all that was wrong in American politics. Although outright thievery on the scale Tweed had practiced was long past, the organization remained committed to self-preservation as its highest ideal, with official patronage as its chief source of sustenance. Grand Sachem John Kelly and his loyal braves soon found Governor Cleveland loath to meet their needs. The conflict reached a head in the spring of 1883 when Cleveland sent the state senate a long list of New York City appointments with Tammany names conspicuously absent. In response, Grady and other Tammany senators joined with Republicans to block the nominees' confirmation. Cleveland countered with a fiery message accusing his opponents of "overweening greed for the patronage," and Grady in turn denounced the message as "an insult to the dignity" of the senate. The hostility between the governor and Tammany Hall, previously latent, now stood open for all to see.[11]

Later in the fall state election campaign, Cleveland intervened behind the scenes with Kelly and other city Democratic leaders to block Grady's renomination for the senate. Kelly's publication of Cleveland's letter against Grady created a sensation, and the breach between the governor and Tammany was complete and irreparable. Overall, however, the outcome in the New York elections in 1883 suggested an uncertain popular verdict regarding Cleveland's first year as governor. The Democrats lost both houses of the state legislature, but in statewide races, all but one candidate on the party's ticket won election. Although the *New York Times* concluded that the result heralded Cleveland's "departure from political life," this report of his demise soon proved premature.[12]

Indeed, as the presidential nominating season of 1884 approached, the plucky new governor of New York attracted increasing attention, largely because national Democrats faced an array of candidates who sparked little enthusiasm among the party faithful. Delaware blueblood Thomas F. Bayard had earned respect for his unquestioned integrity and his able exposition of Democratic doctrine in the Senate, but his aloof personality warmed few hearts, and an 1861 speech he had given upholding the legality of secession provided irresistible grist for the Republican opposition. Former House Speaker Samuel J. Randall won plaudits as an effective advocate of states' rights and limited government, but his fervent protectionism ran counter to dominant party opinion on the tariff, and his colleagues' refusal to reelect him to the Speakership in 1883 punctured his presidential prospects. The new Speaker, John G. Carlisle, attracted no more than favorite-son support from his native Kentucky. Similarly, Indiana's former senator, Joseph E. McDonald, though widely respected, failed to catch on beyond the borders of his home state. Allen G. Thurman of Ohio, who had first entered Congress in the days of James K. Polk, enjoyed affectionate regard as the "Old Roman" of the party, but his seventy years made him unlikely to lead a revitalized Democracy to victory.

Much greater sentimental support clung to the party's other leading septuagenarian, Samuel J. Tilden, whom many Democrats longed to see take the chair denied him in the disputed election of 1876. Tilden's age coupled with his frail health after a debilitating stroke made him an unrealistic candidate, but as long as he left his name in play in the winter and spring of 1884, he remained a potent factor in Democrats' calculations. In that period, Cleveland's friends trod carefully in New York while spreading the good word about their robust and clean candidate to party leaders around the country, many of whom already saw him as a good prospect for the vice presidency. In early June, Tilden issued a formal declination. Although all candidates hoped to inherit his support, Cleveland had the inside track, especially with the aid of state party chairman Daniel Manning, the longtime fugleman of the Tilden Democrats. The governor's friends touted their man as the heir to Tilden's mantle of "reform," an argument that had particular force after the Republicans nominated the scandal-tainted James G. Blaine. Allegations of influence peddling hung about Blaine, and independent Republicans, as they had in Cleveland's mayoral and gubernatorial races, looked to the governor as a worthy alternative. In contrast to Blaine, Cleveland's Democratic backers declared, he was "an upright man of business," and "no governor ever stood better in the moral confidence of the citizens of New York."[13]

Yet not all New Yorkers agreed. As the national convention drew near and the Tilden support made Cleveland the odds-on favorite, the braves of Tammany remained alienated. But they could muster only a minority of the New York delegation, and Cleveland's friends enforced the unit rule to control the state's entire vote. The Tammany men carried their resentment to the Chicago convention, where they claimed that the delegation's majority stifled their individual judgment. In the course of nominating and seconding speeches, ex–State Senator Thomas Grady rose to denounce Cleveland as a "friend of absolutism [and] of centralized autocratic government" who could not carry New York. The speech shocked most delegates and spurred a memorable response in a seconding speech for Cleveland by Wisconsin delegate Edward S. Bragg. Mocking the sham grievances of Tammany, whose "study has been political chicane in the midnight conclave," Bragg claimed to speak for the rising generation of Democrats who favored Cleveland. "They love him, gentlemen, and they respect him, not only for himself, for his character, for his integrity and judgment and iron will, but they love him most for the enemies that he has made." Grabbing the bait, Grady shouted, "on behalf of his enemies I reciprocate that sentiment, and we are proud of the compliment." This bit of political theater could not have inured to Cleveland's benefit more if his own men had scripted it. Cleveland led the first ballot and easily cinched the nomination on the second. With a sentimental nod to the "old ticket" of 1876, the convention nominated Tilden's running mate, Thomas A. Hendricks, for vice president.[14]

The national convention provided a perfect curtain-raiser for what Cleveland's managers hoped would be a campaign focused on their candidate's sterling record of honesty and opposition to machine politics. But ten days later a Buffalo Republican newspaper published the Halpin story. The revelation hit the campaign hard, and the Democrats particularly feared the reaction among the so-called Mugwumps. These were reform-minded independent Republicans who had rallied to Cleveland against Blaine on the character issue. Following Cleveland's command to "tell the truth," his managers responded quickly, emphasizing the solicitude he had shown for the mother and child. They gave wide publicity to a report by Kinsley Twining, a minister and noted religious editor, who had traveled to Buffalo to investigate Cleveland's private life there. Twining depicted the "illicit connection" with Halpin as an aberration— "a culpable irregularity"—rather than an instance in a larger pattern of lechery. Cleveland, Twining wrote, "is a man of true and kind heart, frank and open, so intensely devoted to his business duties that it is impossible that he should be a debauchee." Other sympathetic investigators cast the matter in a similar light, and many Mugwumps satisfied themselves that this taint on Cleveland's private life did not override the clear ethical superiority of his public record over Blaine's. One group of Massachusetts independent Republicans argued that the choice in the election was "between the representative of honest government on one hand, and on the other the betrayer of official trusts."[15]

In a less lofty counterattack, some Democrats circulated the story that Blaine's wife had given birth to their first child three months after their marriage. As the campaign degenerated into one of the foulest in history, Blaine labored to elevate its tone. Breaking with precedent, he took a seven-week speaking tour, during which he emphasized economic issues, especially the Republicans' tariff protectionism. Cleveland, never a comfortable campaigner, made few speeches and said little about substantive issues. The Democratic platform had straddled on the tariff, and Cleveland did not meet Blaine head-on regarding the question. Instead, he advocated a reduction of unnecessary taxation "without depriving American labor of the ability to compete successfully with foreign labor." More at ease with the character issue, Cleveland portrayed his Republican opponents as "a vast army of office-holders, long in power" and "corrupt to the core." Following the pattern of his mayoral and gubernatorial campaigns, he aimed to "impress upon the people that the issue involved in the pending canvass is the establishment of a pure and honest administration of their government." In a bid for support among civil service reformers, he argued that a key way to curb abuse of the patronage power was to amend the Constitution to limit chief executives to a single term. "The eligibility of the President for re-election," he declared, was "a most serious danger." That assertion, of course, would prove embarrassing in 1888.[16]

Blaine's campaign stumbled at the very end, when he failed to rebuke a Presbyterian minister who, in his presence, characterized the Democrats as the party of "rum, Romanism, and rebellion," a not-so-veiled slur against Irish Catholics whom Blaine had tried to woo. The same day Blaine attended a much-publicized dinner of wealthy capitalists, thereby undercutting his arguments that the protective tariff mainly benefited labor. A week later Cleveland won one of the narrowest presidential elections in history. In the national popular vote, his plurality was just 25,685 out of a total of more than 10 million. In the electoral college, New York's 36 votes gave him the winning edge. Cleveland carried the Empire State by the slimmest of margins, 1,047 out of a total popular vote exceeding 1 million. Although an outcome so precarious defies precise explanation, Blaine's diminished popularity among Catholics after the "rum, Romanism, and Rebellion" incident, opposition to his candidacy by Roscoe Conkling and other factional opponents in New York, Republican defections to the Prohibition ticket, and bad weather in Republican upstate regions all helped the Democrats. Nonetheless, in the aftermath, plenty of claimants came forward to assert that their efforts had carried Cleveland through. Tammany had announced support for the ticket in September, less out of a newfound love for Cleveland than to secure a place at the patronage trough in the event of his victory. The Mugwumps, many of whom lived in New York, insisted that their abandonment of Blaine for Cleveland had made the difference. In the nation at large, Cleveland's biggest bloc of votes came from the South, where Democrats saw his victory as at last restoring their political legitimacy after decades of bearing the taint of rebellion. But Cleveland had no coattails in the congressional elections. Although the Democrats retained control of the House, their majority declined by more than a dozen seats, and in the Senate they lost two seats and remained in the minority.[17]

Two years earlier, Cleveland had interpreted his landslide in the gubernatorial race as a direct call from the people, leaving him essentially unbeholden to any political agency as he set about to fulfill his duties. Paradoxically, his razor-thin victory in 1884 had a similar effect. Many men had labored for his election, but no one could make exclusive claim to having secured the result, which seemed to turn on luck as much as anything else. Indebted to no particular individual or entity,

Cleveland once again could picture himself as his own man, obligated only to serve the interests of the people. Although he relished his victory, he approached his impending burdens with characteristic sanctimony. "I look upon the four years next to come," he wrote to a friend, "as a dreadful self-inflicted penance for the good of my country. I can see no pleasure in it and no satisfaction, only a hope that I may be of service to my people." Moreover, the scurrilous campaign left him embittered and further alienated from politics as usual. Beset by the professions of "pretended friends," he was hard-pressed to know "who shall be trusted." "I wonder," he wrote, "if I must, for the third time, face the difficulties of a new official life almost *alone?*" Such solipsistic self-righteousness might fuel a commendable assertiveness in a chief executive, but it did not bespeak the softer arts of persuasion and compromise that a successful president would need to consummate a program.[18]

A TROUBLESOME TIME IN THE WHITE HOUSE

Cleveland had not campaigned on behalf of a well-articulated program, but he inclined toward a set of notions that had characterized his party for decades. Philosophically, he adhered to the state-oriented, small-government traditions of the Democratic Party. He tended to accept classical liberalism's belief that government should not interfere with the immutable laws of economics. He opposed Republican policies of high tariffs, subsidies, and other programs to foster economic growth, which he believed represented corrupt perversions of the true purposes of government in the interest of privileged classes at the expense of the commonweal. But Cleveland had said little about these matters during his campaign, and some question exists as to how well developed his ideas actually were before he entered the White House. After an interview with the president-elect, *New York Evening Post* editor Horace White concluded that Cleveland's understanding of national issues was "extremely defective," and *New York Herald* reporter Charles Nordhoff similarly found him "curiously ignorant of federal questions and politics." Cleveland had won election on little more than his sterling public character and a promise of good government. Now, however, grim necessity demanded that he translate his hazy notions into policy. As Nordhoff presciently observed, he was "bound to have a troublesome time."[19]

As with all presidents, the first major difficulty Cleveland encountered was the distribution of patronage. The first member of his party to win the presidency since 1856, he confronted hordes of hungry Democrats who had been shut out of federal jobs since before the Civil War. During the campaign, however, without engaging in specifics, Cleveland had encouraged civil service reformers to believe that he was a stout defender of their cause. He had won the support of many of them, and now after his victory, for which many reformers immodestly took credit, they wanted specifics. They particularly feared that he would be unable to withstand his party's pressure for a "clean sweep" of Republican appointees to make way for Democrats. As the prominent independent Republican Carl Schurz warned him, "If you should do things not up to the mark, people will be apt to say: 'He is after all not as good as we thought he would turn out to be.'"[20]

Cleveland sought to clarify his position in a public pronouncement two months before taking office. In late December the officers of the National Civil-Service Reform League sent him a letter citing "widespread anxiety" that the change in party control of the executive would aggravate patronage "abuses." In a carefully worded response, Cleveland pledged a "fair and honest enforcement" of the Pendleton Civil Service Act that Congress had passed the previous year. Moreover, he took the occasion to put Democrats on notice that appointments to positions not covered by the act would be based on "sufficient inquiry as to fitness" rather than "persistent importunity or self-solicited recommendations on behalf of candidates." But on the all-important question of what to do about Republicans currently holding office, he straddled. Such officials would not be dismissed simply to make way for Democrats, but, he warned, incumbent Republicans would lose their jobs if "instead of being decent public servants, they have proved themselves offensive partisans." As it played out in practice, Cleveland's "offensive partisanship" formulation satisfied neither the reformers nor Democratic Party regulars.[21]

The reformers' disenchantment began with some of the new president's cabinet selections. Thomas F. Bayard, the new secretary of state, had a reputation for probity, and William F. Vilas in the Post Office Department and William C. Endicott in the War Department had stood in the Democratic Party's reform wing. But two southerners Cleveland appointed, L. Q. C. Lamar for interior secretary and Augustus Garland for attorney general, were weak choices, and reformers objected outright to the other two secretaries. They regarded Daniel Manning, Cleveland's close political adviser whom he chose to head the Treasury Department, as *"the Machine incarnate."* Navy Secretary William C. Whitney, who had Standard Oil connections and had contributed $25,000 to the 1884 campaign, struck Mugwumps as a crafty political manipulator with "no other distinction than his money." As a result of such appointments, E. L. Godkin told Cleveland, "we independents may have to go into the Canvas of 1888, seriously, if not fatally discredited."[22]

Cleveland chafed under such criticism, which he considered unjust. He still claimed to follow reform precepts in handling lower-level offices. The first months of his administration did not bring a mass dismissal of Republican subordinates, although he nearly always filled vacancies with Democrats. Reformers generally applauded this initial restraint. Five months after Cleveland's inauguration, George William Curtis told the Civil-Service Reform League's annual meeting that its cause now enjoyed "astonishing progress" because "at last a President is able as well as willing to resist the party pressure for spoils."[23]

And party pressure for spoils abounded. At the time Cleveland assumed office, out of the 126,000 federal employees in Washington and around the country, only 16,000 fell under the Pendleton Act's protections. Many party leaders believed that most of the remaining 110,000 positions should go to Democratic cadres who had borne the hard labor of the 1884 campaign. Despite his admonition against "persistent importunity," Cleveland soon found himself inundated with requests, recommendations, and complaints. And the protests came not just from disappointed office seekers or disgruntled machine men. No less a figure than Samuel J. Tilden reminded the administration of the political importance of the tens of thousands of officeholders dotted around the country, such as the "little postmasters" who "act as agents and canvassers" for their party. "The immense power of this influence is now wholly on the side of the Republicans," Tilden wrote. "To allow this state of things to continue is infidelity to the principles and cause of the administration."[24]

The political potential of the patronage was hardly news to Cleveland, and despite his reform avowals, he moved to correct what he considered the political imbalance in the federal bureaucracy. Three and a half months after taking office, he wrote to his best friend that he was "much comforted by the reflection that I may serve the country well and still serve my party." By then he had replaced 70 percent of the nation's internal revenue collectors, and he had begun a review that within two years resulted in a turnover in three-quarters of the postmasterships. Many of the dismissed incumbents had served four years or more, but Cleveland also told Treasury Secretary Manning that "those who have been guilty of offenses against our political code should go without regard to the time they have served."[25]

It did not take Republicans long to label Cleveland's "offensive partisanship" rationale as simply a ruse to justify replacing Republicans with Democrats. In cases that required Senate approval of nominees, Republicans began to demand that the administration provide the letters and other papers that supposedly documented the charges of wrongdoing leveled against incumbents. As some Republicans frankly conceded, they aimed to force Cleveland to admit that at least some removals were politically motivated and not based on demonstrable offenses. The president steadfastly refused to produce the documents, and the Senate Republicans eventually backed down. Cleveland thus scored a point for the independence of the executive, but the Republicans had nonetheless managed to highlight the apparent hypocrisy of the president's civil service professions. As Carl Schurz put it, Cleveland's refusal to provide information was not "that sort of moral courage which the reform of the public service stands in need of." Speaking for many Mugwumps, Schurz began to fear that "this 'reform Administration' will end like its predecessors: sit down between two chairs—do just enough to disgust the enemies of reform and not enough to satisfy its friends."[26]

Schurz's prediction proved near the mark. By 1888, although many civil service reformers still gave the president the benefit of the doubt, many others saw little reason to rally to his bid for reelection. "To me," Philadelphia reformer Henry C. Lea wrote, "a man like Cleveland, who steals the livery of God to serve the devil is infinitely more despicable than men . . . who make no pretense of political virtue." And yet to his dismay, Cleveland discovered that he made few allies when he began distributing the largesse to Democrats, for he had insufficient positions to satisfy the numerous supplicants. Moreover, he found it "mighty hard to get along with the Democrats of a locality when different factions are tattling and finding fault with each other like a mess of schoolboys." In many areas, whichever way he tilted in appointments, he made enemies. Thus, patronage recognition might strengthen one faction over another, but it had little effect in building a new Cleveland organization. The push for office continued almost unabated into 1888, when some local party leaders underscored their pleas by asserting that unless the administration made speedy changes in federal offices, they could not ensure support for the president's reelection. One Cleveland supporter from Hornellsville, New York, wrote that it was the "greatest annoyance ... seeing the letter carriers who distribute the mails here about the city clad in their uniforms and working against us." In the end, Cleveland's patronage policy not only disappointed reformers. It failed to unite his party, and it alienated significant blocs of Democrats who would express their anger by opposition or indifference to the president's fortunes in 1888.[27]

Cleveland's patronage woes dovetailed with another issue that plagued his reelection bid—his treatment of veterans. After the Civil War, in an effort to aid veterans unable to support themselves, Congress had passed legislation stipulating that in federal appointments disabled veterans "shall be preferred." Every time the administration fired an ex-Union soldier or sailor to make way for a Democrat, Republicans were quick to charge that Cleveland had violated the spirit and sometimes the letter of the law. Among the most effective Republican spokesmen on this issue was Senator Benjamin Harrison of Indiana, himself a former Union general with strong ties to veterans' groups. In March 1886, in an impassioned Senate speech, Harrison rose to the defense of one Isabelle De La Hunt, a Union veteran's widow who had been eking out a living as postmistress in Cannelton, Indiana. As in many other cases, Cleveland had fired Mrs. De La Hunt on the grounds of "offensive partisanship," although, as in other cases, the administration refused to specify the charges against her. On the floor of the Senate Harrison dramatized the "pathos and indignation" of her heartless dismissal and insisted that "there is not a Democratic Senator here who would not scorn to be the author of such treatment." Republican Party committees reprinted Harrison's speech and distributed thousands of copies to veterans around the country.[28]

But the De La Hunt affair was soon overshadowed by other presidential actions that convinced thousands of veterans that Cleveland had little interest in their welfare. This feeling grew out of his handling of the pension issue. In 1862 Congress instituted pensions for Union veterans disabled during their military service and for the widows and children of men who died from service-related injuries or illnesses. In the ensuing years, the Pension Bureau examined claims and granted tens of thousands of pensions. In the 1880s the aging and increasing infirmity

of the veteran cohort, coupled with aggressive advocacy by pension at-
torneys, led to mounting applications. By the time Cleveland took office,
the rolls listed more than 300,000 pensioners. Cleveland regarded the
stipulation that the disability must have originated in the service as the
legal linchpin of the program, and he was not alone in thinking that a
troubling proportion of pension claims rested on dubious grounds and
some on outright fraud. He had no intention of dismantling the pension
system, whose benefits he acknowledged, but far more than his Republican predecessors, Cleveland drew attention to its flaws. "Meritorious
claims should be speedily examined and adjusted," he told Congress,
but "it is fully as important that the rolls should be cleansed of all those
who by fraud have secured a place thereon." Concerned that pension
expenditures had grown to constitute one-third of federal outlays, he
warned that "every relaxation of principle in the granting of pensions"
taught a "demoralizing lesson . . . that as against the public Treasury the
most questionable expedients are allowable."[29]

To superintend the work of reform, Cleveland appointed John C.
Black as commissioner of pensions. Himself a wounded veteran and a
pensioner, Black was personally popular with ex-soldiers. As commissioner, he reorganized the Pension Bureau and instituted cost-cutting
measures. Still, during his tenure the number of pensions increased,
but so did the number of veterans who failed to get satisfaction from
the bureau and turned to Congress for help. Cleveland's term thus witnessed a substantial increase in the number of special pension bills
introduced by congressmen to grant pensions to specific individuals.
Previous presidents had routinely signed such bills, but Cleveland felt
duty bound to examine each one personally. Although he approved more
than he rejected, he vetoed hundreds of them. The merits of most of
these measures may have justified his decisions, but the image emerged
of the president burning the midnight oil and poring over the details of
individual pension claims just to prevent a few dollars per month from
going to some veteran or widow whose case did not meet the absolute
letter of federal pension rules. Such cases might be "pitiable," Cleveland
said, but "unfortunately, official duty can not always be well done when
directed solely by sympathy and charity." "I can not forget that age and
poverty do not themselves justify gifts of public money." Few veterans
warmed to such legalistic lecturing, nor did they appreciate Cleveland's
sarcasm or attempts at humor in several of his veto messages. In one
case he wrote, "The number of instances in which those of our soldiers

who rode horses during the war were injured by being thrown forward upon their saddles indicate that those saddles were very dangerous contrivances."[30]

Insisting that he sympathized with the suffering veterans, Cleveland suggested a revision of general pension legislation so that "relief may be claimed as a right, and . . . granted under the sanction of law, not in evasion of it." A month later, in January 1887, a two-to-one bipartisan majority in Congress passed the Dependent Pension Bill, which would have authorized a pension for every veteran who had served at least three months and who suffered from a disability that prevented his laboring to support himself, regardless of the origin of the disability. Cleveland vetoed this bill, arguing that it would aggravate, not relieve, what he perceived as the evils of the pension system. The "tremendous addition to our pension obligation" would sabotage efforts to reduce taxes. And, he said, "the race after the pensions offered by this bill would not only stimulate weakness and pretended incapacity for labor, but put a further premium on dishonesty and mendacity."[31]

Though a seeming betrayal of his own call for revision of the law, Cleveland's veto pleased two important constituencies. Mugwumps hailed it for underscoring their ideas of laissez-faire and frugal government. "Of all your vetoes," Horace White wrote to the president, "that of the Pauper Pension bill is the happiest & weightiest." The veto also appealed to the South, where ex-Confederates disliked paying taxes to fund benefits they could not share. Indeed, on the bill's passage in the House of Representatives, southerners cast all but three of the seventy-six votes against it. After Cleveland's message, a party journalist from Kentucky reported to the White House that he had received a large number of letters from throughout the region "indorsing the President's veto of the Pauper Bill. He has made hosts of new friends and captured many that had gone to the Disgruntled Land."[32]

But these signs of approbation had only limited significance for Cleveland's reelection chances. Indeed, the veto had negligible influence in reassuring independents who were put off by Cleveland's civil service lapses, which most reformers considered a more important issue. And as for the South, Cleveland was, in the idiom of twenty-first-century political analysis, simply playing to his party's base. More important, the veto did little to garner support in the critical doubtful states of the North and especially in the Midwest, where veterans and their organizations wielded significant power. In the House vote, the bill received yea votes from more than fifty northern Democrats, including all the Democrats from Indiana and all but one from Ohio. After the veto, the House Pension Committee chairman, Indiana Democrat C. C. Matson, submitted a unanimous report that characterized Cleveland's "strained interpretation" of the bill "as an excuse rather than a reason" for rejecting it. All the committee's Democrats and Republicans joined in a call for the House to override the veto to demonstrate that Americans were not willing "to allow the defenders of the nation's honor and life to live in their declining years in misery and want." The override failed, but the political damage was done. As one old soldier from Ohio wrote to Republican senator and presidential aspirant John Sherman, "Cleveland['s] veto of [the] Pension Bill yesterday has raised the big[g]est howell [sic] that has ever been since the passage of the Kansas-Nebraska Bill. The Simon pure Copperheads even are sick. They foresee that Cleveland has damned the party for the future."[33]

Four months later, Cleveland made matters worse. In June 1887 he endorsed a recommendation from the War Department that captured Confederate battle flags, heretofore stored in the department's attic, be returned to the southern states. Conceived as a gesture toward sectional rapprochement, the flag order struck many northern veterans as hallowing the rebellion they had struggled mightily to defeat. The reaction of veterans' groups such as the Grand Army of the Republic was swift and fierce. The GAR's national commander told a gathering in New York, "May God palsy the hand that wrote that order. May God palsy the brain that conceived it, and may God palsy the tongue that dictated it." Cleveland beat a hasty retreat, claiming to have discovered on further examination that the flags could not be legally returned without congressional action. But the criticism continued and grew so virulent that Cleveland felt compelled to withdraw his earlier acceptance of an invitation to attend the upcoming GAR national encampment in St. Louis. He did so, he said, not out of fear for his personal safety but to avoid insults to "the people's highest office, the dignity of which I must protect."[34]

Democratic strategists quickly grasped the disastrous political consequences of the uproar. Traveling in the Midwest, Pension Commissioner Black telegraphed the White House that the flag order had "provoked deep feeling. . . . The public mind seems unprepared for the sentiment of such a course." In Ohio, Congressman James Campbell, who had voted for the Dependent Pension Bill, denounced Cleveland's flag order as "foolish" and unnecessary. "I owed one of my elections to Congress to the preference of my soldier comrades," Campbell told reporters. "I can't go back on them." Campbell had been contemplating running for governor in 1887 but decided against it because "this doesn't seem to be a Democratic year." From Leadville, Colorado, a group of party stalwarts sent Cleveland the scrawled message, "As Democrats who sup[p]orted you in the last Presidential Campaign, we are sorry to see that you are politically damned, and only seen as a representative of rebellion, a viper, and an untrustworthy man." Some in Cleveland's inner circle thought that the vituperation would eventually inure to the president's benefit, and Navy Secretary William C. Whitney advised "let[ting] the solicitude for his personal safety grow." Even so, in a letter to a Gettysburg reunion, Cleveland could not help lashing out against "frenzied appeals to passion" and "the traffic in sectional hate."[35]

Republicans grabbed the opportunity Cleveland had handed them. Prompted by veterans' groups, midwestern Republican governors dashed off telegrams to the White House condemning the return of any rebel banners taken by the citizen-soldiers of their states. Republican campaigners in 1887 hammered Cleveland for his order, none more powerfully than Ohio Governor Joseph B. Foraker, who told John Sherman that "this flag business will do us much good politically." Running for reelection, Foraker excoriated the president for treating the flags "as though they were not still the emblems of treason."[36]

And yet Foraker and other Republicans insisted that something more important was involved than simply reviving the passions of war for political advantage. At the heart of the southern question was the continued suppression of blacks' right to vote, a degradation of representative government perpetrated by white southerners and condoned by northern Democrats. As Foraker put it, "That the South was made 'solid' by bloody and fraudulent methods is as indisputable an historical fact as the war itself." To interfere with the people's "lawfully expressed will" was "moral treason" and a mockery of "our boasted free institutions." Republicans could not escape the conviction that Grover Cleveland would never have been elected president except for the suppression of the black vote in several states of the South and that his remaining in power depended on his continued collusion in that crime. In his inaugural address Cleveland included a few remarks designed to calm black Americans worried at the ascension of a Democratic president to power, but white southerners knew that they had little to fear from his administration with a Justice Department headed by an Arkansas lawyer who had served four years in the Confederate congress. Attorney General Augustus Garland gave only tepid support to the one significant voting rights case brought by federal prosecutors during his term. The flag order, as one Republican wrote to John Sherman, demonstrated "in a most convincing way the fact that the 'South is in the saddle.'"[37]

Later in the year Cleveland took another step to shore up his southern base by nominating his secretary of the interior, Mississippian L. Q. C. Lamar, to a seat on the Supreme Court. Lamar was one of three southerners the president had taken into his cabinet, and he now proposed to transfer the sixty-two-year-old former Confederate colonel to the nation's highest court. Lamar's age, poor health, and marginal legal expertise suggested that his southern connection was the determining factor in Cleveland's selection. Again Republicans pounced. Lamar's taking a seat on the Supreme Court bench might "appeal to the sentiment of universal reconciliation," said the New York Tribune, but the fact remained that he had "never uttered a word against the murders, midnight whippings and other bloody deeds of the bulldozing period—all of which he saw and part of which he was." Lamar won confirmation on a narrow vote, with two western Republicans and an independent from Virginia joining the Democrats.[38]

Although in various ways Cleveland sought to project himself as an apostle of sectional reconciliation, his actions and attitudes seemed in practice to tilt toward the South. As he looked ahead to 1888, he could not forget that in 1884 in each of three southern states (Tennessee, Virginia, and West Virginia), he had defeated Blaine by a margin of less than 4 percentage points—by just 2.2 percentage points in Virginia. Had Blaine carried Virginia and Tennessee, he would have won the election. Thus, Cleveland labored to appease his base, but in doing so he opened the way for Republicans to depict him as the captive of an unrepentant South. That image alienated elements in the North, where the election of 1888 would ultimately be decided.[39]

If civil service, patronage, pension woes, and sectionalism haunted Cleveland's plans for reelection, so did the money question, about which the Democratic Party stood hopelessly divided. In the pre–Civil War decades, the Democratic followers of Andrew Jackson had, with few exceptions, espoused hard money and distrusted any schemes to manipulate currency values either by banks or by the government. This bent continued into the war years, when Democrats in Congress generally opposed the Legal Tender Act, which authorized the emission of greenback paper currency unbacked by specie, and the National Banking Act, which empowered federally chartered banks to issue banknotes based on their holdings of U.S. bonds. But the party had always harbored a largely western agrarian and producerist minority that favored more permissive monetary policies. In the postwar years this group grew more vocal. They still distrusted the national banking system and the eastern bondholders who profited from it, but they now embraced greenbacks as the government-issued currency best designed to protect the interests of "the people," especially debtors and farmers, against the rich. This notion took form in the so-called Ohio Idea, advocated most notably by the party's 1864 vice presidential nominee, George H. Pendleton of Ohio, which called for the government to pay U.S. bonds with greenbacks rather than gold. In 1868 the Democratic national convention endorsed the idea in its platform but rejected Pendleton's presidential candidacy in favor of hard-money advocate Horatio Seymour of New York. The spectacle of the financially orthodox Seymour running on an essentially inflationist platform symbolized the division—largely along geographic lines—that plagued the Democrats' approach to the currency question for years to come.[40]

During the 1870s debate regarding paper currency turned mainly on the question of when and how the government should proceed to pay coin for the greenbacks. In 1875 the Republican Congress passed the Specie Resumption Act, stipulating January 1, 1879, as the day for specie payments to begin. Soft-money Democrats labored for repeal of the measure, but their efforts were opposed by hard-money Democrats who, despite misgivings about this specific legislation, favored resumption. The Treasury successfully resumed specie payments in early 1879. In addition, the 1870s witnessed the rise of the silver question, which also divided Democrats. In early 1873 Congress removed the silver dollar from the government's coinage list, but hard times in the wake of the financial panic later that year fueled calls for the "remonetization" of silver. Western Democrats such as Missouri Congressman Richard Bland led this effort, taking as their goal the unlimited coinage of silver at a ratio of sixteen to one with gold. Inflationists of both parties secured House passage of such a bill in late 1877, but in February 1878 hard-money Senate Democrats joined their counterparts in the Republican Party to limit such coinage to $2 million to $4 million per month. The resulting Bland-Allison Act did not satisfy soft-money Democrats, who continued to advocate free coinage. They failed, however, to undo what had emerged as a reasonably stable monetary structure that comprised gold coin, limited silver coin, a finite volume of greenbacks backed by an adequate specie reserve, and national banknotes.[41]

With this quasi-settlement of the money question in place, the return of prosperity at the end of the 1870s momentarily robbed the issue of much of its impact in the early 1880s. In 1884 the conservatives in control of the Democratic convention secured approval of a platform plank supporting "honest money, the gold and silver coinage of the Constitution, and a circulating medium convertible into such money without loss." The Republican platform contained an equally brief reference to the question. Cleveland saw no need to push the issue in his campaign and ignored it in his few brief speeches.[42]

On the eve of his inauguration, however, hard-money supporters forced the silver question once again into public view. Outgoing Republican Treasury Secretary Hugh McCulloch warned that the government's acceptance of silver in payment of customs duties, coupled with its practice of using only gold to meet its principal obligations, had led to a declining gold reserve in the Treasury, which could eventually jeopardize the redemption of greenbacks and subvert the gold standard. Although the decline stemmed in part from an economic downturn and changes in tariff legislation, McCulloch insisted that the remedy was to suspend silver coinage. Hard-money Democrats agreed, introduced a suspension measure in Congress, and urged President-elect Cleveland to endorse it. From the party's opposite end, however, ninety-five House members claimed that two-thirds of Democratic representatives opposed demonetization of silver and entreated Cleveland not to adopt that policy. Thus pressed by both sides, Cleveland showed his hand. Enlisting the help of ultra-hard-money journalist Manton Marble in drafting his response, Cleveland called for "a present suspension of the purchase and coinage of silver" as the only way "to prevent the increasing displacement of gold." Otherwise, hoarding of gold would lead to contraction, depression, and "prolonged and disastrous trouble." These dire admonitions availed nothing, however, for two days later the House killed the silver suspension measure, with Democrats voting two to one against it. Thus, even before Cleveland took office, as Senator Benjamin Harrison observed, his "silver letter has produced a wide and bitter break in his party in Congress."[43]

The ensuing four years did not close the breach. Cleveland retreated to generalities on the issue in his inaugural address, but in his first annual message in December 1885 he again called for suspension of silver coinage under the Bland-Allison Act. Silver bills inundated Congress, some calling for suspension and others demanding free coinage. None had any chance of passage. A vote in the House on a free-coinage bill in the spring of 1886 showed Democrats in favor, 98 to 70, thus illustrating the Democrats' persistent division as well as the unwillingness of many to follow Cleveland on the issue. In his second annual message, Cleveland again recommended a cessation of silver coinage, but as the *New York Commercial and Financial Chronicle* predicted, what he had to say "about the white metal will have just as much influence on Congress as it will have on the inhabitant of the moon." An upturn in the nation's economy defused the inflationists' threat, but clearly, Cleveland could not look to the money question as an issue around which to rally his party for his bid for a second term.[44]

Foreign affairs played a minor role in the first three years of Grover Cleveland's administration; hence at the dawn of the election campaign of 1888, he had not compiled a record of noteworthy energy or achievement to present to the electorate. He gave priority to domestic concerns and never articulated a grand design or strategy in international relations. To head the State Department, he chose the moralistic, lawyerly, and unjingoistic Thomas F. Bayard, whom he had defeated in the 1884 convention. Like all nineteenth-century politicians, Cleveland believed in the sanctity of the Monroe Doctrine, and picking up on the program of the previous Republican administration, he worked with Congress to fund an expansion of the navy. Yet he terminated the Republicans' efforts to obtain reciprocal trade agreements with Latin American nations, and he killed a treaty with Nicaragua for exclusive U.S. rights over a prospective canal through that country. On the sensitive issue of Chinese immigration, he instructed Bayard to work for a new restrictive treaty with the Chinese government. Similarly, when controversies arose over the rights of American fishermen in Canadian waters and of Canadian fur sealers in the waters off Alaska, Cleveland sought diplomatic solutions with Great Britain, which managed Canada's foreign relations. Only after the presidential election year was at hand did Cleveland begin to pursue these matters vigorously, with an eye to the political potential of a more robust conduct of foreign policy.[45]

A WINNING ISSUE?

As the fall of 1887 approached, Cleveland and his allies had reason to worry about their chances for gaining another four years in power. They needed an issue that would galvanize Democrats and allow the president to present a coherent and attractive alternative to the Republican economic program. As they surveyed the field of battle for the next year's election, they came to believe that the party's brightest prospects lay in raising the accustomed banner under which a majority of Democrats (though not all) had linked arms and marched for decades: a reduction of the tariff. This seemingly bland issue held the potential to appeal to a wide spectrum of interests: farmers who resented high prices on manufactured goods, commercial interests in New York and other cities who would profit from freer trade, factory owners who sought lower duties on the raw materials they purchased abroad, liberal reformers in whose creed free trade stood as a fundamental principle, white southerners who had for decades regarded a low tariff as an article of faith, and, indeed, all American consumers who wanted lower prices. Moreover, Democratic strategists believed that "tariff reform" would appeal to Americans as taxpayers who resented the large surpluses of tariff-generated revenue piled up in the Treasury and withdrawn from the currents of trade. On this last point, the evidence seemed unmistakable. The federal government had run an unbroken string of surpluses for more than twenty years, reaching as high as $145 million in 1882 and projected to exceed $100 million for fiscal year 1888, or 30 percent of total receipts.[46]

And yet the fate of tariff revision thus far in Cleveland's presidency suggested that the issue did not guarantee surefire success in the coming reelection campaign. Cleveland had alluded to the tariff briefly in his inaugural address and at greater length in his first annual message. In December 1885 he argued that taxation should be "scrupulously limited to the actual necessity of expenditure," although adjustments to import duties should be so devised that American industries would "not be ruthlessly injured or destroyed." In the spring of 1886 the House Ways and Means Committee prepared a bill for substantial tariff reductions, and the president lobbied wavering representatives on its behalf. Nonetheless, the House refused to take the bill up for consideration, by a vote of 140 to 157. Standing by the president and the committee were 135 Democrats, but 35 protectionist Democrats, led by former Speaker

Samuel J. Randall of Pennsylvania, joined the Republicans in killing the bill. Randall, who had represented a Philadelphia manufacturing district for more than twenty years, offered his own bill, which lowered some import duties but called for three times as much revenue reduction by cutting or eliminating internal taxes. The Ways and Means Committee reported Randall's bill adversely, and it went nowhere. Although tariff discussions figured largely in the off-year elections in 1886, the outcome offered no clear verdict on that question or on the administration generally: Democrats lost more than a dozen seats in the House but gained three in the Senate, thereby reducing the Republicans' majority in the upper chamber to two. When the lame-duck second session of the Forty-ninth Congress convened in December, Cleveland again called for tariff reduction in a longer and more pointed passage than in his 1885 message. Still, the House refused to consider the reduction bill, with Randall and twenty-five other Democrats continuing to defy the president.[47]

In his 1886 message Cleveland warned that without revision to the revenue laws, the nation would soon "be confronted with a vast quantity of money, the circulating medium of the people, hoarded in the Treasury when it should be in their hands." Matters reached a crisis of sorts the following summer when the country's money markets suffered a severe stringency that threatened to spark a general panic. The Treasury Department responded by redeeming mature bonds and making advance payments of interest on others, thereby pumping money into the economy. But this action was a temporary expedient, not a permanent solution. Moreover, the stock of mature bonds was soon exhausted, and any further redemption would require the government to purchase these securities at a substantial premium. "It does not seem wise," Treasury Secretary Charles S. Fairchild observed, "to continue taxation beyond the ordinary needs of Government, and then resort to the buying of bonds for the mere purpose of redistributing the circulating media among the people."[48]

The Treasury operations relieved the scarcity of cash somewhat, but the episode confirmed Cleveland's determination to insist on tariff reduction. In September 1887 he held a series of conferences at Oak View, his summer home in northwest Washington, D.C., with Fairchild (who had succeeded the deceased Manning), House Speaker John G. Carlisle of Kentucky, incoming Ways and Means chairman Roger Q. Mills of Texas, and William L. Scott, a wealthy businessman who represented the Erie, Pennsylvania, district in the House and was one of the president's closest congressional advisers. Conspicuously absent was Samuel Randall. Cleveland and his allies aimed not to conciliate the party's protectionists but to overawe them in a drive to make tariff reduction the centerpiece of the administration's legislative agenda and the primary focus of the president's reelection campaign. Carlisle was convinced, as he had written to Cleveland, that "a failure to reduce the revenues at the next session will . . . be fatal to the party, as well as injurious to the country." Cleveland even contemplated calling the new Fiftieth Congress into special session but decided to wait until the regular session in December to allow time to consolidate opinion among congressional Democrats. In the meantime, Carlisle and Mills began to prepare a suitable bill, and Scott outlined a program to urge key party leaders in such states as New Jersey, North Carolina, and Virginia to work on recreant members from those states. "We have got to take Mr. Randall by a flank movement," Scott wrote to Cleveland, "and if possible draw his supporters from him one by one."[49]

In the absence of sophisticated polling developed in the twentieth century, political leaders in the nineteenth century often used state and local elections both to gauge and to mold public opinion regarding party policies and actions. Cleveland and his allies tested their tariff project in the elections held during the fall of 1887, particularly in the president's home state, whose support would be central to his reelection. A few weeks after the Oak View conferences, the New York Democratic state convention adopted a platform that opened with a strongly worded plank that decried unnecessary taxation as "unjust taxation" and "demand[ed] that Federal taxation be straightway reduced by a sum not less than $100,000,000 a year." In the words of the *New York Times*, the platform exerted "a very wholesome effect upon the party in other States and upon the party leaders who are likely to determine the policy of the majority in Congress." For their part, New York Republicans acknowledged the need for tariff adjustments but insisted that they be made "in the interest of protection" and not by "free-trade propagandists." Although the state offices at stake had nothing to do with the tariff, the issue loomed large in the ensuing campaign.[50]

Cleveland made no campaign speeches in 1887, either for candidates or for the tariff project. In midsummer he took a vacation trip to towns where he had lived as a boy in upstate New York. More important, in the fall he took a three-week trip through the West as far as Omaha and back through several cities in the South. In keeping with the dignity of his office, the speeches he gave were nonpolitical and often mere recitations of the virtues of the places he visited, apparently lifted from an encyclopedia. His aim was not to win converts to a policy but to build a personal relationship with the people. He immeasurably enhanced his chances of gaining their esteem by taking along the beautiful twenty-three-year-old Frances "Frankie" Cleveland, whom he had married in the White House the previous year. The trip won Cleveland extensive daily press coverage and, according to the *New York Times,* deepened his fellow citizens' impression of his "trustworthiness." It did not, however, silence Samuel Randall, who treated Atlanta to a rousing protectionist speech a week before the president's visit to the city.[51]

Whatever impact Cleveland made with this tour, his deepest political concern focused on the election in New York. So eager was he for a good showing by Democrats that he bowed to Tammany pressure and publicly endorsed the Hall's unsavory candidate for district attorney—John R. Fellows, a known gambler and former associate of Boss Tweed—over a reformer backed by independent Democrats and Republicans. The endorsement shocked Mugwumps such as Carl Schurz, who thought Cleveland had sacrificed "the high dignity of his office" on behalf of a "dead beat" politician. But the move galvanized the braves, many of whom assured the White House that it had turned the tide in the Democrats' favor. "Nothing that the President has done," one wrote to the White House, "has pleased 'Old fashioned Democrats' like myself as his letter in favor of Col. Fellows & our whole ticket." Fellows won a decisive victory, as did the entire Democratic state ticket.[52]

The Fellows business notwithstanding, Cleveland's allies viewed the New York outcome as a triumph for their chief and a ringing endorsement of his reelection. Navy Secretary Whitney wired Cleveland that the victory represented "a strong undercurrent." From Indiana, William H. English, the party's vice presidential nominee in 1880, wrote that the "glorious victory" in New York "has probably determined, and wisely determined, the political character of the Government for many years to come." "The political outlook never seemed so auspicious," upstate editor Henry Stowell wrote to Cleveland's secretary and political adviser, Daniel Lamont. "Democrats everywhere are jubilant, because they realize its effect upon the canvass next fall." As the *New York Times* reminded its readers, the state party had "committed itself boldly to the revenue reform policy of the Administration." Now the election outcome indicated "plainly that Mr. Cleveland, as the Democratic candidate for President, would carry the State of New-York with ease and certainty," making his national victory "equally assured."[53]

Buoyed by these results, Cleveland set about preparing his third annual message, due for delivery to Congress in early December. He quickly decided to devote the entire paper to the tariff and surplus to make the issue "very prominent." Although his mind was fairly set, he received abundant advice, some of which he had solicited and a good deal he had not. Carlisle and Mills welcomed the emphasis as a boost to their legislative efforts in the coming session. Henry Watterson, editor of the *Louisville Courier-Journal* and one of the nation's strongest voices for freer trade, hailed the opportunity to underscore the Democratic Party's longtime commitment "to the reduction of the war tariff." John P. Townsend, a founder of the New York Free Trade Club, wrote to Cleveland that the recent election victories demonstrated that tariff reformers had "a good fighting case" on which to "make an open fight" in 1888. "Is it not good politics to commit the Democratic party now on this side[?]"[54]

But the counsel was far from unanimous. Speaking for many skeptical party members, former Governor George Hoadly of Ohio answered the president's call for his opinion with a frank admonition that if Cleveland followed Watterson's advice, "success would be converted into defeat." In the recent Ohio elections, the two parties had squared off against each other on tariff planks similar to those issued in New York, but the Ohio Democrats had lost by a margin wider than that by which the New York Democrats had won. The defeated candidate for governor reported to Cleveland that the labor vote had "hurt us in all the cities." Hence, Hoadly cautioned against "alienating large bodies of workmen, whose ignorance is crass, who are thoroughly organized, and whose employers are extremely jealous of any danger of loss of profits." He agreed with Cleveland about the tariff but warned that "it takes time for our countrymen to recover from a blow, and the danger is that thousands of them will be swept off their intellectual bearings for a period long enough to endanger the results of the next Presidential election."[55] The president also consulted prominent Philadelphia publisher A. K. Mc-Clure, who similarly noted that "we have strong prejudices to combat" and urged Cleveland to "open the way for the support of the protection Democrats & for the acceptance of a new tariff bill without apprehension in business circles." McClure hoped in particular to conciliate his townsman Randall, though with little prospect for success. While Cleveland labored over his message, Randall worked behind the scenes with iron and steel industry lobbyist James M. Swank to assemble a list of House Democrats who might be persuaded to stand by protection.[56]

Despite the widespread press speculation about what Cleveland planned to say, his December 6 message had a stunning effect. He paid scant attention to the warnings of Hoadly and others and, leaving all other questions aside, presented a vigorous statement of the necessity for tariff reduction. He began by outlining the dangers incumbent in the burgeoning Treasury surplus, recounting the Treasury's operations to avert the "absolute peril" of the recent monetary stringency. In the absence of any additional matured bonds to be redeemed, he rejected more bond purchases as too expensive and resting on dubious statutory authority. Increased expenditures to relieve the Treasury glut were also out of the question, being marks of "reckless improvidence" and "the demoralization of all just conceptions of public duty." Indeed, one of the great evils of the surplus was its invitation to "schemes of public plunder." The only acceptable solution was a reduction of revenue derived from either import duties or internal levies on tobacco and alcohol. He saw no justification for cutting the internal duties on these latter items, which were not, "strictly speaking, necessaries." Instead, he declared, "our present tariff laws, the vicious, inequitable, and illogical source of unnecessary taxation, ought to be at once revised and amended."

Besides the monetary implications of the present high tariff, Cleveland insisted that it unfairly burdened consumers with high prices not only on imported goods but on competing domestic products as well. The government should give due care to preserving American manufacturers, he conceded, but they did not deserve tariff rates "which, without regard to the public welfare or a national exigency, must always insure the realization of immense profits instead of moderately profitable returns." Labor was entitled to its "full share of all our advantages," but, he claimed, employees in protected industries constituted less than 15 percent of the workforce, and they should "not overlook the fact that they are consumers with the rest." He particularly appealed to farmers as buyers of manufactured goods. He singled out sheep farmers (a strong interest group in favor of maintaining high rates on wool), noting that notwithstanding the enhanced income for their clips, the tariff on finished products required them, like everyone else, to pay high prices on woolen goods. In addition, Cleveland voiced the popular notion that a high tariff fostered trusts, which allegedly also maintained artificially high prices. Cleveland insisted that he did not mean that manufacturing interests should "forgo all the benefits of governmental regard," but he reminded them that if the dangerous condition of the nation's revenue was not corrected, "financial panic and collapse" would "afford no greater shelter or protection to our manufacturers than to other important enterprises."

Without offering specific rates, the president outlined a general approach for reduction. Congress should eliminate duties on articles that did not compete with American products. Duties on luxuries, which presented "no features of hardship," could remain. Levies on necessaries should be "greatly cheapened." Further, he advocated cutting or eliminating duties on raw materials, which would reduce the prices of finished goods, making them more accessible to domestic buyers and more attractive in markets overseas. Cleveland knew full well the controversy his message would ignite, but he gamely (and vainly) sought to place it in a nonideological framework:

> Our progress toward a wise conclusion will not be improved by dwelling upon the theories of protection and free trade. This savors too much of bandying epithets. It is a *condition* which confronts us, not a theory. . . . The question of free trade is absolutely irrelevant, and the persistent claim made in certain quarters that all the efforts to relieve the people from unjust and unnecessary taxation are schemes of so-called free-traders is mischievous and far removed from any consideration for the public good.[57]

Cleveland's message was technically a report to Congress and a recommendation for legislation, but the kind of measure he proposed had virtually no chance of passing the Republican-held Senate. More important, the message was the opening gun of the campaign of 1888, during which Cleveland hoped to win a second term and carry with him a Congress in tune with his conception of the nation's interest.

Among observers inclined to agree with Cleveland, the reaction was electric. In a letter to the president, Henry Watterson exulted that the message was "of a piece with all I have written on the subject." Henry George sent congratulations, and Brooklyn reformer R. R. Bowker called the message "a superb stroke of the genius of common sense." The Mugwump journal the *Nation* labeled it "the most courageous document that has been sent from the Executive Mansion since the close of

Grover Cleveland. (Library of Congress)

the war." Arkansas Congressman C. R. Breckinridge assured Cleveland that his words would "instruct all classes of people . . . in the hut as well as in the mansion." Secretary Whitney, who had previously questioned the timing of the move, reported from New York that it was "looked upon by every one as a conscientious & courageous thing & splendidly executed." "Further than that," Whitney added, "it looks as though it was a winning issue."[58]

But Republicans were more than eager to pick up the gauntlet Cleveland had thrown down. The next day a cabled abstract reached Paris, where James G. Blaine was stopping during an extended European tour. The titular leader of the Republican Party wasted no time in presenting his reaction. He did so in an "interview" with the New York Tribune, for which he himself wrote the questions as well as the answers. Never shy about twisting the English lion's tail, Blaine noted that the British press welcomed the president's message as "a free trade manifesto" that promised "an enlarged market" for British goods in America. In response, he defended tariff protection as a great boon to Americans, especially to labor, including the producers of raw materials. Should import duties be slashed, he said, workers in factories would lose their jobs and be forced to become "tillers of the soil," in competition with existing farmers for a shrinking urban market for their produce. In direct contrast with Cleveland, Blaine regarded wool growers as an interest "we should earnestly encourage." He also warned that injury to the "home trade in raw materials" would cripple the railroads, and as a consequence, "the financial fabric of the whole country will feel it quickly and seriously."

To reduce the revenue, Blaine proposed eliminating the tax on tobacco, thereby appealing at once to southern growers and to the millions of workers nationwide who considered tobacco a necessity, not a luxury. He would leave the alcohol tax in place, principally because of the "moral side" of the issue. (Blaine was an avid analyst of election statistics. In the recent election in New York, the Prohibition Party had garnered nearly 42,000 votes, more than twice the margin by which the Democrats had surpassed the Republicans. The vast majority of Prohibition votes had come from Republican defectors.) With an eye to temperance advocates, Blaine warned that repealing the whiskey tax would undermine local and state efforts at control, such as high license. Whiskey, he said, had "done a vast deal of harm." He "would try to make it do some good" by using the tax revenue to build needed coastal defenses. Such construction projects would not only do a "great service to the country"; they would also "give good work to many men."

But it was the defense of protectionism that Blaine most wished to stress. Taking aim at Cleveland's base, he said that the southern states "above all sections" stood to gain by developing their "enormous resources. . . . They cannot do anything without protection." He conceded that increased foreign trade was desirable but insisted that it was "vastly more important not to lose our own great market for our own people in the vain effort to reach the impossible." What the president's message showed more than anything, he solemnly concluded, was that "the Democratic party in power is a standing menace to the industrial prosperity of the country."[59]

The press accorded Blaine's interview as much attention as it had given Cleveland's message. Indeed, Republicans regarded the statement as virtually the pronouncement of a government-in-waiting. "That is a magnificent document you print today," John Hay wrote to the *Tribune*'s owner, Whitelaw Reid. "What a tremendous contrast between the penny-cracker of the man inside, and the roar, as of great guns, from the man outside. If brains were votes, how easy our battle would be." On the editorial page, the *Tribune* spoke of "the weakness and unsoundness of Mr. Cleveland's arguments in favor of free trade" compared with Blaine's "characteristic boldness" in offering "suggestions which are full of originality and practical statesmanship." The *Iowa State Register* of Des Moines averred that Blaine's "interview will be more widely read than the message and will carry a strong and convincing answer to the dangerous doctrines which Mr. Cleveland has put before the country."[60]

Cleveland's message and Blaine's response appeared to herald a rematch of their 1884 fight. But both men seemed determined to avert a replay of the scandalfest of that year and offer the American people a clear choice of policies regarding their economic well-being. "If the Democrats adopt the recommendations of the message, what will be the result?" asked New York Republican Party boss Thomas C. Platt. "Probably a tariff fight next year. That is what I hope to see." Michigan Congressman Julius Burrows said that Cleveland's report was "as good a campaign document for the republicans as we could wish. He has presented the issue in excellent shape, and upon that basis we shall be glad to meet him." As a result of the message, Wisconsin Republican Senator John C. Spooner assured a constituent, "our chances for carrying the country are infinitely better than they were a month ago."[61]

Republicans generally shared this glee, for the message had done more to unite Republicans than Democrats. Indeed, many Democrats agreed with Spooner that the president had in fact squandered the bright prospects that the recent electoral victories had generated for his party. "Our fat friend at the White House has settled his own hash for 1888," a Pennsylvania Democrat wrote to Randall. "I hope he will be nominated so that no worthy Democrat may have to take the defeat he so well deserves and has rendered inevitable." Representative Randall told reporters that Congress would move to reduce taxation by $60 million or more, "but not on the exact line of the President's suggestions." Some decrease would come through cuts in import duties, but a "large part of this reduction will be in the repeal of internal taxes which the President does not seem to favor." Like Blaine, Randall would eliminate the tobacco tax, but he would also reduce taxation on some distilled spirits. Similarly, respected Virginia Senator John W. Daniel believed that Cleveland had erred in not calling for a cut in internal levies. "Consumers are not alone to be considered in tax reduction," Daniel told reporters. "Planters and producers are as much entitled to regard." Randall and Daniel represented a minority among Democrats in Congress, but a minority large enough to play havoc with Cleveland's hopes for a united front. As Kentucky representative James B. McCreary observed, "There is a contrariety of views among the members of the party, each wedded to his own, and so long as this spirit is maintained the wise words of the President will be unheeded." Among Democratic newspapers, Cleveland's severest critic was Charles A. Dana's *New York Sun,* which charged that Cleveland had presented "precisely that sort of an argument" as would be expected of "the author of any free trade textbook," and for that reason he had received the "hearty approbation of free traders and free trade journals, and of those alone."[62]

Cleveland was deeply disturbed that the *Sun* and others were "bandying" the very epithet he had hoped to avoid. Less than a week after submitting the message, he sat down to write a response—in the same form Blaine had used, a feigned interview with a reporter—to rebut his opponents' efforts "to brand the message as a Free Trade document." He told his phantom interlocutor that "a careful reading of the message would fail to sustain the interpretation put upon it by those who willfully misrepresent it." His purpose, he avowed, was to urge Congress to "reduce the taxes, to stop discussing abstract theories and fighting men of straw, and to deal promptly with the situation *as it exists.*" Cleveland labored over this "interview" through at least two drafts but apparently never used it.[63] Instead, the White House told reporters that the president's daily mailbag was filled with letters of support. Cleveland grew even more discouraged at reports of slim prospects for speedy action on the question in Congress. "The longer the low-tariff men have hesitated," said the *New York Times*, "the weaker they have seemed to become." The *Sun* predicted that "a measure based upon the recent recommendations of the President would be absolutely certain to fail in Congress."[64]

Twelve days after the message, the frustrated president confessed to Secretary of State Bayard, "I am fearful almost to conviction that our people in Congress will so botch and blunder upon the tariff question that all the benefit of the stand already taken will not be realized." Hence, Cleveland pressed Bayard to expedite treaty negotiations with China to stop the illegal immigration of Chinese workers. His purpose was frankly political: "The present condition should be remedied, or an attempt in that direction made at once and by us—that is *our party*. . . . If my fears [about the tariff] should appear to be well founded, a proper movement upon the Chinese question would furnish a compensation in the way of another string to our bow. And the quicker something in this direction is done the better."[65]

While Bayard proceeded to act on the Chinese question, tariff matters moved slowly. After a prolonged disputed election contest, Speaker Carlisle announced the House standing committees in January. To head the Ways and Means Committee, whose job it was to prepare a tariff bill, he selected Roger Q. Mills of Texas. Mills had attended Cleveland's Oak View conferences and was one of the Democratic Party's foremost advocates of tariff reduction. Although the chairman had already drafted legislation, he and the like-minded Democratic majority on the committee took three months to hammer out a detailed bill, which they did not introduce until early April.[66]

BUMPS IN THE ROAD TO RENOMINATION

Although Cleveland encountered opposition to his plan to make tariff reform the centerpiece of his reelection campaign, he had little to fear about his chances for renomination. Few Democrats showed much disposition to reject the only man they had placed in the White House since 1856. Of the two main groups that might act on their disenchantment with Cleveland, neither had more than an extremely remote chance of blocking his renomination: protectionist Democrats who opposed the doctrine of the annual message, and machine-oriented men who believed Cleveland had toyed too long with civil service reform and then had delivered too little patronage when he stopped. The favorite of the first group was Randall; New York Governor David B. Hill curried favor among the latter. Neither had any real hope of unseating Cleveland, but the manner in which the president and his allies squelched these potential challenges fueled a deep resentment that haunted Cleveland's campaign in the fall.

Randall was the beau ideal of those Democrats who believed that the president had gone too far in his December message. "The disfavor with which the message is received by farmers and workingmen," a former House colleague from Ohio wrote to Randall, "shows that Mr. Cleveland cannot be nominated unless it be to invite defeat." But this view reflected frustration more than clear analysis, as Randall well knew. The Cleveland forces knew it too, but they were nonetheless determined to undermine Randall's stature in the party and minimize his power to interfere with their tariff plans. At a meeting of the Pennsylvania Democratic State Committee in January, Congressman William L. Scott, aided by the distribution of administration favors, wrested control of the state party organization from Randall. Scott installed a Cleveland ally as state chairman and secured passage of a resolution endorsing the president's reelection and specifically commending his tariff message. This was overkill and served only to stiffen Randall's resolve. "I am governed by my own convictions maturely formed and honestly maintained," Randall told reporters. "My vote never has been and never will be controlled by the vote of a State Committee." Randall prepared and introduced his own tariff bill, providing a rallying point of opposition to Cleveland and discouraging the closing of ranks through compromise. Crushing Randall's influence in his home state did little to hurt Cleveland's chances in that state, which was reliably Republican. But roughing up the congressman weakened the president's bid for support among protectionist Democrats elsewhere, most critically in northeastern doubtful states. One Pennsylvania Democratic county chairman pleaded with the White House to "treat Mr. Randall with every consideration as he has strength in New York and New Jersey which the administration will need." Nonetheless, at the Pennsylvania state convention in May, Scott's forces blocked a compromise plank on the tariff and even expelled several Randall delegates from the hall.[67]

The president's troubles with Governor Hill were of a different sort, although Cleveland's response was much the same. Hill had been Cleveland's running mate on the state ticket in 1882 and had succeeded to the governorship when Cleveland ascended to the presidency in 1885. Later that year Hill had won election in his own right, and in 1888 he would be up for reelection. The two New York leaders were cut from different cloth. Both were committed Democratic partisans, but whereas Cleveland tried to project an image of rising above mere partisanship, Hill wore his party colors with unabashed devotion. He adopted the practice of beginning each political speech he made with the proud declaration, "I am a Democrat," which carried an implicit condemnation of Cleveland's dalliance with Mugwumps and civil service reformers. Hill was, of course, anathema to these latter groups, and Cleveland himself considered the governor "a whelp, personally and politically." But among some machine Democrats in New York and elsewhere who seethed over perceived patronage slights by Cleveland, Hill seemed an attractive candidate to replace the sanctimonious president on the ticket in 1888. Hill's supporters argued that New York was indispensable to victory in 1888, and in light of the baggage that weighed Cleveland down, Hill was likelier to deliver the state for the Democrats. Hill himself occasionally took leave of his otherwise hardheaded political sense and fantasized that he might take the nomination away from the president.[68]

Machinations on Hill's behalf did not catch Cleveland unawares. When the administration began to use patronage to strengthen its position, it tilted in New York State against the governor's minions. In August 1887 the factions squared off in a contest to fill a vacancy on the party's state committee, and the Cleveland forces prevailed by a vote of 18 to 13. After that, Hill's long-shot chance at the presidential nomination seemed dead, but the president's tariff message gave it new life. Cleveland's factional opponents were joined by some Democrats who thought the tariff stance hurt the party's chances and necessitated the selection of another standard-bearer in 1888. As the new year opened, Cleveland was "quite fully convinced that schemes are on foot for an anti-Administration control in New York," and he instructed his friends that "a move ought to be made towards organization for the sake of the best interests of the party." Hill's threat was apparent at a meeting of the state committee called in late January to elect the New York member of the national committee. More than thirty ballots could not break a 17–17 deadlock between the forces of Cleveland and those of Hill. Wishing to avoid further evidence of opposition, Cleveland and his advisers decided to let the national committee fill the vacancy and finally succeeded in getting their own man in.[69]

Buoyed by the state committee vote, Hill allowed his opposition to Cleveland to become more open. In a Brooklyn speech honoring the memory of Samuel J. Tilden, the governor praised the late New York leader for never assuming "to be better than his party" or forgetting "the obligations which he owed it." In contrast, Hill gave a pallid endorsement of Cleveland's administration as "in the main satisfactory." In a thinly veiled swipe at Cleveland's tariff message, he declared, "We all stand upon the National Democratic platform of 1884, and until the party makes another platform we will adhere to the principles there enunciated." In addition, Dana's *New York Sun* reminded its readers of Cleveland's 1884 "self-declared platform in favor of the single-term idea," which, the paper charged, he was "now preparing to repudiate for the sake of personal ambition."[70]

All this was too much for Cleveland. He considered the state committee tie vote a "fiasco" and was deeply annoyed by Hill's subsequent activities. "I confess," he wrote to a friend, "I cannot quite keep my temper when I learn of the mean and low attempts that are made by underhand means to endanger the results to which I am devoted." He and his advisers stepped up the pressure on their lieutenants in New York to shore up their sagging lines and challenge the Hill men more aggressively.[71] When another state committee vote—this time to select the site of the state convention—showed the success of this new assertiveness by the Cleveland men, Hill moved toward an accommodation. Through an intermediary, he offered to go to the party's national convention in St. Louis at the head of the New York delegation in the president's behalf. Cleveland refused. He could not afford to give the impression that he held New York's support by the grace of David B. Hill. Moreover, if Cleveland should encounter some hitch in the balloting, he did not want Hill to be on hand to capture the attention of straying delegates, as James A. Garfield had done at the Republican convention in 1880. The Cleveland men cracked the whip and kept Hill off the delegation altogether.[72] Once again, as in the treatment of Randall, this was overkill. The pro-Cleveland *New York Times* called Hill's exclusion an "absolute defeat and repudiation by his party," while the *Sun* said that Cleveland had trampled the governor "under his feet." Happy to pour salt on the wounds, the Republican *Tribune* likened the whole episode to "a public flogging." The vengeful Hill would not forget this public humiliation.[73]

THE MILLS BILL

While this drama in New York unfolded in the winter and spring, other states lined up behind Cleveland's renomination. Even so, the president continued to receive warnings about the political risks raised by his tariff stance. Smith Weed, a party strategist and longtime Tilden adviser, warned Lamont that northeastern manufacturers who had been "favorably disposed" toward Cleveland were "terribly stirred up by the message," and the question now was "how to quiet that feeling." Lamont frankly admitted to Weed that Cleveland "regrets that he did not talk with you about the tariff" before issuing the document. Perhaps most telling was the outcome of the spring state elections in Rhode Island, where incumbent Democratic Governor John W. Davis lost his bid for reelection. The state convention had adopted a platform that was, in essence, a synopsis of Cleveland's message, and its impact was fatal. "Able orators were imported into the State," Davis reported to Cleveland, "and 'revenue reform' as advocated by us was denounced as 'free trade' which mill operatives and others have . . . learned to look upon as predetermined ruin to them." Davis lost by 8 percentage points.[74]

The preliminary handling of the revenue reduction measure—the Mills bill—by the Ways and Means Committee did not help matters. Early in the year Mills laid his draft before the committee. The majority Democrats refused to hold hearings, and they also barred the committee's Republicans from the meetings where they perfected the measure, often in consultation with tariff reformers such as R. R. Bowker, David A. Wells, and Edward Atkinson. On one occasion Samuel Randall attended a dinner with committee members and wound up getting into a shouting match with William Scott. Randall dismissed Mills's panel as a "one horse committee" uninterested in the views of labor. The closed-door proceedings only added to the resulting bill's vulnerability, opening the way for critics to depict it as the product of secret machinations in which Mills and his colleagues were in the thrall of free-trade theorists.[75]

In early March Mills presented the bill to the whole committee and to the press, and a month later he formally introduced it in the House. The bill was not quite the campaign document Cleveland might have desired. Its authors claimed that it would reduce the revenue by some

$78 million. Of this sum, $24 million would come from cutting internal taxes through the elimination of levies on some forms of tobacco and on fruit-based brandies. This provision directly contravened Cleveland's December recommendation, but it did not go far enough to satisfy either Randall or the Republicans. The remainder of the reduction would come from expansion of the list of duty-free imports ($22 million) and a decrease in the rates on other items ($32 million). The most remarkable aspect of the tariff section of the bill was its clear sectional tilt. Including Mills (from Texas), six of the eight Democrats on the Ways and Means Committee represented southern states, and they showed a keen solicitude for the interests of their constituents. Should the bill become law, there would be no change or only minor reductions in customs duties on foreign commodities that competed with southern products such as sugar, iron ore, bituminous coal, tobacco, and rice. In contrast, items that southerners used were slated for substantial cuts. For instance, the bill would reduce the duty on hemp bagging for cotton by 75 percent and eliminate altogether the levy on metal ties for cotton bales. Northern manufacturers generally faced larger reductions on such commodities as glassware, crockery, woolens, paper, tinplate, steel rails, and other metal products. Midwesterners encountered similar cuts or abolition of duties on lumber, salt, hemp, and flax. In one of its most controversial provisions, the bill put wool on the free list.[76]

With an overall average rate reduction of 7 percent, the bill seemed far from drastic, but the steep reduction or elimination of duties on some key commodities provided ample ammunition for Republicans and others who wished to tar it with the "free-trade" brush. "I am glad that it is as bad as it is," James Swank of the Iron and Steel Association confided to Randall; a bill that would "only moderately reduce duties" would be harder to defeat. Representative William McKinley of Ohio, a member of the Ways and Means Committee, described the bill as "but the beginning of a tariff policy marked out by the President," to be followed by further legislation to put the tariff "on a purely revenue basis," which, in its effect on American industry, would be tantamount to free trade. More colorfully, Julius Burrows of Michigan, McKinley's colleague on the committee, labeled the bill a "'lump of deformity' . . . adopted by the Democratic party and nursed by the harlot of free trade." Focusing on the bill's sectional bias, the venerable William D. "Pig Iron" Kelley, the committee's ranking Republican and Randall's Philadelphia colleague, called the measure "an anachronism" whose provisions "would have been nicely adapted to the era during which the exigencies of slavery demanded the maintenance of free foreign trade and the repression of mining and manufacturing throughout our broad domain." When Mills introduced the bill, the *New York Tribune* predicted that "within forty-eight hours half of the Democratic members will be frightened by passionate protests from constituents, whose industries Mr. Mills proposes to prostrate or destroy." In fact, however, most of Mills's colleagues defended the measure in marathon sessions from mid-April to mid-July, in what became known as the Great Tariff Debate of 1888.[77]

As discussion of the Mills bill took center stage both in Congress and in the nation at large, doubts about the political utility of the tariff strategy continued to plague the Cleveland camp. Some worried Democrats thought that Cleveland should intervene to derail the Mills bill, and Weed urged him to choose a running mate who was not "ultra on tariff." The president still met with reformers such as Wells and Atkinson and found their company and advice "always improving." Yet by mid-April he conceded that he would be willing to accept a "modification" of the internal tobacco tax, a means of revenue reduction he had opposed in his message. He made that concession privately, however, fearful that any public statement "explaining my message to Congress . . . would now be greatly misrepresented and misconstrued, and might do more harm than good."[78]

Cleveland was aware that the Mills bill, despite its authors' claims to moderate reductions, had served not to mollify but to further incite "the bulls that are roaring 'free trade.'" A growing number of Democrats began to distance themselves from this specific measure. In late April and early May, party conventions in three key northern swing states—Indiana, Connecticut, and New Jersey—issued platforms that avoided any mention of the Mills bill. The Hoosiers called for "revision and reform" of the tariff as recommended by Cleveland, but Democrats in the other two states, which had large industrial sectors, ignored the December message. Instead, they pointed to the declarations of the 1884 national platform as correct Democratic doctrine on the revenue question. Four years earlier, the national convention had called for revenue reduction, but it devoted much more space in the platform to insisting that the effort "be cautious and conservative in method" so as not to "injure any domestic industries. . . . [M]any industries have come to rely upon legislation for successful continuance, so that any change of law must be at every step regardful of the labor and capital thus involved." As spring wore on, reaffirmation of the 1884 platform emerged as a rallying point for Democrats who wished to steer the party away from the dangers of tariff radicalism and close the gap between its Cleveland and Randall wings.[79]

By mid-May Cleveland had come to see the wisdom of this approach. As New York Democrats prepared for their state convention in New York City, the president himself drafted the platform for the delegates to adopt. After only minor tinkering with the language, the convention adopted Cleveland's draft, without officially recognizing its source. In it, he cited the 1884 national platform and the 1887 state platform, and he also included "an explicit approval of the doctrines" contained in his annual message. But in speaking of the need to relieve the country of its onerous tax burden, neither Cleveland nor the convention invoked the word *tariff* or the Mills bill. In the closed-door sessions of the resolutions committee, a proposal to include an endorsement of the bill, which Cleveland's men opposed, provoked a prolonged and heated discussion before it was finally defeated. The *New York Herald* hailed the state convention's work as "loyal and harmonious," but the platform angered tariff reformers. In the words of the *New York Times,* "nothing but sheer ignorance of the sentiments of the people or gross incompetence to find them out can account for the faint-heartedness and consequent bungling" with which the convention had treated "the burning question of the time."[80]

THE DEMOCRATIC NATIONAL CONVENTION

Cleveland was determined to exercise a similar moderating influence on the handling of the tariff issue at the national convention three weeks later in St. Louis, where the stakes would be much higher. Once again he prepared a draft platform for the convention to adopt. He solicited suggestions from others and used a few phrases from the drafts they submitted, but as a text in Cleveland's own hand shows, the platform was largely his own composition. Its authorship, however, was kept secret. Determined to take control of the deliberations at the convention, Cleveland and Lamont reached out to some of the party's protectionist champions, though not to Randall, for assistance. Most important, to convey the draft to St. Louis they commissioned Maryland Senator Arthur P. Gorman, one of the party's most prominent protectionists and chairman of the national executive committee during Cleveland's successful

1884 campaign. Working with Gorman was William Scott, representing moderate tariff reform. Their labors took on added urgency just before the convention met, when Oregon Democrats went down to defeat in state elections after having made a fight focused largely on the tariff issue and based explicitly on Cleveland's message.[81]

Once they arrived in the convention city, Scott and Gorman encountered trouble in carrying out Cleveland's plan. In a narrow vote, Henry Watterson defeated Gorman for chairman of the committee on resolutions. The opening paragraph of Cleveland's draft reaffirmed the 1884 platform, but it made no mention of his message to Congress or the Mills bill. Gorman's introduction of the draft sparked heated controversy in the committee, which labored over it in tumultuous marathon sessions. Watterson wanted no mention at all of the 1884 platform, which he considered a "straddle" on the tariff issue. After a five-hour meeting on the convention's second day, the committee voted, 25 to 19, to accept the text as submitted by Gorman, but Watterson and his allies threatened to take the question to the floor of the convention. A panicky Scott wired Lamont at the White House that the low-tariff men were insisting on a specific reference to Cleveland's message, "and I fear I cannot stop them otherwise." "Don't see how we can oppose that," Lamont responded. Cleveland thus found himself in the anomalous position of having key Democratic leaders demanding that the party endorse a policy statement he himself had issued but from which he was now attempting to draw back.[82]

When the committee reconvened in the evening, Gorman and Scott offered compromise verbiage to break the impasse. The endorsement of the 1884 platform would remain, followed by the statement that the party "endorses the views expressed by President Cleveland in his last annual message to Congress as the correct interpretation of that platform upon the question of tariff reduction; and also endorses the efforts of our Democratic Representatives in Congress to secure a reduction of excessive taxation." In addition, on the convention floor, Scott introduced a resolution separate from the platform, endorsing and recommending "the early passage of the bill for the reduction of the revenue, now pending in the House of Representatives," that is, the Mills bill. Watterson was satisfied, and the convention adopted the platform and resolution by voice vote. Although subsequent portions of Cleveland's draft and the final platform contained "straddling" passages calling for the reduction of "unjust taxation" without endangering "our established domestic industries," most observers focused on the all-important first paragraph and Scott's resolution, and here, Cleveland's attempt to bring his party back from the brink of "free trade" had met with less than complete success. Scott insisted to Lamont that their program had been "carried out as nearly as any reasonable man could expect or hope for." But, as Gorman later noted, "the convention was composed of gentlemen who were carried away by sentiment and it is simply wonderful that we were able to prevent more radical measures being adopted." Acting through intermediaries, Cleveland had failed to secure the plank he wanted and wound up creating a good deal of confusion. As the *New York Times* said of Gorman and Scott's performance, "this little game is not easy to understand."[83]

Although some advisers had suggested that the platform deal only with the tariff, Cleveland favored the insertion of other topics, perhaps to divert attention from the tax question. The document denounced trusts, favored "a firm and prudent foreign policy," and claimed that since the Democrats had assumed power the government had paid more in veterans' pensions than during any previous comparable period. As Cleveland had hoped, Bayard had negotiated a treaty with China to exclude the immigration of laborers, and the platform chided the Republican Senate for delaying its approval. On the touchy issue of patronage and the civil service, Cleveland's draft had praised the launching of reforms "whereby fidelity and efficiency in the discharge of official duty, instead of the claims of partisanship alone, have become the requirements in making appointments and promotions." Such language would appeal more to reformers than to party regulars, and the final version omitted it and merely commended the president for elevating "the public service to the highest standard of efficiency, not only by rule and precept, but by the example of his own untiring and unselfish administration of public affairs." In a gesture toward allaying the ill will still lingering after the Civil War and Reconstruction, Cleveland's text claimed that his administration had steadfastly maintained "the equality of all our citizens before the law, without regard to race or color." But the plank the convention adopted read, "without regard to race or section." In truth, Cleveland had done little for African Americans, and the insertion of the word *section* showed the unwillingness of his party, dominated by its southern wing, to rise above deeply ingrained resentments.[84]

In uniting with Watterson to present the platform to the convention, Gorman insisted that "every Democrat in this broad land can stand" on it, but he also conceded that "local interests warp the judgment" of some and that "absolute uniformity of opinion . . . is impossible." On this latter point he spoke truly, as reactions to the document revealed. According to the *Indianapolis Sentinel*, "The most ardent tariff reformer could not have asked of the convention a more clear, explicit, or emphatic definition of the principles and policy of the party." The *Washington Post*, however, decried the tariff plank as "a straddle pure and simple." The Mugwump *Springfield Republican* was satisfied that the platform "defines the issue in a way not to be mistaken, and for that reason it gives the party a good start on solid ground." The Democratic *New York Sun*, no friend of the president, crowed that the platform showed that "the Convention and Mr. Cleveland have put their love of free trade out to roost; and may its sleep be peaceful and undisturbed!" From the Republican vantage, however, as represented by the *New York Tribune*, the tariff plank marked "the explicit commitment of the Democratic party to the cause of free trade." The *Tribune* recognized that "the President had become alarmed, and was willing to have his party attempt some evasion," but in caving in on the endorsement of his message and the Mills bill, Cleveland demonstrated that "the Southern Free Traders are his masters." Protectionist Democrats agreed. "Cleveland surrendered to Wat[t]erson and the South on the tariff," former Ohio Congressman A. J. Warner wrote to Randall. As a result, "the Republicans have the issue at last just as they have wanted it. Who can fail to see that to place ourselves in this position was as unwise as it was unnecessary?"[85]

If Cleveland's men were outfoxed on the tariff plank, their handling of the president's formal renomination exhibited an amateurish flavor. In the first place, the protracted proceedings of the resolutions committee delayed the anxiously awaited presentation of the platform until the day after the presidential nomination, thereby robbing that event of some of its climactic impact. Of course, the convention's choice of a nominee was never in doubt, but the matter of who would place Cleveland in nomination was not settled until a few days beforehand, thus leaving little time for preparation of an effective address. Cleveland forbore selecting some leading Democrat whose own prominence might have given his candidacy a boost. In the absence of clear direction from Washington, a petty fight for the honor broke out among the factions of the New York Democratic Party. At one point three different men seemed in the running to make the speech, but Cleveland and Lamont finally opted for Tammany's recommendation of Daniel Dougherty. A well-known party orator originally from Philadelphia. Dougherty had performed the same service for Winfield Hancock in the 1880 convention. But he had lived in New York for less than a year and thus would not even be able to vote in the fall election. His selection, according to one account, left "smothered bitterness" among Tammany's foes. Honored but hurried, Dougherty asked Lamont to send him talking points at his St. Louis hotel. In his brief address, Dougherty sang Cleveland's virtues and called for "reform, revision, [and] reduction of national taxation," but he reassured the nation that "to lower the tariff is not free trade." Though reporters rolled their eyes at Dougherty's weakness for "the ancient Websterian school of oratory," he nonetheless hit his mark, igniting a frenzied twenty-four-minute demonstration during which, for the first time since 1840, Democrats screamed their lungs out for the reelection of a president. After seconding speeches, the delegates approved Cleveland's renomination by uproarious acclamation.[86]

The convention's last great responsibility was the nomination of a candidate for the vice presidency, and once again the Cleveland men seemed to falter. The death of Vice President Thomas A. Hendricks in 1885 had left the party with no incumbent. During the spring attention had focused on a handful of potential running mates, most notably Governor Isaac P. Gray of Indiana. But Gray faced bitter factional opposition within the Hoosier Democratic Party that could jeopardize the ticket's chances in that key midwestern swing state.[87] At last, a week before the convention, Cleveland signaled his preference for a man who had shown no interest in the position, former Senator Allen Granberry Thurman of Ohio. It was an odd choice. Thurman would turn seventy-five a week after the November election. He had come of age in the time of Jackson, and his trademark red bandanna, which he used after taking snuff, evoked the politics of a bygone era. He was seven years older than the oldest man ever elected to the vice presidency, Elbridge Gerry, who had died in office. The memory of Hendricks's death, coupled with Thurman's less than robust health, might have given Cleveland pause. Indeed, a year earlier Thurman had emphatically declined the president's offer of a position on the Interstate Commerce Commission. At that time he told Cleveland that he had "long ago, after mature reflection, resolved to pass my remaining days in private life. . . . [T]he time has come when I can best obtain happiness, or at *least* contentment, in the society of my family, my friends and my books." Now, however, Cleveland would not be deterred, and Thurman acquiesced.[88]

Armed with the sword of integrity, Grover Cleveland attacks the heights of protection. (Library of Congress)

A few days before the convention met, a newspaper boom generated support for the Old Roman. At St. Louis, William Scott took chief responsibility for coordinating the effort, although the congressman denied acting on orders from the administration. More than Scott had expected, the last-minute push for the Ohioan proved disruptive. Several states had already planned to support Gray or other candidates, and they now had to scramble to shift their allegiance. Not all delegates did so willingly, including many from Thurman's own state who had come prepared to vote for Gray. Cleveland had not discussed Thurman's candidacy with Ohio's member of the Democratic National Committee, who told reporters that Thurman had "stated repeatedly that his only candidacy now was for a seat in heaven." One Buckeye congressman grumbled, "The democratic party will be obliged to transport the old gentleman about the country to show the people that he is alive." Nonetheless, delegates and reporters alike saw that Cleveland wanted Thurman nominated, and most delegates fell into line.[89]

But if the "who" of Cleveland's vice presidential choice was clear to all, the "why" remained baffling to many. Thurman's age was widely recognized as an impediment, but Cleveland did not regard it as an insurmountable obstacle. His primary aim, of course, was to choose a running mate who would add strength to the ticket. Could Thurman do that? Southerners liked Thurman, but Cleveland could be reasonably confident of carrying the South in November anyway. Moreover, pro-southern speeches that Thurman had made in the 1860s would be grist for northern Republicans in the fall campaign. The Ohioan was popular in New York, particularly among machine politicians who were lukewarm toward Cleveland, but even if the president captured his home state, he would still need to pick up at least twelve more electoral votes to win. Ohio's twenty-three would put him over the top, but the state had not voted for a Democratic national ticket since 1852. Some speculated that Cleveland, influenced by Navy Secretary Whitney, believed that Thurman could unite warring factions in Ohio, but during his long years in Buckeye Democratic politics, Thurman had in fact collected his share of enemies. When rumors of Cleveland's choice arose, former Governor George Hoadly wired the White House that "Thurman's nomination, if made, [would be] disastrous enough, still more so if any executive influence can be supposed to promote it." In St. Louis the Ohio delegates were so divided that they could not agree to place Thurman's name in nomination, and that honor fell to another state. Perhaps Cleveland

Allen G. Thurman, Democratic nominee for vice president in 1888, with a red bandanna in his pocket. (Library of Congress)

hoped to curry favor in neighboring Indiana, whose Democrats admired Thurman and whose fifteen electoral votes, added to New York's, could spell victory. Yet if Indiana was central to Cleveland's calculation, was Thurman likely to be more help there than Gray? Indeed, Gray's men harbored resentment at the way the Cleveland forces had treated their candidate. Thurman was popular in the far western states of California, Oregon, and Nevada, particularly for sponsoring legislation to force the Pacific railroads to repay their government loans and for the leading role he had taken in Chinese exclusion legislation. When Ohio demurred, California proudly put Thurman's name before the convention. Still, the math did not quite work for Cleveland. California and Oregon's total of eleven electoral votes was just shy of the magic number he needed, and he was unlikely to win the three votes of Nevada, whose citizens deeply resented the president's stand against silver.[90]

Thus, Thurman was far from an ideal candidate, but Cleveland could see no better alternative. The predicament was a revealing commentary on the dearth of national leaders in the state-oriented Democratic Party. Some of the most prominent men, such as Secretary of State Thomas F. Bayard and House Speaker John G. Carlisle, were already engaged in work more important than the vice presidency. Samuel Randall's failing health, not to mention his tariff views, disqualified him from consideration. Pension Commissioner John C. Black enjoyed some support, but the pension issue was a dodgy one for Cleveland, and, like Gray, Black confronted serious opposition in his home state of Illinois. In the end, whatever Thurman's liabilities, the Old Roman drew on a well of affection among the delegates at St. Louis, most of whom were willing to ratify the president's choice. On the convention's last day, June 7, Thurman easily defeated Gray and Black, and his nomination was made unanimous amid a roiling sea of red bandannas.[91]

As the raw-throated delegates set off for home, most remained hopeful that the tide was with their incumbent captain. William R. Grace, former mayor of New York, told reporters that Thurman would "add strength to the ticket" in key northeastern doubtful states, the platform offered "exactly what the present needs of the country require," and "the St. Louis Convention was the greatest assembly of great men he had ever seen." But such fulsome exultation could hardly mask the reality that, on balance, the national convention had done little to put Cleveland and his party on the sure route to victory. "We haven't a walk over," one party worker candidly warned Lamont, "but have a hard fight ahead of us." For their part, Republicans took hope from the proceedings at St. Louis. They conceded that Thurman added strength to the ticket in some ways, but he could not deliver Ohio. Most important, as William McKinley put it, the Democratic platform was "entirely satisfactory to republicans. It makes the issue clearly between free trade and protection." On that issue, said Julius Burrows, "we shall go to the people with the perfect confidence that the verdict will be in favor of American industries and American labor." In three weeks, the Republican hosts would gather in Chicago to choose the man to lead that fight.[92]

3

THE REPUBLICAN CHALLENGER
IF NOT BLAINE, WHO?

Most contemporaries and later historians gave Grover Cleveland credit for making the tariff question the central issue during the presidential election campaign of 1888. It was a challenge that most Republicans were delighted to accept. Indeed, for years many Republicans had pushed to make the tariff the key point of contention between the two parties. Protectionism, they had come to believe, was a policy that was right for the country and attractive for the party. At last, one GOP senator wrote after Cleveland's tariff message, "the Democratic party has come out from ambush and its attitude of duplicity to a point in the open field where we can get a 'whack' at them."[1]

In the 1870s Republicans had focused primarily on lingering sectional issues, particularly the refusal of white southern Democrats to abide by the Fourteenth and Fifteenth Amendments. Although Democrats derided their opponents for "waving the bloody shirt," Republicans continued to defend the rights of African Americans, especially their right to vote. But as time wore on, the party faced mounting difficulty in convincing northern voters of the importance of civil rights issues, with the result that GOP leaders gave increasing attention to economic questions. In the 1880s the party witnessed an internal struggle between those who gave priority to sectional and racial issues and those who put economic matters at the top of the Republican agenda.[2]

The foremost leader of the latter group was James G. Blaine. A popular story in party lore regarding the 1880 campaign described how, after the Republicans had narrowly lost the September elections in Maine but had run well in manufacturing towns, Blaine had stormed into national party headquarters insisting that party workers "fold up the bloody shirt" and "shift the main issue to protection."[3] Four years later in his campaign against Cleveland, he called the tariff question "the controlling question of this campaign." Thus, long before Cleveland's message, Blaine had insisted that "the question of questions . . . which dominates all others is this: 'Shall the American idea of a tariff for the protection of American labor and American industries be maintained as the settled policy of the United States?'"[4] As 1888 approached, Blaine still held sway as the party's leading spokesman on the issue, and a renomination for the presidency seemed his for the asking. But would he ask?

THE BLAINE FACTOR

James G. Blaine had stood as a dominant figure in American politics for more than two decades. First elected to the House of Representatives in 1862, he quickly rose to prominence and served as a popular and effective Speaker from 1869 to 1875. Tall, attractive, and well-spoken, he easily acquired a following that was immense and intensely loyal. For decades he traveled widely during election seasons, preaching Republican doctrine and charming campaign audiences. Blessed with a phenomenal memory, he could greet untold numbers of party cadres by name and treat them with a familiarity that helped fasten their political fortunes to his own. "I love Blaine as much as you can possibly," Iowa party leader James S. Clarkson once wrote to another Blaine supporter. "I will die unsatisfied and with lessened faith in American sense and appreciation if he is never President." "Had he been a woman," another contemporary wrote, "people would have rushed off to send expensive flowers."[5]

Yet, in the party's factional squabbles, Blaine had also made enemies, including most notably New York Senator Roscoe Conkling, with whom he shared a deep mutual hatred. The two men were among the long list of candidates for the Republican presidential nomination in 1876, but Blaine was the clear front-runner. Just weeks before the convention, however, allegations that he had taken a bribe from a railroad helped derail Blaine's candidacy. The nomination went to Rutherford B. Hayes, and Blaine moved up to the Senate. (A nominating speech at the 1876

James G. Blaine, Republican nominee
for president in 1884.(Library of Congress)

convention likened Blaine to a plumed knight, and the sobriquet stuck.) He ran for president again in 1880, but in the convention that year, when his forces deadlocked with those of former President Ulysses S. Grant (managed by Conkling), the Blaine delegates turned to dark horse James A. Garfield. Garfield won and made Blaine his secretary of state, a position he vacated soon after Chester A. Arthur succeeded Garfield.[6]

Out of public office for the first time since the 1850s, Blaine turned to writing. The first volume of his chronicle, *Twenty Years of Congress,* appeared in the spring of 1884 and contained a long chapter devoted to the history of the protective tariff and its benefits to the nation. Finally winning the Republican presidential nomination in 1884, he lost narrowly to Cleveland. The party's reform wing, known as independents or Mugwumps, had been contemptuous of Blaine since 1876; they abandoned the ticket and backed Cleveland. In New York, which Blaine lost by a razor-thin margin, Conkling had quietly knifed his old enemy. Conkling's own county, reliably Republican in presidential contests since 1856, went Democratic in 1884, giving Cleveland 1,223 more votes than it had given the Democratic nominee in 1880, a figure that was greater than Cleveland's statewide margin over Blaine.[7]

Blaine's near miss in 1884 made him the instant front-runner for the Republican nomination in 1888. In the interim he took steps that seemed designed to further that eventuality. He campaigned for Republicans around the country, spreading his own message and adding to his vast store of IOUs among party politicians. In 1886 he published the second volume of *Twenty Years,* which he followed the next year with a collection of his speeches and state papers. Always good newspaper copy, his comings and goings, his public appearances, and even the state of his sometimes precarious health attracted wide attention. His loyal supporters—dubbed Blainiacs—wanted him again in 1888, but his persistent detractors gagged at the prospect. Still a colossus in American politics, he was at once the Plumed Knight of fawning oratory and the Tattooed Man of scathing cartoons.[8]

Blaine well understood the ambivalent character of his standing in the nation and the party, and he experienced mixed feelings of his own about running again and even about serving as president. In the summer of 1887 he set off on an extended tour of Europe, in part to be absent when speculation about the nomination heated up. In October he wrote to the *New York Tribune*'s Whitelaw Reid, one of his closest allies, that he felt "very strongly disinclined to run." "In the first place & *radically*," he went on, "*I do not feel that I want the office—conceding the election.* In the next place I do not want the turmoil & burdensome exactions of a canvass." As a candidate once defeated, he wrote, he would not think of seeking the nomination unless it came unanimously or nearly so, and the appearance of other men already in the field made that impossible. "Above all," he insisted, "I abhor the idea of becoming a chronic candidate." Still, he left the door open a crack: He would pull out at the proper time, he told Reid, "if the friends entitled to be consulted—of whom you are chief—shall agree with me." A month later he seemed more inclined to enter the fray when he sent Reid a draft of an editorial for the *Tribune* sharply critical of Conkling's leadership of the New York Republican Party. Because Conkling "cherishes no ambition except for revenge," Blaine told Reid, it was time to "destroy his power for evil."[9]

Reid wisely laid aside Blaine's draft as likely to precipitate "a needless row." Nonetheless, the editor took heart from his friend's apparently renewed fighting spirit, even more so after Blaine's response to Cleveland's tariff message. "There has been," Reid wrote to Blaine, "since the publication of your interview, an extremely rapid development and concentration of public sentiment. Nobody now considers the nomination of any other Republican candidate probable." With Blaine as the party's nominee, the party could carry New York "by a reasonably safe majority," and "warm hopes are entertained by a good many of our friends" for taking Indiana, New Jersey, and Connecticut and even making inroads in the South in Virginia and West Virginia. According to Reid, even Henry Cabot Lodge and Theodore Roosevelt, two rising party stars who had opposed Blaine in the 1884 convention, now preferred his selection because they thought it would be "the strongest nomination possible" and because "they are particularly eager to beat the Mugwumps with you." "Few doubt that the nomination will come to you with substantial unanimity," Reid concluded, invoking the talismanic condition that Blaine had cited as the sine qua non for his candidacy.[10]

But despite the hints that he might be willing to run, Blaine did not share Reid's optimism. Many candidates would be in the field, he wrote after the turn of the year, and he could win the nomination "only after a contest." He did "not feel like entering the northern scramble," nor did he wish to "become a bidder for Southern delegations" that would, "as usual, be up at auction." (Southern delegates at Republican conventions, especially impecunious African Americans, not infrequently looked to presidential candidates or their representatives for help with convention expenses.) Moreover, Blaine worried that the party would not be able to raise the funds necessary to wage an effective campaign in the fall. He reminded Reid of the reluctance of manufacturers to make large contributions in 1884. As a result, he had been forced to chip in $65,000 of his own money, "a larger fraction of my total property than I wish it were." Cleveland, he predicted, would have a much larger fund in 1888. Again, Blaine pleaded, "the one rule I have cherished since 1884 was to run for President if called upon by an undivided unanimous party; and not to run with a divided party even though the larger half was in my favor." Deep down, he thought he deserved a renomination. "Jefferson and Jackson, after good runs the first time, were unanimously renominated," he reminded a confidant, and "I came very much nearer victory than either of them in the first trial." Still, he insisted to Reid, he had "not the slightest feeling of disappointment" at declining to run, but instead felt "a great sense of relief."[11]

At the end of January, Blaine issued a formal withdrawal in the form of a letter written in Florence, Italy, and addressed to B. F. Jones, Republican national chairman. It appeared in American newspapers in mid-February. As a declination, it was not quite absolute. Blaine did not say that he would refuse a nomination, but only that his name would "not be presented" to the convention. Moreover, he included a brief account of recent party history that put his own contributions in a highly favorable light. The party had suffered devastating losses in 1882 and 1883, he noted, but then "the spirit of the Republican party in the National contest of 1884 rose high, and the Republican masses entered into the campaign with such energy" that the outcome depended on a single state (New York) where the party lost by less than "one-eleventh of 1 per cent." Blaine did not have to mention who had led the comeback of 1884. His private pessimism to Reid notwithstanding, he declared that the party had continued to gain popularity, and now, because of Cleveland's tariff message, the Republicans showed "irresistible strength" in the coming clash between protection and free trade. In that fight, he promised to work for the party "not less earnestly and more directly, as a private citizen than as a public candidate."[12]

The shock waves from Blaine's bombshell reverberated across the political landscape. If Blaine had seemingly answered the question of whether he would run, now the regnant query was, "Is he sincere?"

Within his family circle, the evidence suggests that he was. Mrs. Blaine reassured her daughter that the letter "has to go, and we shall all be happier for being spared a summer of suspense with the chances of defeat in the autumn." Mary Abigail Dodge, Mrs. Blaine's cousin who was traveling with the family, wrote to Stephen B. Elkins, a West Virginia coal and railroad magnate who had masterminded Blaine's nomination in 1884, that Blaine was "unchangeably convinced that he should decline the nomination and that he should decline it now." But Dodge also repeated Blaine's mantra about a call of the party unanimously tendered, and she added, "His nomination, to have any superiority over others in securing votes at the election, which is the only thing a nomination is for, must seem to the party so desirable as to preclude the mention of any other name before the convention." This passage in Dodge's letter, written with Blaine's knowledge, could seem as much an instruction as an observation and could leave a Blaine enthusiast like Elkins perplexed about Blaine's true intentions. Was he angling for a draft?[13]

In the initial public reaction to the "withdrawal," many Democrats and Mugwumps suspected just such a scheme by the man they had long decried as a wily trickster. Indiana Democratic Senator Daniel Voorhees dismissed the letter as simply "a very urgent appeal for the nomination." Other Democrats, though, welcomed it as putting a strong potential rival to Cleveland out of the way. Republicans in general were inclined to express belief in Blaine's "sincerity," many with genuine regret, others with disguised relief.[14] Blaine's political intimates, an ocean away from their chieftain, were not quite sure what to make of it. William Walter Phelps, a wealthy New Jersey congressman and a passionate Blaine man, felt bereft. For more than twelve years he had labored for Blaine, "shaping all political & social matters to aid his fortunes." Now, he wrote to Reid, "it's as if I went out of business." Reid was less despairing. Three days after the publication of the withdrawal, Reid told a fellow journalist that New York Republicans were "settling down to the view that Mr. Blaine's letter leaves things much as they were before." The *Tribune* continued to guardedly boom Blaine, and Reid worked behind the scenes to engender a sense of inevitability about his nomination. Phelps enlisted in this endeavor, as did Elkins. The line they adopted was, as Reid put it, that in the likelihood that no other suitable candidate emerged, "the demand for the re-nomination of Mr. Blaine will again spring up, and he may be placed in a position where it would be infamy to refuse."[15]

THE REPUBLICAN FIELD

Whatever the real intentions of Blaine's Florence letter, it had the effect of removing restraints on the candidacies of other men, and the
field soon became crowded. Most prominent was Senator John Sherman of Ohio, who had tilted with Blaine in the previous two national
conventions. Sherman had made no bones about his candidacy even
before Blaine's withdrawal. During the ballyhoo following Blaine's interview on Cleveland's message, the Ohio senator publicly dismissed
the rumor that he would bow out in Blaine's favor as "absurd." Indeed,
apprehension of a "serious" contest with Sherman formed a large part
of the reason that Blaine announced his own departure from the field.[16]

Sherman, brother of famed Civil War General William T. Sherman,
was a formidable candidate. He occupied a place nearly as prominent
as Blaine's in the minds if not the hearts of Republicans throughout
the country. Sherman first entered national politics in the 1850s on the
wave of revulsion against the Kansas-Nebraska Act, which reopened
western territories to slavery. After six years in the House, he moved
in 1861 up to the Senate, where he served for the next thirty-six years,
except for a four-year stint in the cabinet of Rutherford B. Hayes. Having
served as chairman of the House Ways and Means Committee, chairman of the Senate Finance Committee for twelve years, and secretary of
the treasury, Sherman won renown as the preeminent "financial statesman" of the Republican Party. For more than three decades he took a
leading part in designing every piece of economic legislation passed by
Congress, and in the late 1870s he successfully executed the Treasury
Department's critical resumption of specie payments for Civil War–era
paper currency. After Cleveland's annual message in December, Sherman took to the Senate floor to defend protectionism in a well-received
speech. He characterized the government's surplus less as a danger than
as a mark of "the steady improvement of our financial condition," and
he warned that Cleveland's policy would "break down" the "protective industrial policy built up by the Republican party." The speech was printed
and distributed widely as a campaign document. "The more the people
are educated upon the tariff subject," a Kentucky Republican wrote to
Sherman, "the more certain will be our success in the coming Pres. contest." In an age when economic questions moved to center stage both in
politics and in governance, even men who backed other candidates conceded that Sherman's expertise and experience rendered him, in John

Senator John Sherman of Ohio, the Republican Party's leading expert on finance. (Library of Congress)

Hay's words, "thoroughly fit for power." And on the era's other great issue—what to do about lingering troubles in the South—Sherman had been an eloquent advocate for the civil rights of African Americans. The great black leader Frederick Douglass assured him that "there is no man living with any chance of being president of the U. States whom I would rather see in that quality than yourself."[17]

Nonetheless, Sherman confronted numerous obstacles to his nomination and, should he pass that hurdle, his election. Experienced though he was, at sixty-five he could not boast youthful vigor as one of his assets. More troubling, many men saw him as cold and rigid—the "Ohio Icicle," as some uncharitably put it. His political style invited respect, not affection. And even respect was not always forthcoming, especially in his own state, where he sometimes faced factional opposition. On one such occasion, in 1879, Sherman made a trip home to "mend fences" among his fellow Republicans, thereby adding a new term to the American political lexicon. As the 1888 campaign season got under way, his fences had again fallen into disrepair. Although he demanded and received an endorsement from the state party, it was no secret that many Buckeye Republicans preferred Blaine or even other Ohioans such as Governor Joseph B. Foraker or Congressman William McKinley. Nor could Sherman claim much strength in the key state of New York. In the 1870s, as treasury secretary, he had tangled with the state's Stalwart faction associated with Senator Roscoe Conkling and eventually ousted one of its leaders, Chester A. Arthur, from the lucrative post of collector of customs at the port of New York. The Stalwarts neither forgave nor forgot, and one of them who now headed the New York party apparatus, Thomas C. Platt, was determined that John Sherman would never be president. Sherman's conservative monetary record, particularly his opposition to free coinage of silver, made him equally repugnant to Republicans in the mining regions of the West. He enjoyed considerable support among the beleaguered Republicans of the South and also in Pennsylvania, where Senator Matthew S. Quay held a firm grip on the state party, but his candidacy encountered difficulty achieving much traction elsewhere. This was Sherman's third try for the nomination, and his own acknowledgment that it would be his last gave the effort a tinge of desperation.[18]

Desperation was a sentiment that few observers would have attributed to Iowa Senator William Boyd Allison, another potential nominee who received wide notice even before Blaine's withdrawal. Indeed, it was

Allison's serene nature, his ability to smooth over differences, that won him esteem in the party. He was an adept legislator with an enormous well of patience for conciliating opposing views in the committee rooms and back corridors of Capitol Hill. "He is like a naval engineer," a Senate colleague observed, "regulating the head of steam but seldom showing himself on deck." Allison had cultivated this skill over a long career dating back to 1863, when he first entered Congress. He served four terms in the House, and during his second he took a seat on the Ways and Means Committee. During the Civil War he helped raise troops in Iowa but did not sign up himself, and his lack of a military record counted against him in the presidential politics of 1888. In 1873 he entered the Senate, where he distinguished himself on the Finance Committee and the Appropriations Committee, chairing the latter since 1881. Though less well known than Sherman as a spokesman for the party's economic policies, he had contributed nearly as much in formulating financial legislation, most notably attaching a moderating amendment to the Bland-Allison Act for the remonetization of silver in 1878.

But the very circumspection that greased Allison's relations with congressional colleagues prevented his developing a charisma that might have generated wider popular support. Moreover, his tendency to seek middle ground in legislation led some easterners to doubt his orthodoxy on such issues as the currency and the tariff. On the latter question, they suspected that Allison's attention to the needs of his agricultural constituency in Iowa made him less sympathetic to the protectionist demands of manufacturers in the East. In addition, a vigorous movement for railroad regulation launched by Iowa's Republican governor in the winter of 1888 tended to lower Allison's stock in the boardrooms of New York and Boston. Some analysts viewed Allison as little more than a favorite son in the race. Yet Allison benefited immensely from the campaign direction provided by James S. Clarkson, one of the shrewdest political managers in the Republican Party. The Iowa delegation had stoutly supported Blaine in the three previous national conventions, under Clarkson's chairmanship during the last two. In the spring of 1888 Clarkson boomed Allison indefatigably, although he was not immune to a wistful yearning for the Blaine candidacy that Reid and Elkins sought to resuscitate.[19]

No such affinity existed between the Blaine camp and the backers of another midwestern candidate, Walter Q. Gresham of Indiana and Illinois. Born in Indiana, Gresham served a term in the state legislature in the winter and spring of 1861 before heading off to war as the colonel of a Hoosier regiment. He won promotion to general, but a severe wound in July 1864 took him out of the fighting. He twice ran for Congress in Democratic southern Indiana, lost both times, and in 1869 accepted appointment as federal district judge for the state. During Chester Arthur's administration he served as postmaster general and briefly as secretary of the treasury. Early in 1884 Blaine had intimated that he would back Gresham for president in exchange for appointment to his old job as secretary of state, but Gresham said no. As a loyal member of the cabinet, he supported Arthur for the nomination, although he harbored some veiled hopes that in the event of a deadlock, the convention might turn to him. In the fall campaign, Gresham made only one speech for Blaine, whose supporters later complained that he had done little to push his department's employees to work for the ticket. "The talk about Gresham," Reid said in 1888, "encounters the angry criticism of those Republicans who think that if Arthur's Cabinet had acted as Republicans ought to act, we should have had the missing 600 votes in this State in the last election."

Before Arthur left office, he gave Gresham the federal circuit judgeship for Illinois, Indiana, and Wisconsin. On the bench at Chicago, Gresham gained popularity for a widely noticed opinion against railroad machinations by Jay Gould and for defending the rights of striking railroad workers. As a judge, he enjoyed a growing reputation as a friend of labor and, by extension, the downtrodden generally. Mugwumps and reformers liked him, too, especially for his implementation of the Pendleton Civil Service Act under Arthur and for his criticism of machine politics in general. They also warmed to his tariff views, which favored moderate customs duties. For most Republicans, however, such views raised alarm. As one Indiana legislator put it, the popularity Gresham had earned among workers for his court decisions was more than offset by his not being "regarded as sufficiently stalwart on the question of a protective tariff, a question of the most vital importance to the laboring man." The problem was compounded by the support Gresham received from the *Chicago Tribune,* one of the nation's most influential papers; its publisher, Joseph Medill, had long been associated with the party's low-tariff wing. The free-trade taint and Mugwump support simply aggravated the ill will that Blaine's backers felt for the judge. Although he won the support of his adopted state of Illinois and pockets of Republicans in several other states, one party leader expressed the view of many that Gresham "can't be nominated unless Blaine's friends are the most forgiving Christians yet discovered in politics."[20]

In the fluid situation after Blaine's withdrawal, the Republicans suffered no dearth of favorite-son candidates. The hopes of these men rested on the possibility of a deadlocked convention casting about for a nominee likely to unite the party's various factions while being beholden to none. Connecticut proposed Joseph R. Hawley, who was serving his second term in the Senate. An early advocate of abolitionism, Hawley was a founder of the Connecticut Republican Party. He had served ably as a general during the Civil War, after which he became an effective spokesman for party ideals, both as editor of the *Hartford Courant* and as a forceful orator. He served a term as governor in the late 1860s and a couple of terms in Congress during the 1870s, but it was his successful management of the nation's centennial celebration in the mid-1870s that brought him national recognition. In 1881 he went to the Senate, where he won respect as a leader who was solid and dependable but not flashy. One of his strengths as a candidate was his residence in a doubtful state, albeit a small one. Should he miss the presidential nomination, which was likely, he would be a strong contender for the second spot, especially if the head of the ticket hailed from a western state.[21]

The Republicans of Michigan were hopeful that the party would turn to their ex-governor, Russell A. Alger, as the ideal western candidate. A Union army veteran like Hawley, Alger had risen from private to major general and had seen action in numerous battles. After the war he helped organize the Grand Army of the Republic in Michigan and was prominent in the national GAR. He had a strong hold on the affections of northern ex-soldiers. Because Republicans anticipated a "business campaign" focused on the tariff, Alger, who had made a fortune in the lumber business, cast himself as the candidate who knew most about the practicalities of economic issues. Moreover, his ample wealth gave him the wherewithal to court delegates outside Michigan, especially in the South. His "barrel" would also be an asset for the fall campaign. Rumor had it that if Blaine were really out of the running, Alger had found favor as an acceptable alternative by "Boss" Thomas C. Platt of New York, who, though not quite a kingmaker, would have great influence over the selection of a nominee. In reality, however, Platt played his cards close to the chest, and Alger failed to rise much above favorite-son status. Few other men had nearly as much confidence in Alger's chances as he himself displayed.[22]

Even less promising were the prospects of men whose candidacies represented little more than compliments paid them by their states in advance of the real bargaining at the national convention. Governor Jeremiah Rusk of Wisconsin had won election to several local offices in the 1850s, fought bravely in William T. Sherman's army during the war, and sat in Congress for three terms in the 1870s. Respected as an advocate for the interests of farmers and veterans, he had held the governorship since 1882. In May 1886 he dispatched the state militia to quell labor rioting in Milwaukee, thereby earning the admiration of conservatives and the deep distrust of labor. Pennsylvanian Edwin Fitler, a wealthy cordage manufacturer, was in his first (and only) term as mayor of Philadelphia. His popularity in the City of Brotherly Love was genuine, but he was hardly known elsewhere. Neither Rusk nor Fitler had any chance to win the presidential nomination.[23]

Only slightly more plausible was the nomination of Chauncey M. Depew of New York. Depew was a graduate of Yale, where he had affiliated with the nascent Republican Party in the 1850s. During the Civil War he served for two years in the legislature and two years as the state's secretary of state. After the war he forsook public office for corporate law, and by 1885 he had risen to the presidency of the New York Central Railroad. An adept and entertaining public speaker, Depew gained wide renown for his performances on both the after-dinner circuit and the Republican stump. Nonetheless, his railroad associations rendered his candidacy anathema to Republicans in the so-called Granger states of the West. Depew himself considered his nomination impossible and was more than willing to bow out in favor of Blaine, if the Plumed Knight would accept. Ultimately, Depew's candidacy served as a device for holding the New York delegation together and protecting it from raids for other candidates, especially Sherman, while the Blaine situation sorted itself out.[24]

The anemic candidacy of William Walter Phelps performed the same function for another doubtful state, New Jersey. Scion of a wealthy New York mercantile family, Phelps moved to New Jersey in the late 1860s and began to take part in Republican politics. He served a term in the House of Representatives in the 1870s and later was briefly the minister to Austria-Hungary in the Garfield administration. By 1888 he had been back in the House for six years. Phelps had no real chance of winning the presidential nomination, but if his idol Blaine was truly out and the nomination went west, he keenly hoped to be tapped for the vice presidency.[25]

As the Republican preconvention campaign got under way in earnest, everything hinged on the Blaine question. Would he ultimately consent to run, and if not, to whom would his powerful backers turn? No one understood the centrality of the Blaine factor better than Benjamin Harrison and his supporters. As a candidate for the presidential nomination, Harrison fell into the same category occupied by Gresham and Allison. He was not as prominent as Sherman, nor had he been on the national political scene nearly as long. But neither was he a mere favorite son. His residence in the key doubtful state of Indiana gave him an important edge, but his résumé listed many other attributes that made him an attractive choice for Republicans determined to take back the White House.

No candidate could boast a pedigree more distinguished than Harrison's. His great-grandfather had signed the Declaration of Independence, and when Benjamin was seven years old, his grandfather, William Henry Harrison, served briefly as the ninth president of the United States. His less ambitious father was a farmer of shaky financial standing, with a desultory political career that peaked with two terms in Congress in the 1850s. Benjamin Harrison was born in 1833 in his grandfather's house at North Bend, Ohio. Like Cleveland, he was raised a Presbyterian, but unlike Cleveland, he remained a regular and devout practitioner of that faith until his death. He attended Presbyterian-dominated Miami University at Oxford, Ohio, and for a time considered entering the ministry. At Miami he excelled in the classroom and honed his skills at public speaking. As a fellow student later recalled, Harrison "never seemed to regard life as a joke nor the opportunities for advancement as subjects for sport." He took an early interest in questions of political economy, and in his graduation oration, "The Poor of England," he examined the operation and impact of that nation's poor laws. Described by a classmate as "a protectionist at the age of nineteen," Harrison was no devotee of laissez-faire.[26]

After graduating in 1852, Harrison read law with a prominent lawyer in Cincinnati. He married in the fall of 1853 and passed the bar early the next year. In the spring of 1854 he moved to Indianapolis, which he called home for the rest of his life. After a slow start, he built a flourishing legal practice that won him prominence and, eventually, high fees. With no substantial monetary inheritance from his family, Harrison was in essence a self-made man. He was proud of his heritage, but he rarely traded overtly on his illustrious name. "Fame," he wrote to a friend, "is truly honorable and fortune only desirable when they have been *earned*."[27] Harrison joined the Republican Party and in 1857 won his first political office as city attorney. Three years later he was elected reporter of the state supreme court, a job he held until early 1862, when he entered the Union army as colonel of an Indiana regiment. Harrison earned a reputation as a competent military organizer and a courageous if not particularly distinguished soldier. He remained in uniform for the duration of the war and left the service as a brevet brigadier general. As a politician in the postwar decades, he closely attended the interests of his brother veterans.

After completing a second term as court reporter in early 1869, Harrison concentrated on his law practice and quickly moved to the head of the Indiana bar. During election seasons he frequently took to the stump and won plaudits as a forceful exponent of Republican Party doctrine. Defending the party's Reconstruction efforts in the South, he gave no quarter in denouncing the "dastardly outrages" that whites committed against African Americans in their drive to retake control of the former Confederate states. When depression plagued the country in the wake of the panic of 1873, Harrison advocated a "sound currency" and condemned Greenbackism and other inflationist schemes that he believed could lead to further economic disaster. In 1876, after the Republican candidate for governor withdrew in the face of conflict-of-interest allegations, Harrison agreed to step into the breach and campaigned tirelessly before narrowly losing the October election. Immediately afterward he set off on a multistate speaking tour for presidential nominee Rutherford B. Hayes, thereby extending his reputation beyond the borders of Indiana. One observer described Harrison the stump speaker as "all energy, nervous and wiry, . . . putting a full point to each sentence with a rapid motion of clenched fists."[28]

Harrison's Democratic opponent in 1876 had been James D. Williams, a rural congressman nicknamed "Blue Jeans" who cast himself as the people's advocate against the aristocratic Republican. Harrison's personality lent itself to the charge that he had scant sympathy for the little man. Never comfortable as a mixer among people outside his immediate family or small circle of associates, he often appeared aloof and cold. His occasional defense of well-to-do clients fed the notion that he was a champion of the "kid-gloves" set. This image was compounded by his actions during the Great Railroad Strike of 1877. Triggered by wage cuts, the strike began in the East and reached Indianapolis in late July. As a private citizen, Harrison served on a Committee of Arbitration that sponsored open discussion with the workers, yet he also headed a local militia company formed to maintain order and incidentally to help suppress the strike. In subsequent court proceedings on contempt charges, Harrison favored making examples of lawbreaking strikers, but he also called for short sentences for those convicted. Harrison's defense of order pleased citizens who shared his fear of social upheaval, but despite his attempted evenhandedness with the strikers, many workers remained unconvinced that he understood their interests.

Even so, the episode did not impede his rise to prominence among Republicans. After the death of Senator Oliver P. Morton in late 1877, Harrison emerged as the paramount leader of the party in Indiana. At the 1880 national convention he led a well-timed switch by the Hoosier delegation to James A. Garfield, and in the fall he campaigned vigorously for the ticket. Garfield hoped to reward Harrison with a cabinet post, but Harrison preferred a seat in the Senate. Federal Judge Walter Q. Gresham momentarily thought of contesting for the Senate seat, but he had a slim chance. Gresham's long service on the bench had prevented his playing the kind of overt political role at which Harrison excelled. In January 1881 the Indiana legislature handily elected Harrison to the Senate.

Early in his term, Harrison spent considerable time fielding patronage requests from his fellow Hoosiers. Nonetheless, during his six years in Congress he won praise as a competent legislator and an able advocate of Republican Party doctrine. As chairman of the Committee on the Territories, he labored for the admission of Dakota and other western territories to the Union, but the Democratic House of Representatives blocked the entry of these Republican-leaning areas. He advocated federal aid to education, aimed primarily at the South's illiterate population, but again this legislation failed to win approval from the House. The House also killed Harrison's bill to pension all dependent veterans, although he had more luck securing approval of the 101 special pension bills he sponsored. Like many other Republicans in this era, Harrison believed that the nation could derive substantial benefit from activism at the national level, but if his Senate service showed him anything, it was the exasperating frustration inherent in the period's frequently divided government. On the party's premier issue, the tariff, he enthusiastically toed the orthodox line. Not only did he believe in protectionism, but he also saw the issue as a way to win favor from labor and counter his "kid-gloves" image. "The wages of American workmen should be carefully and kindly considered" in setting customs duties, he declared. "The cry of the free trader is for a cheaper coat, an English coat, and he does not seem to care that this involves a cheapening of the men and women who spin, and weave, and cut, and stitch."[29]

In 1880 some Republicans had seen Harrison as a remotely possible dark horse for the party's presidential nomination. Four years later his Senate service and growing national reputation rendered his prospects a bit more tangible. The main Republican contenders in 1884 were the incumbent Chester Arthur and Blaine. Should the convention deadlock, Harrison's chances lay in winning the support of Blaine's backers, as Garfield had done in 1880. But this strategy ran directly counter to a similar one pushed by the backers of Walter Gresham, who was a poten-tial heir to Arthur's support. At the convention, after Blaine's managers complained that Harrison would deprive the Maine leader of needed votes, the Hoosiers did not present Harrison's name, and the majority of them voted for Blaine. Afterward, the senator wrote to his manager that he was "glad to have you give our state an advanced place in secur-ing the nomination of Mr. Blaine."[30] Harrison campaigned vigorously for Blaine in the fall and also served as his lawyer in a libel suit Blaine brought against the *Indianapolis Sentinel,* which had published scur-rilous stories about his marriage. Although Blaine eventually dropped the suit and lost the election, Harrison's men would not let the Plumed Knight's minions forget the valuable services Harrison had rendered.

Harrison's last two years in the Senate coincided with Grover Cleve-land's first two years in the White House. The Hoosier senator continued to gain notice as he stepped forward as a vocal critic of the president's policies. On matters of patronage, he condemned the administration's removal of officeholders on vague charges of "offensive partisanship" as a species of "hypocrisy" that sacrificed Republicans to Cleveland's "false pretensions." "The President proclaims Civil Service from the house tops," Harrison wrote to Hoosier reformer William Dudley Foulke, "while his assistants are openly disregarding the spirit of the law with-out any rebuke from him." When Congress passed a version of the de-pendent pension bill that Harrison had sponsored, Cleveland vetoed it, as he had hundreds of private pension bills. These vetoes, Harrison declared, were "tipped with poisoned arrows" and showed Cleveland's callous indifference to the well-being of the nation's veterans.[31]

Despite his growing reputation, Harrison found himself in an uphill struggle when he sought reelection to the Senate. In the winter of 1885 the Democratic majority in the Indiana General Assembly had configured the state's legislative districts in a reapportionment that Harrison described as "A Bill to Prohibit the Election of a Republican United States Senator from Indiana." In the election of 1886 Harrison waged a desperate campaign in favor of Republican candidates for the legislature, which would choose the state's next senator. He carried on a voluminous correspondence, raised funds, and took an extended speaking tour, denouncing the gerrymander and expounding national themes such as tariff protection and what he considered Cleveland's mistreatment of veterans. In the end, the Democrats won a slight plurality of seats in the legislature, where, after a prolonged struggle, they secured the support of a Greenbacker to elect a Democrat by a majority of a single vote. In the November elections, however, the Republicans' state ticket had been victorious, along with seven of thirteen congressmen. Most significant, in the aggregate tally for legislative candidates, the Republicans had received a total of 10,000 more votes than the Democrats. The result not only showed the GOP and Harrison as victims of the gerrymander but also demonstrated Harrison's superb organizational skill and his ability to amass votes in the face of formidable odds. National party leaders, including Blaine, had followed the Indiana contest closely, and Stephen B. Elkins congratulated Harrison on his "splendid fight." Although the national election was two years away, senate colleague Preston Plumb of Kansas assured Harrison that having waged "so magnificent a fight . . . puts you in the line of Presidential promotion."[32]

Harrison lost his Senate seat, but as he himself recognized, he had "come out of it with more friends & reputation than ever before." After the close of his term in March 1887, he returned to the full-time practice of law, which he much enjoyed, but at age fifty-four he was not quite ready to leave public life for good. He told one Republican gathering in Baltimore that although he was "an expiring statesman" he was also "a rejuvenated Republican." "I do not mean to quit the politics into which I was born." He continued to receive encouragement regarding his presidential prospects. During the summer he took a family vacation in Deer Park, Maryland, where Elkins, who owned a neighboring

Benjamin Harrison. (Library of Congress)

cottage, related his belief that if Blaine were out of the running for the 1888 nomination, Harrison would have an excellent chance. Harrison also heard from Wharton Barker, a Philadelphia banker, publisher, and would-be kingmaker, who fancied that he had brokered Garfield's nomination in 1880. In August Barker told Harrison that if Blaine remained in the race, he and John Sherman "will destroy each other and your nomination will follow as a matter of course." And Plumb repeated to Harrison his "strong conviction that your name is one which ought to be taken into careful account from the stand-point of availability. Of course the capacity goes without saying."[33]

Harrison took this flattering counsel in stride, but the Republican defeat in the 1887 state election in New York gave such notions a new relevance and weight. D. S. Alexander, a former Indiana attorney now practicing law in Buffalo, wrote to Harrison that the election had left Empire State "party managers *badly rattled*. . . . N. Y. Republicans are looking anxiously outside of this state for success in 1888. They recognize already *the great importance* of Indiana and are asking 'who can carry that state?'" Democrats controlled the federal, state, and New York City patronage, a circumstance that many Republicans saw as an insuperable obstacle for their party in 1888. As one put it, "the Angel Gabriel['s] name on the Republican ticket couldn't defeat the devil or Jeff Davis in New York." In any calculus that left New York out of the Republican equation, Indiana would become indispensable, and many regarded Harrison as the best man to win the Hoosier state. If he were teamed with Hawley and carried Connecticut or Phelps and carried New Jersey, Harrison could win the presidency without New York's electoral votes.[34]

Despite the compelling force of such calculations, however, Harrison's chances for the nomination remained dependent on Blaine's fate—either his withdrawal from the race or his faltering in the convention. In either contingency, Harrison recognized the necessity of retaining the good opinion of the Plumed Knight and his supporters. When the *Chicago Tribune*, no friend of Harrison, alleged that in 1884 he had made public a letter from Blaine regarding his libel suit against the *Indianapolis Sentinel*, Harrison promptly wrote to Elkins to deny the charge and to assure Elkins that he blamed the *Tribune* for the error. "I am not mad at you or at Mr. Blaine," he noted. Harrison also assured Elkins that if Blaine were nominated, the *Indianapolis Journal*, the state party organ, would give him "cordial support." In the early jockeying before Blaine's withdrawal, Harrison carefully maintained a noncandidate status. He tried to dampen any overt enthusiasm among his Indiana supporters that might offend the party's eastern power brokers. To one Republican who asked permission to introduce a resolution of endorsement at a local party gathering, Harrison replied, "I am very grateful for your goodwill. I have, however, said to all friends and must say to you that I will not in any way promote any movement to make me a Presidential Candidate." But behind the scenes he sought to "direct our work into quieter & more effective channels." His close political adviser, Indiana Attorney General Louis T. Michener, headed a small committee that managed a discreet canvass, fielding inquiries and softly touting their man's merits. Their aim, Michener later wrote, was "to have an unseen management that would produce a 'spontaneous movement.'"[35]

The moment to unleash that movement arrived with the announcement of Blaine's withdrawal in mid-February. The next day the *Indianapolis Journal* began openly to boom Harrison as "a man having the elements of character, the resources of ability, [and] the experience which long training and discipline give, to make a model candidate to lead the party to national success." Following the political etiquette of the day, Harrison continued to refrain from pushing his own cause too overtly, but he delivered a few well-received speeches that signaled his appeal as a forceful advocate of party doctrine. He told audiences that the continued denial of blacks' right to vote in the South was a "dominant question" because it blocked the operation of "a free and fair tribunal" for the determination of all other questions. If blacks had been fairly represented in Congress, for instance, the dependent pension bill could easily have passed over Cleveland's veto. Further, Harrison charged that the president's tariff ideas jeopardized the nation's economic well-being. Because of Cleveland's annual message, he argued, the "paralyzing shadow of free trade" threatened to halt the nation's "march of prosperity." In these speeches, Harrison aimed to leave no doubt that it was time for a new president, and he did not have to say that, in his opinion, he was the Republican best equipped to save the country from these perils.[36]

VYING FOR DELEGATES

With the acknowledged front-runner Blaine apparently sidelined, not only Harrison's candidacy but also the general campaign for national convention delegates entered a new and aggressive phase. John

Sherman quickly claimed the title of new front-runner. Laboring in his behalf were several capable lieutenants, including industrialist Mark Hanna of Cleveland, former Ohio Governor Charles Foster, and ex-Senator Warner Miller of New York. Former Illinois Congressman Green B. Raum, long an ardent advocate of blacks' civil rights, was particularly proficient at persuading southern delegates to enlist in Sherman's cause. By late spring, this southern support, added to Ohio's 46 delegates, led Sherman's men to claim more than 300 first-ballot votes for the senator, nearly three-fourths the number needed to win. This proved to be an exaggeration. Indeed, despite his impressive showing, before the convention met, Sherman was unable to position himself as the putative nominee.[37]

In March, Iowa Republicans braved a late-season blizzard to gather in Des Moines, where they gave their expected hearty endorsement to William Boyd Allison. Among the men chosen as delegates at large was James S. Clarkson, who boomed Allison in his newspaper, the *Iowa State Register,* and took the lead in pushing the senator's candidacy in other states. As a longtime member of the national committee, Clarkson had a wide acquaintanceship in the party. He wrote numerous letters and traveled widely on Allison's behalf. The senator showed up on many delegates' lists of second and third choices, but try as Clarkson might, he failed to garner much support for his candidate beyond the Iowa delegation. Nor did Allison's cause benefit when a group of railway executives, meeting in Chicago a few weeks before the Republican convention, denounced new rate regulations issued by the Iowa Railroad Commission. Although Allison bore no responsibility for the commission's actions, his undeserved reputation for Granger "radicalism" became more firmly embedded in the minds of many eastern Republicans. As Whitelaw Reid put it, "Allison could not carry New York—partly because he has made no great impression upon the Eastern mind and partly because the impression he has made is particularly unsatisfactory to Wall Street and the money centres generally."[38]

Paradoxically, Russell Alger's great wealth and success as a capitalist had a similar impact on his quest for delegates. Alger easily won the endorsement of the Michigan state convention at Grand Rapids in early May, but he had little appeal among Republicans who believed that the party was burdened by an image of servility to business. Moreover, the Michigan delegates, though enthusiastic for Alger, tended to be political amateurs poorly equipped to win support for their candidate from other states. Neither of the state's two Republican senators nor any of its six Republican congressmen were chosen to go to the national convention. "The weakness of the Alger delegation for effective work," said one observer, "lies in the absence from it of all the republicans of the State who have anything approaching a national reputation" or "any experience in national politics." Alger might be able to "purchase" support at the convention, but that was hardly the basis on which to build a successful national candidacy.[39]

Many Republicans who hoped to refurbish the party's image rallied behind Gresham, with his reputation for sympathy for farmers and workers. In the midst of the preconvention campaign for delegates, Gresham issued an evenhanded ruling in a railroad strike case that won praise from management and labor alike. "He has," said a newspaper touting his candidacy, "demonstrated repeatedly that the weak and the poor have just as good a chance for justice in his court as the wealthy and the powerful." Although he had lived in Illinois for only three years, Gresham enjoyed strong backing there, including that of the state's two most powerful Republican newspapers, the *Chicago Tribune* and the *Inter-Ocean.* The principal objection came from U.S. Senator Shelby Cullom, who had his own aspirations to be Illinois' favorite son and considered Gresham an outsider, "not entitled to recognition as a citizen of our state." Few Illinois Republicans agreed, however. The judge's managers secured the support of the state's delegates to the national convention, where they remained loyal to him from the first to the last ballot. Gresham attracted handfuls of delegates from several other midwestern and western states, but his backers' efforts to gather support in his native Indiana had little chance against his old rival Harrison.[40]

The battle with Gresham was a key element in Harrison's campaign, which national party leaders, especially the Blaine men, watched closely. The winter and spring witnessed a pas de deux between the Blaine and Harrison camps that continued until the last day of balloting at the national convention. After the publication of Blaine's Florence letter in mid-February, Harrison lost no time in issuing his reaction, couched in the most complimentary tones:

He certainly was not actuated in taking this step either by fear of defeat in the convention or at the polls. He has given his own reasons and I have no doubt sincerely. Mr. Blaine will continue to be a leader whether his name is on the ticket or not. The letter breathes the same intelligent and earnest devotion to the principles of the republican party that has always characterized him.[41]

These honeyed shafts hit their mark. Elkins immediately wrote to Harrison and revealed that for two years he had considered the Hoosier "the strongest leader we had next to Blaine." But Elkins also noted that because of "the confusion incident to the conflicting claims of a number of candidates, Blaine may yet be nominated." Harrison poured on more honey, telling Elkins that he had always believed that Blaine could be nominated "easily." But the wary Hoosier also frankly warned Elkins that if Blaine were nominated after his ostensible withdrawal, "his letter will prove to have been a great mistake," for it would be hard to convince other candidates "that they have not been injuriously dealt with." "Such a nomination," he wrote, would generate "more opposition than if he had taken the nomination without a word of protest." Moreover, "Mr. Blaine's friends will practically surrender their influence in naming another candidate, if they hold off & only establish tentative relations." Harrison welcomed "relations" with Blaine's allies and indeed could not hope to be nominated without their help, but he also understood that Blaine's friends, if not Blaine himself, might try to string him along in a double game with Blaine's nomination as its ultimate goal.[42]

Blaine made no direct contact with Harrison during the preconvention campaign, but he clearly recognized Harrison's virtues as a potential nominee, as demonstrated by a confidential assessment of the field of candidates that Blaine sent to Elkins soon after his declination. Sherman should not be nominated, Blaine said, because of opposition to him "at critical points" (that is, New York) and also because he was "not in sympathy" with the Blaine wing of the party. Gresham, too, was "not acceptable." Blaine dismissed the judge as a "disciple" of Robert Ingersoll, the nation's foremost religious agnostic, but more important, Gresham was "a demagogue and iconoclast on the Bench. His unjust hostility to corporations would array the capital of the country against him before the canvass would be a month advanced." Similarly, Blaine wrote, Allison "has a tariff record which would destroy the effort of the party to make a campaign for protection." Blaine also ruled out the several favorite-son candidates "for various reasons" he did not bother to specify. Thus, Blaine concluded, "the one man remaining, who in my judgment can make the best run, is Ben Harrison. I could give many reasons, but forbear." Blaine did not admit to Elkins that he thought he might regain his old job as head of the State Department in a Harrison administration, but that this prospect had occurred to him and formed part of his calculation is more than plausible.[43]

Elkins might have taken this "sacredly private" missive from Blaine as a request to go all out for Harrison, but he did not quite do that. In communications with Harrison and his manager, Louis Michener, he continued his strategy of encouraging the Hoosier's candidacy while noting that Harrison's access to the Blaine men's support depended on Blaine's truly being out of the running. Soon after Blaine's Florence letter, Michener wrote to Elkins that the letter "takes him out of the range of possibilities" and added, "we think we have the right to make some modest claims upon the friends of Mr. Blaine, such as yourself, for instance, because of the high character of our candidate, and the very material support given to Mr. Blaine at a critical juncture in the last National Convention." Elkins replied that he was "neither unmindful [of] nor ungrateful" for "the kindly aid" the Harrison men had rendered in 1884. "Gen. Harrison knows that I feel favorably disposed towards him," Elkins wrote, "and that next to Mr. Blaine he has always been my choice." After Elkins received Blaine's assessment of the candidates, he assured Michener that he was "doing, in a quiet way, all the work that I possibly can in Harrison's behalf" and cited "the necessity of the General and his near friends always having a kind word for Blaine." Still, Elkins told the Hoosiers, "there is a strong current running towards Blaine, and he may be nominated by acclamation." In truth, Elkins was one of the main forces behind that "strong current." On the same day he wrote to Michener, he thanked Whitelaw Reid for taking his advice and printing a pro-Blaine interview by Chauncey Depew in the *New York Tribune*. The pronouncement would "have great effect & weight throughout the country," Elkins told Reid. "The movement towards Blaine is gaining in strength."[44]

Thus, Elkins cultivated good relations with the Hoosiers for three reasons. First, the Harrison candidacy could serve as a temporary repository for tacit Blaine support that could be sprung for the Plumed Knight under the right circumstances at the convention. Elkins frankly told Harrison that it would be "good policy generally whenever a district wants to send a delegate who is, or has been, a Blaine man, uninstructed and untrammelled by pledges or promises." Second, Harrison's candidacy in Indiana could prevent that pivotal state from going to an anti-Blaine candidate such as Gresham, who, with support from Illinois, Wisconsin, Minnesota, and other states, could ride to the nomination on a wave of a midwestern movement. And third, in the event Harrison rather than Blaine were nominated, he would be a formidable candidate in the fall campaign and, in the event of victory, a president sympathetic to Blaine's approach to issues and amenable to his advice on patronage.[45]

But the relationship was not a one-way street. Harrison and Michener well understood what Elkins and his allies were doing. As Harrison later wrote, he "was not unaware of the fact that they were trying to bring about his [Blaine's] nomination." The implicit Blaine strategy envisioned a multiplicity of candidates competing in the national convention and, after a lengthy deadlock, the delegates turning to Blaine with a unanimous or nearly unanimous nomination that he could not refuse. Harrison's chances, in contrast, lay in the likelihood that anti-Blaine delegates (especially those of John Sherman) would refuse to fall in with the scheme. The Hoosiers knew that the Blaine contingent would be the largest at the convention, and they were determined to be in a position to capture it at the crucial moment when the Blaine plan collapsed. Hence, through the winter and spring, Harrison and Michener were more than willing to go along with Elkins's game. They welcomed his aid, and they responded promptly to his advice. Ultimately, they believed, the Harrison tail would wag the Blaine dog.[46]

Early on, Elkins warned the Hoosiers that Harrison's record on Chinese immigration could hurt him among West Coast Republicans, who had always been strong backers of Blaine. The Indiana senator had voted against the Chinese Exclusion Act of 1882 on the grounds that the measure went beyond the class of laborers whose immigration the United States could legally suspend under an existing treaty with China. In late February the *New York Herald* published an article detailing Harrison's votes and claiming that he had "steadily resisted all legislation to restrict Chinese immigration." As a result, the paper asserted, Pacific state Republicans would regard Harrison's nomination as "a virtual abandonment of the campaign in California, Oregon, and Nevada." Elkins urged Harrison and Michener to send him information to counter the charges. Both men responded, Michener in greater detail. He noted that on key votes on the legislation in 1882, most Republican senators, including fellow presidential candidates Sherman, Allison, and Hawley, had voted as Harrison had done, presumably on the same grounds. In addition, when the issue of tightening limits on the immigration of Chinese laborers arose in 1886, Harrison had voted in favor of restrictive legislation, both as a member of the Foreign Relations Committee and in the Senate. Elkins passed Michener's letter on to the *New York Tribune,* which printed it nearly verbatim over a pseudonym. The issue subsided, and Oregon Senator John H. Mitchell, a leading anti-Chinese Republican, assured Harrison that he believed the former senator had done "all that could be done in the matter of restriction and at the same time maintain the integrity of existing treaties" and stated that opposition to Harrison's candidacy based on the Chinese issue was "not only untrue but unjust."[47]

In the preconvention campaign, no state drew more attention than Indiana. From the start, eastern leaders advised Harrison that it was "very important that you have the solid Indiana delegation" and that "the country must not hear of Gen. Gresham." As in 1884, the state witnessed a fierce struggle between the forces of the two Hoosier leaders, but the balance of power had shifted by 1888. Gresham no longer wielded the political leverage he had held as postmaster general, and Harrison, after his tenacious fight to retain his Senate seat, had a firm grip on the state party organization.[48]

Gresham was popular among many Hoosiers, but his managers concluded early on that the most they could hope for was an uninstructed delegation to the national convention in Chicago. An uninstructed delegation would deny Harrison the certainty of thirty first-ballot votes, and it would signify to national party leaders Harrison's weakness in his own state. If Harrison could not command his own state party, these leaders would reason, how could he win Indiana for the Republicans in November?[49] As part of this strategy, the Gresham men provided Harrison's Chinese immigration voting record to the *New York Herald.* But Harrison's supporters were prepared with attacks of their own. On the tariff issue, some branded Gresham with the odious "free trader" label. Indeed, they questioned whether he was truly committed to the Republican cause in general. After his "one weak speech" for Blaine in 1884, some said, all he deserved was "a severe chastening" until he had "again earned the respect of the party."[50]

The bitterness between the two camps grew so intense that the Gresham men abandoned their hope for even an uncommitted delegation and adopted the strategy of accepting a favorite-son endorsement of Harrison. Convinced that the judge had more support outside the state, they believed that once the Harrison men realized that their candidate could not win the nomination, "they will feel bound to join in a friendly spirit a move for Gresham." But getting the Harrison organization to accept delegates "friendly" to the judge proved enormously difficult. In Gresham's own hometown in southern Indiana, the Harrison men alleged that "Gresham was [for] Free Trade and [they] told all manner of lies about him" before railroading through a slate of Harrison delegates to the district convention. Indeed, throughout the state, Gresham supporters found that they had to be exceedingly discreet to have any chance at all of being chosen.[51]

The Harrison organization showed its muscle in the April district conventions that named delegates to the national convention. Ten of the thirteen districts instructed their delegates to vote for Harrison, one "commended" his candidacy, and another had already selected Harrison delegates in February. Of the twenty-six delegates chosen, seven at most, but probably no more than four, could be regarded as Gresham men. Even these delegates publicly vowed to cast an initial vote for Harrison "if there is a reasonable show for his nomination." The *Indianapolis Journal* anointed the group a "solid Harrison delegation," and Michener told Republicans elsewhere that all the delegates would "stand by him loyally and sincerely." At the May 3 state convention, the Harrison men repeated their triumph, electing all four delegates at large and passing instructions for the delegation to vote and work "earnestly and persistently" for the former senator. As Harrison's wife, Caroline, noted after the state convention, Michener was "laughing all over" at the result.[52]

Even after this impressive showing, however, the Gresham men continued to belittle Harrison's strength in Indiana. They adopted the tactic of telling eastern Republicans that Gresham supporters constituted a majority of the delegates and that they had only "consented" to the Harrison instructions to avoid a quarrel in the state convention. Such tactics foreclosed any chance that the Harrison delegates might switch to Gresham in the national convention. *Indianapolis Journal* editor Elijah W. Halford, himself a delegate, complained to Gresham's manager, Charles W. Fairbanks, that he had never before seen "so persistent, outrageous, and untruthful an attempt made to misrepresent the facts." Traveling in the East, Michener urged Halford to get out "a *special edition* to be sent out to all the men on our lists" to counteract "the persistent lying in favor of G." Three days later the *Journal* editorialized, "Indiana Republicans have but one choice for President."[53]

The Harrison people particularly hammered at Gresham's tariff views. Michener told eastern protectionists that Gresham believed in "sugar coated free trade." Wharton Barker, who published the protectionist journal the *American,* wrote to Gresham that he had "no advocate among the known Protectionists of the nation." He asked the judge to "please let me know what rate of duties you advocate for iron ore, pig iron, steel, steel rails, and wool." Gresham thought Barker's letter "insolent" and did not reply. Although the *Chicago Inter-Ocean* claimed that Gresham was "as good a protectionist as Blaine or Sherman," and Joseph Medill insisted that he "would stand on the Republican platform," Gresham himself refused to discuss the subject publicly. As the national convention approached, Barker confidently assured the Harrison men that they "need not have any future fear from Gresham. The high tariff men will not have him." Further, Barker wrote to Harrison, "the Iron and Steel men are satisfied that your nomination is wise."[54]

BLAINE DREAMS: FATE OR FANTASY?

While the struggle with Gresham unfolded, Harrison and Michener continued to pay court to Elkins. At the district convention held in Indianapolis, Michener secured passage of a resolution declaring that Hoosier Republicans would never forget Blaine's "able services, and that in retirement he is still the recipient of our love and confidence." Michener sent a copy of the resolution to Elkins and also wrote that he regarded Blaine as "the greatest Statesman of the present day." If Harrison were nominated and elected, Michener wrote, "no good friend of Mr. Blaine's will have any occasion to regret it, and I do not use this language lightly, for I understand its full import, and mean it to be understood in that light." Elkins did not need much imagination to see that Harrison would be amenable to Blaine's entry into his cabinet. Elkins reciprocated the goodwill with assurances that "Harrison is growing daily" because "the logic of the situation is in his favor." He told Harrison that he was doing "quiet work" in his behalf and "talk[ing] daily with leading republicans on the strength of your position." Yet Elkins nearly always coupled his encouraging reports with reminders of the contingent nature of Harrison's position. Blaine "may be nominated," he told Michener at one point, "but if he is not, in my judgment Harrison is bound to be and it is the wisest and safest thing to do." After the Indiana state convention, Elkins "heartily" congratulated Michener on "the great enthusiasm expressed in favor of General Harrison." But he also wrote,

"Everything now points to Blaine's nomination. This however may all be changed."[55]

The Harrison camp well knew that this support for Blaine was not entirely spontaneous. "I think the indications now are," Harrison wrote to Barker, "that a movement will be made to name Mr. Blaine." How to react to that effort was "a very grave question," Michener said, for after Gresham's defeat in the Indiana convention, Michener was convinced "that the only thing to be feared was the Blaine movement." Barker advised Harrison "not [to] permit the Blaine men the advantage they would have if they could say you would go on the Blaine ticket as Vice President." In fact, throughout the spring, Harrison and Michener had insisted that Harrison would not accept second place, thereby signaling their unwillingness to enter into any alliance aimed at nominating Blaine. Even Harrison's wife, who usually stayed out of political discussions, wrote to her son that "the Blaine men, Mr. Elkins among the rest, are very foolish to think of nominating Mr. B. after his declination. It will be sure to make trouble for the party."[56]

Nonetheless, with little more than a month remaining before the national convention, Elkins still harbored fond hopes that the national convention would eventually choose Blaine. A typically cryptic letter from Blaine hinted that Elkins might have reason to hope that his idol would accept. "My letter declining to be nominated for the Presidency was in all respects wise for myself," Blaine wrote to Elkins. "I hope it may prove wise for the Party, but the multitude of candidates & the growing difficulty of concentration causes me to doubt a little on the latter. But I trust a wise result will be reached." In mid-April the death of Roscoe Conkling aroused fear among Sherman's supporters that the demise of Blaine's old nemesis would "revive the spirits" of the "hungry and brainless crowd" pushing Blaine. Indeed, in early May an increasingly confident Elkins sent Whitelaw Reid his estimate of Blaine's growing strength on the first ballot to be taken in Chicago. He counted 349 votes for the Plumed Knight, or 84 percent of the number needed to win. A week later Elkins told Reid that fresh reports pushed his estimates even higher.[57]

Reid found these numbers gratifying, for throughout the spring he had worked as assiduously as Elkins in Blaine's behalf. In numerous letters Reid wrote that Blaine had been sincere in his withdrawal, but he also insisted that the Florence letter contained nothing "absolutely inconsistent with his accepting a nomination." Indeed, he told one correspondent that Blaine, a notorious hypochondriac, had written the letter "partly, perhaps, because at Florence he had a twinge of rheumatism." The more time that passed, Reid said, the clearer it became that the men he termed the "volunteer candidates" were "all lacking in strength at some critical point." For different reasons, neither Sherman nor Allison nor Gresham could carry New York, and whereas Chauncey Depew might win New York, his railroad connections would likely cost him key midwestern Republican states. Reid did concede, however, that "there is a very kindly feeling here towards Ben Harrison." The ex-senator would offer geographic balance to a ticket headed by Blaine, but "if it should be thought impracticable to nominate Blaine, a good many of the Blaine people hereabouts would be likely to take Harrison for second choice." Yet Reid sought to project that outcome as only a remote, if acceptable, possibility, telling one California Republican in late April that "the chances are about three out of four in favor of the nomination of Blaine." And should the party choose him, Reid said, no one in the United States was "so big that he can refuse the greatest office on earth without making himself ridiculous or worse. I certainly do not believe Mr. Blaine would."[58]

As Reid's comments suggested, New York would play a pivotal role in the nomination. After Blaine's withdrawal, Depew enjoyed something of a boom, but he had no real chance to take the prize. Many New York leaders, including Depew himself and Thomas C. Platt, favored Blaine, but in light of the Florence letter, they thought it best to keep the state's options open. When the state convention met in mid-May, it did not select Depew as a favorite son for the presidency but instead chose him as a delegate at large to Chicago. There he would be joined by Platt and Senator Frank Hiscock, and also by ex-Senator Warner Miller, who supported Sherman. Although the state convention made no endorsement, Reid figured that of the seventy-two New York delegates, ten or twelve would go for Sherman while the rest would at heart favor Blaine. "I begin to think," Reid confided to William Walter Phelps, "Blaine will be nominated, will accept and will be elected."[59] Even Allison's hardheaded manager Clarkson said, "Anyone is blind and deaf who travels over the country and does not see that the great majority of the people are determined that Blaine shall be the nominee." Elkins told Clarkson that "New York will demand" Blaine, and "if nominated Blaine will not decline." Indeed, so encouraged was Elkins that he suggested to one of

PREPARING FOR A TEN STRIKE

James G. Blaine prepares to bowl over other Republicans for the presidential nomination. (New York Daily Graphic, May 23, 1888)

Sherman's managers, Charles Foster, that the other candidates should come together in a meeting and, failing to agree on any of them, defer to Blaine. "Feeling Blaine's nomination would come," Elkins asked Foster, "why not make it unanimous by having Sherman declare in advance for him[?]"[60]

While the Blaine men indulged in such fantasies, the Harrison men remained cool. Though conceding that "nothing can beat Harrison but a movement in favor of Blaine," Michener thought it "best for us to say nothing at all against Mr. Blaine and thus avoid any complications." "My notion," he told Barker, "is that Mr. Blaine will by letter or interview check his friends in their mad career." He was right. In mid-May Blaine, who was in Paris, wrote Reid a letter for publication that he hoped would reinforce his earlier withdrawal and arrest the efforts of his "most valued friends" who had seen it as "not absolutely conclusive." After his Florence letter, he told Reid and the nation, "if I should now, by speech or by silence, by commission or omission, permit my name, in any event, to come before the Convention I should incur the reproach of being uncandid with those who have always been candid with me. . . . Assuming that the Presidential nomination could by any possible chance be offered to me, I could not accept it without leaving in the minds of thousands of these men the impression that I had not been free from indirection, and therefore I could not accept it all." Privately, Blaine wrote to Reid that it would be "a stupendous blunder both for the party and myself to nominate me after my Florence letter." He urged Reid to "cool the ardor of those who would inconsiderately rush me into the canvass whether or not & rush me to defeat." Reid printed the Paris letter in the May 30 issue of the *Tribune*. An accompanying editorial called it "an act of magnanimous self-abnegation rare in political history."[61]

The letter stunned Blaine's partisans. "The general feeling is disappointment and discouragement," Elkins wrote to Reid. Even the battle-hardened Tom Platt confessed that he was "pained and disappointed beyond measure. It just makes me sick & discouraged." Moreover, the letter hardly clarified the situation for the New York delegation. Two days after its publication, Platt, Depew, and others met at Reid's house but could not agree on a plan of action. New Yorkers were "not quite decided," Reid said afterward, but were "eager to hear and consider carefully everything that can be said for or against any nomination." The candidates' agents were, of course, equally eager to fill their ears. "The Grand Old Party is pretty well represented in the city now," observed the *New York Herald* in early June, "every man with a boom as big as a teacup having dozens of friends at work on the New York delegation." While representatives of Alger, Gresham, and Allison prowled the hallways of the Fifth Avenue Hotel, the Republicans' principal New York haunt, Sherman himself held court in room number 38. Although, as the *Herald* put it, the Ohio senator "proved to a number of delegates that he is not a load of ice," he made no headway with Platt. The boss was certain that he did not want Sherman, but he remained unsure as to which of the other candidates would best serve New York's interests.[62]

Despite the plethora of candidates, Blaine loyalists found it "difficult," as Elkins put it, "to become reconciled to Blaine's retirement." Elkins remained convinced that "over-persuasion" by friends of other candidates regarding the "'insincerity' feature" had prompted Blaine to write the Paris letter. Without that pressure, Elkins believed, Blaine would have "remained silent and received the nomination." Reid, who in early June was floating tickets of Harrison and Phelps or Depew and Harrison, by midmonth was telling correspondents, "My table groans under the letters insisting that Blaine must be nominated, which seems to me impossible, unless the other candidates are made to realize that feeling. If Sherman, Harrison, and Allison would unite in a letter to Blaine requesting him to accept the nomination, the Convention would name him like a flash."[63]

That idea had even less viability now than when Elkins had first broached it with Sherman's man Foster a month earlier. In fact, Sherman's friends now asked Elkins to endorse their man, which he refused to do. "Sherman isn't ready to get out yet," Phelps told Reid, "even for Blaine." And neither was Harrison. After the Paris letter, Michener insisted to Elkins that "a great many of the old Blaine Guard are coming to the support of Harrison." "With your help," he added, "we shall be able to get the greater part of the Blaine delegates, and thus nominate our man." As his own power to control the situation ebbed, Elkins clearly saw the need to secure his footing with the Hoosier candidate. He pressed Harrison to meet him at Deer Park, and after Harrison declined, Elkins bowed to the Hoosiers' wishes and swung by Indianapolis on his way to the Chicago convention. He told Michener that he would bring "some *very* important information" regarding New York, where party leaders "rely somewhat on my seeing our friend before I get to Chicago." "Platt is in a doubtful state," he noted, and "has promised to wait until my conference" with Harrison.[64] But if Elkins expected specific promises about appointments in a Harrison administration, he was disappointed. The candidate would say no more than that he would try to "treat the Republican leaders in all the States fairly—to please them if I can."[65]

Even before Elkins's visit, Michener had headed for Chicago, accompanied by Harrison's law partner John B. Elam. Harrison had given them instructions that comported with his own discussion with Elkins. They had full authority to speak in his behalf, but he also directed them to make no explicit promises regarding patronage. Those instructions were soon put to the test when Senator Matthew S. Quay, the leader of the party in Pennsylvania, approached the Hoosiers with a proposition to switch his allegiance to Harrison in exchange for the promise of a cabinet post for his state. Quay had agreed to back Sherman but was "ready to leave him any *moment* if Penn[sylvania] can make a nomination by doing it." The Pennsylvanians even drafted a letter for Harrison to sign, stating that he thought their state "entitled to representation in my Cabinet." Michener and Elam thought well enough of the offer to dispatch the proposed letter to Harrison in Indianapolis. Harrison categorically refused the deal, noting on the envelope containing the draft, "I said 'no.'" Quay stood by Sherman until the convention's last ballot.[66]

THE REPUBLICAN NATIONAL CONVENTION

In the week before the official opening of the convention, Republicans poured into Chicago, where they quickly found that confusion reigned. Harrison's son-in-law, Robert McKee, reported to the family in Indianapolis, "If any fellow can make heads or tails out of the grand hubbub of claims, counter claims, lies and a few truths that slap him from every side, he is more levelheaded than I am." One thing was certain, though: "There is a tremendous sentiment on all sides for Blaine." Michener and his Hoosier coworkers labored mightily to counteract that sentiment or, more important, turn it their way. They had scant hope for cracking the Blainiac stronghold of California, however. The sixteen Golden State delegates, according to one wag, wanted "Blaine or nothing, and if they had a second choice it would be Mrs. Blaine."[67]

More accessible and more important for Michener's purposes was New York. The New Yorkers arrived in Chicago still undecided about what they would do. On the day before the convention opened, the delegates caucused and concluded that they would formally offer Depew's name in nomination. Depew may have harbored some small hope that lightning would strike, but Platt frankly told reporters that his colleague's candidacy did "not change the situation any." Leaders of the delegation regarded it as little more than a means of holding the delegation together while they continued to negotiate with other camps. A New York Sherman delegate assured his chief that Depew's entering the race inured to the Ohioan's benefit because western delegations would unite on Sherman to defeat the railroad president. But in fact, Platt was considering which other western candidate—Alger, Allison, or Harrison—would have the best chance of beating Sherman. He had already ruled out Gresham and met with the judge in Chicago and frankly told him that his nomination was impossible. The degree to which New York would participate in a potential move to Blaine remained a mystery, but Platt always kept his eye on the main chance. The night before the convention opened, Chicago betting parlors were offering two-to-one odds that the convention would turn to the Plumed Knight.[68]

When Republican national chairman B. F. Jones gaveled the convention to order on June 19, the candidates' agents continued to make extravagant claims, but no one could predict with certainty who would emerge as the party's standard-bearer. What was certain was that Republicans were eager to meet Cleveland squarely on the tariff issue. "Thanks to Mr. Cleveland and his Southern allies," Jones told the assembled delegates, "the Democratic party has thrown off the disguise in which it has heretofore fought its battles in the Northern States, and has boldly declared for British free trade, and against American protection." "The distinctive issue of the present campaign," said temporary chairman John M. Thurston, "is that of the tariff." Moreover, Thurston added, "The Republican party turns to the new South with wide-open arms" and "proposes to break down the barrier of unpleasant memories with the hope of a new prosperity." Although Jones and Thurston sounded the motif for the impending campaign, Frederick Douglass was on hand for the opening ceremonies and struck a cautionary note. He asked the delegates to remember "your black friends . . . now stripped of their constitutional right to vote for the grand standard-bearer whom you will present to the country." "Be not deterred from duty by the cry of 'bloody shirt,'" Douglass urged. "Let that shirt wave so long as blood shall be found upon it."[69]

After the opening ceremonies, routine matters occupied the convention's first few days. The committee on permanent organization presented Californian Morris M. Estee for permanent chairman, and the delegates approved. In a convention so full of contingency, the presiding officer had the potential to wield immense power, and the Blaine men could take comfort that one of their own would have the gavel in his hand. A credentials fight over several seats in the Virginia delegation occupied considerable time. The convention eventually voted against a group more or less identified with Sherman, an outcome that most observers considered a blow to his chances in the main contest. While the supporters of the various candidates angled for position behind the scenes, the delegates were startled by newspaper accounts of a purported interview in which Andrew Carnegie, with whom Blaine was traveling in Scotland, asserted that "if Mr. Blaine is nominated he will not refuse." As John Hay put it, the report "tangled the skein in an extraordinary manner." Nor was the skein straightened much when Carnegie denied the interview but repeated his own long-held belief that his friend "ought—not would—accept."[70]

The real business began on Thursday, June 21, with the adoption of the platform. The chairman of the committee on resolutions was William McKinley, a veteran Ohio congressman who had made the tariff his legislative specialty. The Indiana member of the committee was *Indianapolis Journal* editor E. W. Halford, who did his best to make sure that the platform harmonized with Harrison's views. According to rumor, some western committee members favored recognition of a need for tariff reduction, but they got nowhere. As presented by McKinley, the platform declared, "We are uncompromisingly in favor of the American system of protection; we protest against its destruction as proposed by the President and his party. They serve the interests of Europe; we will support the interests of America. . . . We denounce the Mills bill as destructive to the general business, the labor, and the farming interests of the country."

The document specifically condemned the Democrats' proposal to put wool on the free list. To reduce the surplus, the Republicans proposed repealing tobacco taxes and imposts on spirits used for the arts or mechanical purposes, plus the "revision," by which they meant the increase, of some customs duties "to check imports" and thus reduce revenue. "If there shall remain a larger revenue than is requisite for the wants of the government," they went on, "we favor the entire repeal of internal revenue taxes rather than the surrender of any part of our protective system."

Regarding the surplus in a positive light, the Republicans called for expenditures for a variety of purposes: strengthening the navy, fortifying harbors, rehabilitating the merchant marine, internal improvements, aid to education, and veterans' pensions. They condemned trusts, immigration of Chinese labor, and polygamy in Utah. On the question of civil rights, they insisted on the right of all citizens to vote in elections and to have their votes counted. Harkening to the pleas of western members, the platform committee included a plank that said, "The Republican party is in favor of the use of both gold and silver as money, and condemns the policy of the Democratic Administration in its efforts to demonetize silver." The plank on the civil service repeated the 1884 plank endorsing reform and condemned the Mugwumps for having deserted the party on the issue that year to support a candidate, Cleveland, who broke his reform pledges once in office. In foreign affairs, the document censured the administration for inadequate defense of the Monroe Doctrine and for "its weak and unpatriotic treatment" of the fisheries controversy with Canada and Great Britain.[71]

The convention adopted the platform unanimously. Most Republicans around the country applauded it. The *New York Tribune* called the document "the best and strongest statement of principles since the days of Abraham Lincoln." Most important, said the *Tribune,* "the main issue, Protection or Free Trade, is met with the courage of men who know that their principles have made the growth and prosperity of the country great beyond all precedent." Only the party's small minority of tariff reductionists failed to embrace the platform enthusiastically. Joseph Medill deemed the revenue plank "a dreadful blunder." Gresham even considered pulling out of the race but bowed to objections that doing so would embarrass his supporters. Nonetheless, the tariff plank rendered his diminishing prospects even more doubtful. Democrats responded predictably. "This is the feast to which the republican party invites the tax-payers of the country," said the *Indianapolis Sentinel,* "cheap whisky and tobacco, dear clothing and food and shelter, the indefinite perpetuation of war taxes in time of peace, for the benefit, not of the public treasury, but of monopoly." At least, said the *New York Herald,* the Republicans had "committed themselves squarely upon the one question of which everyone is thinking, and on which the canvass ought to be and will now be made."[72]

Who would lead the Republican canvass was at last the question before the convention. After adopting the platform, the delegates spent the rest of the day listening restlessly to nominating and seconding speeches. All the speakers naturally recited the virtues of their candidates. Most of the speeches, however, also betrayed a partly apologetic tone, gently urging the delegates to overlook certain negatives attached to their candidates. Gresham's advocates admitted that he was "not presented as the first choice" of his home state but claimed that he was "the favorite son of the United States," and they particularly insisted that he was "sound upon the tariff." Iowa's chairman sought to make a virtue of Allison's blandness by portraying the senator as a man of "calm pose of mind who seeks the methods of a judicious conservatism" and is "versed in the details of public business." Declaring that "the accumulation of wealth is a grand thing when it is honestly accumulated," speakers for Alger assured the delegates that he had "acquired not a dollar by any improper or objectionable methods." Similarly, Frank Hiscock of New York granted that Depew was "the President of a great railroad corporation," but he maintained that "there is not a farmer, freighter, mechanic, or common laborer in New York who will vote against him for that."

The addresses in behalf of John Sherman partook of more substance than the others, emphasizing the senator's long record of leadership on such issues as the currency, the tariff, and civil rights. But a seconder from North Carolina probably did Sherman no good by asserting that no one had done more to make the Republican Party "successful in all the campaigns since its organization, except perhaps that wanderer on the hills of Scotland—with that single exception he stands without a peer in the Republican party." This unsubtle reminder of Blaine's superb talents inevitably made one's own candidate pale by comparison. Charles Emory Smith, editor of the *Philadelphia Press* and a Blaine man at heart, had so little to say about the inexperienced Edwin Fitler of Pennsylvania that one observer noted he had "served no purpose except to show how big an ass a bright man can make of himself." Senator John C. Spooner argued that the principal objection against Wisconsin Governor Jeremiah Rusk—that he hailed from a state certain to go Republican—could be leveled against most of the other candidates. That objection, however, did not apply to Harrison, and Harrison's advocates, while touting his personal virtues and accomplishments, made the most of his residence in a doubtful state. "Indiana is the great pivotal State in the coming contest," one of them declared, "and the supreme importance of her fifteen electoral votes must not be ignored by this convention." After more than five hours of speeches, the convention adjourned, and the delegates resigned themselves to the unrelenting importunities of the agents of the various campaigns before balloting began the next day.[73]

Most of those agents had been hard at work for days, none more industriously than Harrison's manager, Louis Michener. Assisting him most closely was William W. Dudley, a seasoned organizer best known in party circles for his no-holds-barred effort in winning Indiana for the party in 1880. Utterly committed to Harrison's cause, Dudley had written to the general a few months earlier, "I love you as a brother and will stand by you as long as I live." Michener also had help from state officials and other prominent Hoosier Republicans, as well as, he later claimed, "10,000 volunteers who came from Indiana" and "thronged the hotels and lodging houses and earnestly, intelligently and persistently presented the arguments" in Harrison's favor. Michener's strategy was "to give no offense to the friends of other candidates," to garner as many first-ballot votes as possible, and, most important, to gather "assurances of 'second choice' support." Other campaigns took a similar approach, but Michener was convinced that his superior candidate gave him the advantage.[74]

As expected, no one placed Blaine's name in nomination, but as a Sherman man wrote to the senator, Chicago reverberated with "too much Blaine talk for comfort." After the nominating speeches, Elkins was claiming that 500 delegates at heart favored Blaine. But Blaine's champions found it difficult to coordinate a semiclandestine effort on behalf of an unnamed candidate in such a way as to minimize offense to other candidates whose support they ultimately would need. At a nighttime meeting after the nominating speeches, Elkins, Platt, Hiscock, Phelps, and others devised a strategy for a deadlock. They saw little prospect for Sherman's withdrawal but doubted that he could assemble enough votes to win. Hence, they would lend support to other candidates to test their strength and demonstrate that none had the numbers to overpower Sherman. In the resulting stalemate the convention would have no alternative but to turn to Blaine. They more or less agreed to tap Harrison first for this dubious distinction, believing that if the strategy failed he would make an acceptable nominee.[75]

As the delegates assembled for balloting on Friday, June 22, John Hay described the scene as "a hot and sizzling cauldron of intrigue and anxiety." The first ballot showed fourteen men receiving votes. Although many of these votes were simply complimentary, the wide dispersal portended well for the Blaine men. Sherman received 229 votes, slightly more than half the number (416) needed to win, followed by Gresham (107), Depew (99), Harrison (85), Alger (84), and Allison (72), with the rest of the votes scattering. Blaine received 35 votes—all 16 from the irrepressible Californians, plus handfuls from twelve other states. Sherman's total included all of Ohio's 46 votes, 29 from Pennsylvania, and 139 from southern states. The senator received votes from only three northern states aside from Ohio and Pennsylvania, hardly the basis on which to mount a Republican campaign. Harrison received 29 votes from Indiana (one defector going to Gresham) and handfuls from nineteen other states and two territories. All 44 of Illinois' votes went to Gresham, who also received 11 from Minnesota, where his low-tariff views were popular, plus small numbers from several other states. Seventy-one votes from New York formed the bulk of Depew's tally. After Fitler withdrew, Sherman moved up to 249 on the second ballot, which proved to be his high-water mark in the convention. Otherwise, the second and third ballots on Friday brought little change, except for Alger's nearly doubling his votes from the South, largely at Sherman's expense. At two o'clock the delegates took a recess until seven.[76]

After his poor showing in the morning session, Depew decided to withdraw. He and New York's other delegates at large, Platt, Hiscock, and Miller, met to determine the state's next move. The meeting quickly degenerated into a heated argument. Platt and Hiscock pushed for Allison, whom Depew adamantly opposed because of Iowa's abusive depiction of himself as a "railroad" candidate. Miller favored Sherman, against whom Platt was implacable. They finally agreed to back Harrison when the convention reconvened and persuaded three-quarters of the delegation to join them. How long they would stay with Harrison remained an open question. At any rate, their decision advanced the Blaine "testing" strategy to the next phase. News reports carried rumors that Michener and his allies, in exchange for New York's support, had promised that a New Yorker would be named treasury secretary in a Harrison cabinet. Whether or not that was the case, the Hoosiers played the New York switch for all it was worth, touting Harrison as the candidate with the greatest support from the key doubtful states. The New York move naturally alarmed the other camps. When the convention met for the evening session, the forces of Sherman, Gresham, Alger, and Allison demanded an adjournment to Saturday. That the Blaine men were not averse to forestalling a Harrison stampede appeared evident in the votes favoring adjournment from many of them, including the solid vote of California and Maine. Indeed, before the adjournment, one of Sherman's men wired the senator that Blaine's son Walker "has been showing me how his father will be nominated tomorrow." Later that night representatives of the other candidates who opposed both Blaine and Harrison met and vowed not to support Harrison in the next day's balloting.[77]

Nonetheless, on the fourth ballot on Saturday morning, Harrison showed substantial gains, having climbed to 216 votes, only 19 behind Sherman. Besides 58 of New York's 72 votes, he received 20 from Wisconsin after Rusk's withdrawal and handfuls from two-thirds of the other states. Many Wisconsin delegates leaned toward Gresham, and the state's switch to Harrison, at Rusk's insistence, helped the Harrison men undermine their Hoosier rival. On this ballot, as on the previous three, William McKinley received a few votes. During the roll call, McKinley rose to declare that his "sense of personal integrity" and "honorable fidelity to John Sherman" would not allow him to permit the use of his name. His small total increased anyway, and skeptics thought his "withdrawal" was designed to encourage a stampede as much as to stop one. On the next ballot Harrison's total declined by 4 votes. This result, coupled with the McKinley votes and the small increases Blaine received on these two ballots, suggested that a break toward someone was imminent. Amid near pandemonium, Sherman's manager Charles Foster moved for an adjournment until four o'clock. The Indiana delegation favored the adjournment, as did most of the other candidates' camps, hoping to get a grip on events before they spiraled out of control. Walker Blaine, who attended the convention with his brother Emmons, later reported to the family, "Everybody thought Harrison beaten and everyone believed that father would be nominated that afternoon."[78]

But even though Blaine's name was on everyone's lips, it was far from certain that he would have everyone's vote. Many of his supporters still believed that for Blaine to accept the nomination, it would have to come as the unanimous or nearly unanimous demand of the delegates. After the recess, Depew predicted that Blaine would be nominated by acclamation at the afternoon session, but this attempt to engineer the inevitable failed. Indeed, those who were against Blaine dug in their heels more deeply. Sherman made it clear that he would not withdraw in favor of Blaine, whose course he considered "dishonorable." In Washington, Sherman sought to enhance his own standing by asking Allison for help, but the Iowa senator said that he would not bow out to Sherman until his total reached 300 votes. Some wished to stop Blaine with

McKinley as a dark horse, but Sherman rejected that idea, telling Mark Hanna in Chicago that McKinley's nomination would be "a breach of implied faith" and that he preferred "defeat to retreat." Moreover, those who pushed McKinley as a compromise choice raised the ire of the Blaine men. When Ohio journalist William Henry Smith suggested that McKinley's nomination offered "the honorable way out" of the impasse, Whitelaw Reid pointedly asked, given McKinley's relation to Sherman and his convention-floor declination, "What would make it honorable under such circumstances to nominate McKinley and yet dishonorable to nominate Blaine? Which nomination would be less galling to the present candidates and especially to Sherman, Harrison, and Allison?" By the time the convention reconvened on Saturday afternoon, the Blaine men had concluded that it was still too early to expect frustrated and weary delegates to rush to Blaine en masse. To prolong the stalemate, many of them favored an immediate adjournment. Michener and the Hoosiers opposed that move, believing that they could still demonstrate Harrison's substantial strength in the afternoon session. But the other candidates were unwilling to give them the chance. The motion to adjourn carried by a substantial majority, and the delegates would not reconvene until Monday morning, June 25.[79]

The weekend recess witnessed intense machinations. After the adjournment on Saturday, Elkins indicated to Harrison supporter Wharton Barker that the Blaine men would consummate their plan to nominate Blaine on Monday. Barker immediately telegraphed Sherman, advising him that he must stay in the race to head off Blaine, and he sped off to Washington to push the point with the senator personally. Sunday morning newspapers carried accounts of an interview in which Sherman not only reiterated his determination to stay in the race but also asserted that if Blaine's friends thought he could be nominated by acclamation, "they are very much mistaken." Sherman followed up with telegrams ordering his men in Chicago not to withdraw—telegrams they were free to exhibit on the convention floor. "Why should I withdraw with [the] largest vote[?]" he demanded. "Let Blaine withdraw. He is now as much a candidate as I." Sherman's determination could affect the Blaine movement in various ways. On the one hand, it could deny the unanimity for Blaine that many Blaine men thought necessary. On the other hand, some of them began to float the idea that a roll-call victory over Sherman would not be considered ethically objectionable, since Sherman had entered the presidential race before Blaine's Florence letter and not after Blaine had supposedly left the field to others. Moreover, Sherman's remaining in the field would forestall a switch to McKinley, which some Blaine men saw as more dangerous.[80]

Thus, on Sunday, the New York leaders began a serious flirtation with Sherman. The senator himself asked them point-blank, "Cannot New York do for me what she did for Indiana [that is, Harrison]? If that is done and I cannot get the nomination I will be content. If not, I will not withdraw but will [accept] defeat as gracefully as possible under the circumstances." The New Yorkers saw their opening and led Sherman's agents to believe that they would go to Sherman on Monday morning. In midafternoon on Sunday, Platt and Hiscock wired Sherman directly that "if any attempt is made to stampede the convention for any Ohio dark horse [that is, McKinley] a large majority of the New York delegation including us will surely vote for you."[81]

But the Harrison men also implored the New Yorkers to stick with Harrison. They insisted that his vote on Monday morning would show a substantial increase. By late Sunday afternoon, Michener informed Barker that "New York is standing by us firmly and will continue. I believe our man will be nominated." In the complicated discussions that day, Platt got the impression, whether warranted or not, that he would receive an appointment as secretary of the treasury in a Harrison administration. According to some later accounts, Elkins made the promise to Platt in exchange for New York's full support for Harrison. Many years later, Elkins admitted taking a carriage ride with Platt and advocating Harrison, but he denied making the alleged promise. In fact, on Sunday, Pennsylvanians for Harrison reported to Barker that Elkins was among those "working like beavers to nominate Blaine." Similarly, a pro-Sherman New York delegate wired the senator that "Elkins [is] now open handed working to try Blaine on 1st ballot" on Monday. Indeed, Elkins continued to play the double game he had pursued all spring. According to news reports, he even asked the Hoosiers to withdraw Harrison and back Blaine, at which suggestion Dudley "read the riot act to Elkins, accusing him of duplicity and trickery." In any event, by the end of the day, the most the Sherman men could get from the New Yorkers was an indication that they would "probably" go to Sherman after testing Harrison's strength on two ballots on Monday.[82]

Sunday evening, rumors circulated through Chicago that Blaine had wired from Scotland an absolute declination. The substance of Sherman's interview adamantly refusing to withdraw had been cabled to

Blaine, indicating that the possibility of a unanimous call from the convention was dead. The indefatigable Michener at last saw his chance to close the deal for Harrison. At a meeting with a group of New Yorkers at two o'clock Monday morning, he urged that when the delegation caucused later that morning, they present a motion for a full vote for Harrison. They agreed. An hour later, Michener and Dudley met with Sherman's managers at their invitation. Foster told them that since their figures showed that Harrison could not win and Sherman would, the Hoosiers should "come to the support of Sherman, and so contribute to his nomination." When the Ohioans produced their numbers, however, Dudley pronounced them "clearly inaccurate," and he and Michener left to pursue votes elsewhere.[83]

As anticipated, the New York delegation caucused at nine o'clock Monday morning. By that time, no doubt remained about Blaine's final, emphatic refusal of a nomination, and realists saw that the contest had come down to Harrison and Sherman. While the New Yorkers met, Michener and Dudley waited anxiously outside the door. Before long they heard a burst of applause, and Platt came out to assure the Hoosiers of a unanimous vote for Harrison. Years later, Michener wrote that Platt had told him that New York would vote for Harrison as long as Indiana did. But in fact, the caucus had decided to vote for Harrison for one or two ballots, after which, if he did not make sufficient gains, New York would switch to Sherman. Foster immediately wired Sherman the news. "I do not think Harrison will gain enough to hold N.Y., but," he added, "the situation is dangerous." Recognizing the absolute importance of increasing Harrison's total vote, Michener and Dudley "at once sent runners to the other delegations to tell them that we were now assured of the entire New York delegation."[84]

When the convention reconvened at 11:07, Charles Boutelle of Maine read two cables from Blaine urging his friends to "refrain from voting for me." Chairman Creed Haymond of the California delegation jumped to his feet to try to block their presentation as out of order, but he was gaveled down. As the voting got under way, Michener and Dudley worked the delegations up and down the aisles, Dudley, who had lost a leg at Gettysburg, hobbling on crutches. But the delegates were still trying to sort out the impact of Blaine's final withdrawal. On the day's first ballot, the sixth of the convention, Harrison picked up only 19 votes over his total on Saturday. He gained in seven states but lost in thirteen others; he received all of New York's 72 votes, but without that state's additional 14 votes, his increase would have been only 5. Fortunately for the Hoosiers' purposes, there was little time to analyze the meaning of the vote, and New York decided to stick with Harrison on the seventh ballot.[85]

The moment of truth was now at hand for Michener and his allies. They received immeasurable help when, before the start of the seventh ballot, Clarkson of Iowa informed Michener that his delegation intended to withdraw Allison at the close of that ballot and that he would try to take as many votes to Harrison as he could. A native of Indiana whose father had worked for William Henry Harrison's Whig nomination in the 1840 campaign, Clarkson felt a sense of kinship with the Hoosiers and their candidate. Armed with Clarkson's promise, the Harrison men fanned out among the other delegations, urging them to join the movement. Michener himself buttonholed the Californians, who had voted solidly for Blaine on all six ballots. It was time, Michener told them, to look out for themselves. If they switched to Harrison now, they could go home boasting that they had "led the break to him, thus contributing largely" to his nomination. The tactic worked. On the seventh ballot, California cast 15 of its 16 votes for Harrison. The Golden State stood fourth on the list of states, and its switch proved an inspiration to others. With 279 votes, Harrison gained 48 on the ballot, at last surpassing Sherman with 230. On the eighth ballot, Iowa kept its promise and gave 22 of 26 votes to Harrison, although by the time the clerk called that state, the drift had already turned his way. Ohio stuck by Sherman with 45 of its 46 votes, but when Pennsylvania was called, Quay at last switched from Sherman to Harrison, bringing the latter's total to 399, not quite enough to put him over the top, but his victory was now certain. Harrison finished the ballot with 544 votes, or 65 percent of the total. Like Sherman, neither Gresham nor Alger withdrew, and Michigan and Illinois each stuck by its candidate through the last ballot. After the chairman announced the result, the delegates took the customary step and rose en masse to make the nomination unanimous. An exhausted Michener wired Harrison, "You are put in command."[86]

The convention moved immediately to the selection of a vice presidential nominee, and it was soon evident that the choice had already been made. At Blaine's behest, Andrew Carnegie had cabled Elkins with the suggestion that the convention take William Walter Phelps along with Harrison, and the New Jersey congressman clearly coveted the honor. But in his negotiations with Michener, Platt had signaled his preference for New Yorker Levi P. Morton. This formed part of Platt's plan to solidify his control of the state's Republican Party. The other main ingredient was to give his backing to Warner Miller for the party's gubernatorial nomination, which aided Platt in prying Miller away from his support for Sherman so that Platt could present a united delegation to Harrison on the convention's final day. Michener and his allies honored New York's request and backed Morton. In the single ballot taken on the vice presidential nomination, the New Yorker easily defeated Phelps, 592 to 119. A former congressman and minister to France, Morton was not well known nationally, but in the fall campaign, as a wealthy banker, he could make up with cash what he lacked in cachet.[87]

Harrison had kept in constant contact with his managers through a private telegraph wire to his law office in Indianapolis. When the good news finally arrived, he "nearly fainted." He quickly pulled himself together and hurried home to tell his wife, but the massing crowd taking chunks of his picket fence showed that the news had preceded him. Before the day was over, the new nominee made four short speeches from his front porch and thereby launched his general election campaign.[88]

CLOSING RANKS

With a convention such as the one the Republicans held at Chicago, replete with intrigue, tumult, broken promises, and dashed hopes, it was not surprising that some feelings of resentment lingered afterward. Most alienated was Gresham, who complained that "evil influences," especially railroad interests, had worked against him. He sat out the fall campaign, insisting, quite properly, that the "proprieties" of his position as a judge prevented his taking an active part.[89]

Sherman bitterly ascribed his defeat to "the weakness of the Ohio delegation, the open purchase of votes by Gen. Alger, and the opposition of a selfish and corrupt clique in New York." Despite his disappointment, however, Sherman was committed to a Republican victory in 1888 and soon wrote to Harrison and promised his "hearty and full support." Many of Sherman's supporters were most dismayed that when the delegates at last made their choice, they did so less on the basis of ability than "availability." As John Hay put it, "Why they should assume that the people have no sense or conscience, that the man universally known as the best man for the place could not get votes as easily as a man universally regarded as second-rate is a mystery I cannot fathom." Harrison understood that Sherman's steadfast refusal to withdraw had

Levi P. Morton, Republican nominee for vice president in 1888. (Library of Congress)

inured to his own benefit. To his credit—and as a shrewd move to ease the path to a united campaign—Harrison accepted Sherman's congratulations with fitting humility. "Your equipment for the presidency was so ample and your services to the party so great that I felt there was a sort of inappropriateness in passing you by for any of us. . . . I shall very much need your service and assistance, for I am an inexperienced politician as well as statesman." An inexperienced statesman, perhaps, but hardly an inexperienced politician.[90]

Ever the enigma, Blaine wrote to Reid wistfully of his "feelings at the close of my personal aspirations for the Presidency." Coming more than six months after Blaine had "withdrawn" from the race, the comment suggested that he had in fact continued to entertain hopes of a united call from the convention until at last it had become clear that Sherman and other candidates would not go along. Anti-Blaine men such as Ohio editor Richard Smith remained convinced that "the despatches from Scotland" had showed that Blaine was "in the conspiracy." For his part, Harrison had no illusions about what had happened at Chicago. He later wrote that it was "more than probable" that Blaine had hoped that his original declination "would not be taken too strictly." Certainly, Blaine's "leading friends in the Convention" had worked for a deadlock that would cause the delegates to turn to him "as the only man who could unite the party. . . . When this denouement did not come and he was compelled to speak again, he did so in a way to set his friends free, & the Convention soon finished its work."[91]

Harrison and Blaine had not been well acquainted before 1888. Harrison had supported Blaine in the past, but he had never been part of the Plumed Knight's inner circle. Now fate had thrown them together in a new relationship. Both recognized that they had to make the most of an alliance if their ambitions were to reach fruition. Blaine frankly confessed to Reid that the eagerness of some observers to announce his political retirement "travels somewhat beyond the record." For Blaine, a Harrison victory posed the bright prospect of his return to the cabinet as secretary of state. Immediately upon learning the result from Chicago, he sent Harrison a gushing telegram, congratulating him "most heartily." Acknowledging the centrality of the tariff issue in the campaign that was about to begin, he assured the nominee, "Your election will seal our industrial independence as the Declaration of '76, which bears the honored name of your great-grandfather, saved our political independence." Harrison graciously returned his "high appreciation of the efficient and

On the day Harrison won the nomination, crowds gathered at his Indianapolis home, with its picket fence still intact. (Benjamin Harrison Home)

conclusive support your very close friends gave to me." But along with the flattery, Harrison made clear that he and the party expected more. "I am now looking forward with great interest to the time when you shall return and give to the campaign the impetus that only your voice can give to it."[92]

Harrison and Blaine's mutual goodwill, whether sincere or feigned, bespoke a party ready for the coming fight with the Democrats. Battles for a presidential nomination in this era were often about the clash of personalities and factions. For many party cadres, as John Hay had suggested, the salient question focused on which candidate was likeliest to win in November. In these nomination contests, principles counted for less, primarily because all the candidates subscribed faithfully to the basic party doctrine. Nonetheless, candidates' views were not inconsequential in the party's quest for the ideal nominee. In 1888 Gresham's tariff notions proved to be a drag on his candidacy, and his managers' efforts to portray him as an orthodox protectionist failed to convince the delegates at Chicago. In contrast, not only Harrison's availability but also his proven talents as an effective exponent of Republican beliefs impressed party leaders. Once the Republicans had chosen Harrison as their nominee, the vast majority stood ready to link arms and contend with the Democrats on the field that Cleveland had laid out in his December message to Congress. Like the Democrats, the Republicans regarded the encounter not as a sham battle but as a vital struggle to determine the direction of the nation's economic future. "The voters need to know what the Tariff means, what it does for them, and what a Democratic victory would involve," declared the *New York Tribune* after the convention. "This year, the Republican party needs to depend upon facts and reasons. There must be argument at the beginning, argument in the middle, and argument to the end of the campaign." Throughout the spring and at Chicago, Republicans had sought an "available" leader, but to a considerable degree, they saw such a leader as one who could expound that economic argument out of deep conviction and make the fight on behalf of protectionism vigorously and with effect. In nominating Benjamin Harrison, they would soon discover, they had found a man more than equal to the job.[93]

THE CENTENNIAL CAMPAIGN FOR THE WHITE HOUSE

As the general campaign opened in the summer of 1888, leaders of both major parties knew that neither could regard itself as the favorite to win the presidency. Republicans and Democrats alike recognized that they confronted an arduous struggle and that winning would require the effective management of party machinery as well as the mounting of a persuasive campaign of education. "This campaign," President Grover Cleveland wrote to a Democratic leader, "is one of information and organization." Although no one could accurately predict the outcome even as the campaign entered its final hours, leaders of both parties agreed in retrospect that the Republicans had, in the end, outfought the Democrats on both these fronts. Republican Party managers outgeneraled their Democratic counterparts in mobilizing their party's cadres, and Benjamin Harrison and his allies proved more adept and persuasive in merchandising their program—principally tariff protectionism—to the nation's voters. But like most presidential elections in the Gilded Age, the outcome was extremely close, and in a campaign filled with dramatic incidents, no one could discount the impact of sheer luck.[1]

ORGANIZING THE CAMPAIGN

Neither party, of course, meant to leave anything to chance. The first order of business after the nominating conventions was the creation of a campaign organization. In assembling the directorate for their campaign, the Republicans had a long list of skilled political managers to choose from. In July the national committee met in New York and elected Pennsylvania Senator Matthew S. Quay as chairman. In addition, the committee made Quay chairman of the executive committee, which had direct responsibility for managing the presidential campaign. Although other men had support for the chairmanship, Quay proved to be an inspired choice. A Republican since the party's birth, Quay had risen rapidly to the top of the Keystone State machine, which he drove relentlessly to make Pennsylvania one of the most reliably Republican states in the nation. As John Sherman assured Harrison, Quay was "a shrewd, able, and skilful political manager." Iowa's James S. Clarkson became the committee's vice chairman and served indefatigably at party headquarters in New York, even while hobbling on a sprained foot. The committee treasurer was William W. Dudley, the veteran Hoosier operative who had helped Louis Michener secure Harrison's nomination and who, in previous state campaigns, had shown a deep understanding of the power of money. The job of secretary fell to J. Sloat Fassett, a mainstay of the New York party who would keep the lines of communication open with that state's boss, Thomas C. Platt. Within two weeks, Clarkson assured Harrison, "Our Committee is perfectly harmonious in its personnel. We all like Senator Quay, & shall all work together in complete accord."[2]

All these men well knew that the daunting task before them would require large amounts of money. They also knew that with the national government now controlled by their opponents, Republicans could not count on filling their campaign coffers with contributions from the army of federal officeholders. That advantage in 1888 would go to the Democrats. Instead, Republicans worked to develop other sources of funds, most notably economic interests that benefited from the protective tariff. Democrats and Mugwumps were fond of quoting a letter allegedly written in May by James P. Foster that called for Republicans to "put the manufacturers of Pennsylvania under the fire and fry all the fat out of them." Later historians cited the letter as evidence of what amounted to an extortionate relationship between Republicans and the nation's industries based on the GOP's tariff policy. (Cleveland's biographer Allan Nevins erred in attributing the phrase "frying the fat" to Quay.) But, read in its entirety, Foster's letter in fact reflected Republicans' frustration at past efforts at raising money. More important, as president of an auxiliary group, the National League of Republican Clubs, Foster was a political novice who, at best, stood on the periphery of the regular party

Senator Matthew S. Quay of Pennsylvania, Republican national chairman.
(U.S. Senate Historical Office)

apparatus. His naïve and, indeed, insulting circular embarrassed the party and no doubt repelled some potential donors.[3]

Quay and other party leaders understood that the hard but delicate work of raising money could not be left to amateurs like Foster. To get operations under way, the chairman himself lent the committee $50,000, and vice presidential nominee Levi P. Morton contributed $20,000. Quay engaged in some fund-raising, but he soon accepted the argument of other party leaders that the best way to tap industrial and commercial interests for contributions was to create a special advisory committee of economic leaders who had the trust of their colleagues in the business world. To head this group, the national committee secured the services of John Wanamaker, whose highly successful Philadelphia department store and other enterprises made him one of the nation's most respected entrepreneurs. Wanamaker's eagerness to aid the cause was heightened by word from Harrison, conveyed through intermediaries and unbeknownst to Quay, that in the event of success, Wanamaker would have a place at Harrison's cabinet table. Assisting Wanamaker were Quay ally Thomas Dolan, a wealthy industrialist whose varied interests included one of the nation's largest woolen mills, and Herman O. Armour of meatpacking fame. Before the end of the campaign, these men collected and deposited with the national committee more than $700,000, well over half the total subscriptions of $1.2 million that Quay listed in his committee accounts. The American Iron and Steel Association, one of the most aggressive of the nation's newly forming lobbying groups, chipped in another $79,000. As Clarkson put it, Wanamaker and his committee did "sagacious & splendid work in organizing ways & means."[4]

Thus, in short order the Republican legions were well led, well fed, and ready to do battle. Though an ardent believer in protectionism, Quay said little in public, leaving that aspect of the campaign to Harrison and other speakers. The chairman concentrated on management. He oversaw the arranging and scheduling of speeches and other campaign events, the printing of campaign literature, and the subsidizing of party newspapers. Most important, he allocated the party's funds to state party leaders and others. Representing the politics of the old school, he put great stock in the power of "organization." Some disagreed with the particulars of his management, but the most important Republican appreciated Quay's skilled and effective leadership. The "only proper course," Harrison wrote to one of the chairman's detractors, was "to stand loyally by our organization and to urge all friends to do the same. I think the great and original source of our strength in this campaign is harmony."[5]

In assembling a team to run their organization, the Democrats were hard-pressed to find men to match their opponents' talent and efficiency. The Democrats' traditional emphasis on state and local governance and politics had produced few effective managers with national stature and experience. Ten days after his renomination, Cleveland wrote to a friend that if anyone had "any very clear ideas" on who should run the national and New York state campaigns, "I am not aware of it." Inertia as much as anything led to the renewed appointment of national committee chairman William H. Barnum, who had held the position for twelve years. A seventy-year-old Connecticut industrialist and ex-senator with protectionist tendencies, Barnum seemed ill suited to mount a struggle for tariff reform. A campaign committee would bear the major responsibility for running the campaign, but after a month, neither that group nor its chairman had been selected. "I confess [that I] cannot see what in the Hell we are to do for the Head of the Com[i]t[tee]," Pennsylvania Congressman William L. Scott wrote to Cleveland's secretary, Daniel Lamont, at the White House. "You cannot find a man that there will not be some objections to him." Scott himself, who was in uncertain health, refused to be considered, as did Maryland Senator Arthur P. Gorman, who had performed the job four years earlier. Finally, in mid-July Cleveland convened a meeting at the White House with Scott, Barnum, Navy Secretary William C. Whitney, and Ohio's national committeeman, Calvin S. Brice. After some prodding, Brice agreed to accept the chairmanship, and the campaign committee formally elected him a few days later in New York, with Lamont on hand to ensure that all went well.[6]

The forty-two-year-old Brice had made millions by manipulating railroad investments on Wall Street and for years had taken part in state and local Democratic politics in Ohio. He had, however, little preparation for directing a national campaign. As one observer put it, Brice "brings to his new found work of political management the confidence of a success unsubdued by experience." Initially he got considerable help from Barnum, but the former senator was ill during much of the fall and wound up playing only a minor role. Brice received more guidance from Lamont, who did as much as he could to oversee the campaign from the White House, frequently visiting party headquarters in New York or meeting with Brice and Cleveland in Washington. Gorman and

*Calvin S. Brice, chairman of the Democrats' national campaign committee.
(U.S. Senate Historical Office)*

Scott, who served on the campaign committee, also advised Brice. A few weeks after he took office, his inexperience showed when newspapers printed the substance of a conversation in which Brice had suggested that the tariff issue was hurting the Democrats and that the president could learn something from Harrison in doing more to further his own chances. Brice issued a public denial of the statements, and Gorman assured reporters that rumors that the chairman would be eased out were untrue. Still, doubts about Brice's leadership lingered. As the campaign entered its final month, Cleveland's friend Wilson Bissell reported to Lamont that "a sort of amateurish air" permeated national headquarters, and "I gained the impression that they have washed fully as much as they will hang out." Like Barnum, Brice had protectionist leanings, and Cleveland may have selected him as campaign chairman to signal a moderation of the party's low-tariff stance, as he had attempted to do with the tariff plank at St. Louis. If so, he added to the confusion over the party's position and irritated low-tariff Democrats. After the newspaper flap, Texas Senator John H. Reagan pointedly told Brice that "the National Democratic Committee and its officers have no right in duty and good faith to the party to change or attempt to change the issue presented to the country by the last annual message of the President, by the action of the democrats in Congress, and by the National Democratic Convention, on the tariff question."[7]

A lack of funds compounded Brice's problems. The national committee had a treasurer, Charles J. Canda, a wealthy banker who had held the job since 1875, but the position was widely regarded as "purely a perfunctory political office." The Pendleton Civil Service Act of 1883 prohibited the direct requisition of campaign funds from federal employees, and the committee was slow to devise methods for soliciting "voluntary" contributions. (By way of example, Cleveland himself sent in a check for $10,000, one-fifth of his annual salary.) Moreover, true to their states' rights orientation, the Democrats centered most of their fund-raising and spending at the state level. Brice endorsed that approach, funneling contributions to the doubtful states of New York, New Jersey, Connecticut, and Indiana, "the states where we are making the fight." But he also argued that he must have money to meet "the total expense of maintaining and operating these headquarters [and] of editing, printing and distributing eight or ten million documents." By mid-September no money from contributions had gone to pay such expenses, and the national committee was $96,000 in debt—$50,000 of it borrowed from a bank, and $46,000 advanced by Brice himself. "I can not undertake to continue the work of the Committee on this plan," he told Lamont, "unless some of our friends . . . relieve me here so that I can have time to look for money." Finally, Brice and Barnum were reduced to issuing an open call "to the People of the United States" for contributions to help defray "the expenses of a canvass of such moment." In early October Scott informed Lamont that "financial matters are looking better here."[8]

THE CANDIDATES' ROLE

Behind the scenes, Cleveland closely monitored the operations of the national committee as well as the committees in key states such as New York and Indiana, but he did almost no overt personal campaigning. Although he often characterized his bid for reelection as a campaign of education, he did little of the educating himself. His only speech was the platitudinous response he gave on June 26 to the committee that officially notified him of his nomination. In this utterance, he forbore discussion of issues and instead reprised the sanctimony that suffused much of his earlier political oratory. Depicting his renomination as a "summons to duty," he declared that his "familiarity with the great office which I hold has but added to my apprehension of its sacred character and the consecration demanded of him who assumes its immense responsibilities." He reserved consideration of more down-to-earth matters such as the tariff for the one substantive statement he made during the campaign, his formal letter of acceptance, which he did not issue until three months after his nomination. Projecting himself as adhering to notions of political decorum, Cleveland stood for the presidency in 1888; he did not run.[9]

The challenger, Benjamin Harrison, had a different conception of his role. Harrison had risen to prominence in large part because of his ability to articulate his party's doctrine on the political stump. Now in the midst of the most important campaign of his life, it seemed a profound waste for him to sit in his parlor and leave the work to others. But Harrison and Republican leaders thought it would be a huge mistake for him to copy the speaking tour James G. Blaine had taken in 1884, which had ended with the Reverend Burchard's disastrous "rum, Romanism, and rebellion" aspersion a week before the election. As Harrison put it, "There is great risk of meeting a fool at home, but the candidate who travels cannot escape him." The solution was suggested by Harrison's encounters with the crowds that had massed at his home upon hearing the news of his nomination. His managers not only encouraged but soon began orchestrating the continued visits by delegations of well-wishers from around Indiana and from other states as well. Although James A. Garfield and other candidates had occasionally addressed visiting groups, none had done so as much as Harrison, who launched a full-fledged front porch campaign.[10]

What began as a spontaneous outpouring soon became a well-managed system. The meetings grew too large for Harrison's front lawn and were shifted to a public park with a dais and seats. The candidate delegated arrangements to a committee that oversaw every detail of a group's visit. The committee insisted that each group designate a chairman, who was required to submit his opening remarks in writing in advance. The committee scrutinized the text for anything potentially embarrassing, returned the edited version to the chairman, and examined it one more time just before the chairman addressed Harrison when the group visited. Harrison responded with a short speech, often geared toward the interests of the callers he addressed. When a thousand members of the Terre Haute Railroad Club visited on August 4, for instance, the candidate spoke of the need for laws for safer construction of railway equipment and for the arbitration of labor disputes, and he also touted the benefits of a protective tariff not only for Terre Haute's factories but also "for the railroads that do the transportation, . . . for the workingmen, who find steady employment at good wages, and for the farmers, who supply their needs."[11]

Harrison often addressed several delegations per day. His long experience as a courtroom lawyer had given him a superb capacity for extemporaneous speaking. Altogether, he gave over ninety speeches to more than 300,000 listeners. More important, his stenographer took down his remarks, which, after a review by Harrison himself, went to the Associated Press for publication in hundreds of newspapers the next day. Nearly every morning of the summer and fall, voters across the nation could read Harrison's words at their breakfast tables. In addition, midway through the campaign, Indiana Republicans compiled some of the more notable of these talks in a pamphlet that the party distributed by the tens of thousands. Harrison found the labor arduous, and typically at the end of a long day of speechmaking he stretched out on a lounge while a family member massaged his head. After several weeks he frankly confessed to his running mate Levi P. Morton that he was "quite tired of hearing my own voice." Nonetheless, he persevered, and his performance remained flawless. Party leaders, many of whom at first feared the possibility of a gaffe, were delighted by these "magnificent utterances." "I have watched Gen. Harrison's course with increasing admiration," one former cabinet member wrote to Michener. "To speak day after day as he has done, to different phases of humanity, varying his short addresses so that no vein of sameness runs through them, never dropping a stitch in his logic to be picked up by his adversaries in unraveling the force of his expressions, leaving nothing for his partisans to explain—why it is marvelous!"[12]

SURROGATES: BLAINE AND THURMAN

In part, Harrison took such a direct role in the campaign because Congress remained in session until the third week in October. Senators and congressmen who normally would have taken to the hustings as surrogates for the presidential nominee were stuck in Washington, mostly dealing with tariff legislation. When they did steal time away, they tended to look after their own interests in their home states. The party's 1884 nominee, James G. Blaine, stepped into the breach and made numerous speeches, although not all party leaders were convinced that he enhanced Harrison's prospects. On the one hand, the immensely popular Blaine could rouse the party faithful to enthusiastic labor in behalf of the ticket, but on the other, he might overshadow the less well-known nominee. After more than a year's absence abroad, the Plumed Knight returned in mid-August to a hero's welcome in New York, where "whistles shrieked and guns boomed" to hail his arrival. Even the pro-Cleveland *New York Herald* declared that "Mr. Blaine might well be proud of the place he holds in the hearts of the people." Republican dignitaries flocked to the city to join the celebration, although some party leaders such as John Sherman did "not exactly like the folly and flummery of this Blaine reception" and stayed away. Blaine showed that he was more than ready to carry his load in the campaign. In his brief response to this welcome, he zeroed in on the tariff issue, noting that the central question was "whether the great mass of American citizens who earn their bread by the sweat of their brow shall be seriously reduced in their emolument" and whether they would "take that fatal step at the bidding of an American Congress and an American President." The event had a powerful impact; one New York Democrat warned Lamont in Washington that, "as it stands today, the Republicans have got us on the run on the free trade issue. Their whole procession last night was an organized cry of 'No, no, no free trade.'"[13]

After the arrival hoopla, Blaine headed for Maine, where he concentrated on leading the party's efforts in his home state's local and state elections in mid-September. But in his first speech at Portland, he committed a blunder that threatened to compromise his ability to help the national ticket. In a passage dealing with Cleveland's annual message, Blaine denied the president's assertion that a protective tariff bred trusts and insisted instead that free-trade England was "plastered all over" with such combinations of capital. But Blaine also declared that trusts were neither "altogether advantageous or disadvantageous," and at any rate, "they are largely private affairs with which neither President Cleveland nor any private citizen has any particular right to interfere." Blaine's comment was difficult to explain, except by his inattention to the issue during his absence from the country. The Republican platform included a plank denouncing trusts, the Republican Senate had earlier in the summer instructed a committee to investigate restrictive combinations, and the day before Blaine spoke, John Sherman had introduced antitrust legislation in the Senate. Democrats pounced. "Blaine's flippant remarks will deceive no one," declared the *Detroit Free Press*. "The people know just what injury these huge financial octopuses will do to them." In a follow-up speech Blaine still contended that the tariff did not generate combinations, but he conceded that state legislatures had the power to regulate trusts while the national government had jurisdiction over interstate commerce. Cleveland no doubt took special pleasure in noting in his letter of acceptance that "no member of our party will be found excusing the existence or belittling the pernicious results of these devices to wrong the people." For his part, Harrison insisted that he had opposed trusts "long before" the Republican convention's pronouncement against them, and he expressed his confidence that "the legislative authority should and will find a method of dealing fairly and effectively with these and other abuses."[14]

Although Democrats (and some Republicans) tagged Blaine as Harrison's Burchard, Harrison had no intention of excluding him from further service. After the Republicans won a resounding victory in Maine, which party leaders took as a portent for November, Blaine set off on a speaking tour for the duration of the campaign. Some Republicans warned

Harrison that too close an association with Blaine might cost him potential support among Mugwumps who had become disenchanted with Cleveland, but Harrison calculated that the charismatic Blaine was doing more good than harm among other, larger constituencies, especially in the doubtful states. After a mix-up between the national committee and the Indiana Republican committee over the number of speeches Blaine would make in Harrison's home state, Blaine threatened to make none there at all. But Harrison soothed his bruised ego, and Blaine kept all his engagements, including a huge rally at Indianapolis with the nominee at his side. In treating the tariff issue, Blaine often accused Cleveland of taking a pro-British, free-trade position, a tactic aimed in part to woo the important Irish American voting bloc. Toward the end of the campaign, Blaine sounded this theme at a meeting of 10,000 "Irish protectionists" in New York's Madison Square Garden, where, one reporter noted, "No pen can describe the madness with which the uncrowned king was greeted." On the last Saturday before the election, Blaine reviewed a huge parade in Manhattan and wired Harrison, "The greatest political procession ever seen in New York has been passing [the] Fifth Avenue Hotel for four hours and seems endless. Our friends are in high heart." Historians of the People's Party of the early 1890s often credit the Populists with generating political enthusiasm in a previously torpid electorate, but scenes such as these and similar ones in other cities and towns demonstrated that the major parties had already perfected techniques to spark popular participation, which the Populists later adapted to their own purposes.[15]

The Democrats could assemble huge gatherings of supporters as easily as the Republicans, but Cleveland's principal surrogate in the campaign, vice presidential nominee Allen G. Thurman, was no match for Blaine. Extensive travel and speaking in poorly ventilated halls or outdoors in all manner of inhospitable weather would tax the strength of any campaigner, but these trials bore particularly hard on the seventy-four-year-old Thurman. In August he opened his campaign before a crowd of more than 12,000 people at Port Huron, Michigan, where he kept his hat on because, he said, "I do not want to break down at the beginning of the campaign." As he did in most of his speeches, Thurman focused on the tariff issue, asserting that the Republicans' protectionism subjected workers to higher prices for all they bought with no compensating increase in wages. He denied that the Mills bill would lead to free trade but then chided the Republicans for being "more afraid of free trade than they are of rattlesnakes." This last comment, which suggested that free trade might not be such a bad thing, was stricken from the printed version of Thurman's speech that party committees distributed as a campaign document. In New York, Brice declared that the Ohioan's "grand and vigorous speech" had demonstrated the "soundness" of his nomination.[16]

After a few more speeches in the Midwest, Thurman headed home to Columbus, where a severe attack of neuralgia kept him off the stump for several days. His next big engagement was set for Madison Square Garden on September 6, but when he rose to give his speech he became ill with "cholera morbus"—acute intestinal distress accompanied by diarrhea and vomiting—and had to be led away before he collapsed. After resting a few days in his hotel, he gamely delivered a speech in Newark, New Jersey, but had to stop halfway through. These episodes early in the campaign turned out to be the most serious Thurman suffered. Indeed, he seemed to build in strength as the weeks wore on. But his escape from further embarrassing incidents was no doubt due in large part to the watchful care his handlers exercised. For the remainder of the campaign, Brice gave Thurman the use of his private railroad director's car, complete with chef and staff, and Thurman took frequent layovers at his home. His son traveled with him and made sure to keep handshaking and interviews to a minimum. "On each one of these trips," the son wrote to Lamont, "he is taking great chances of contracting a bad cold, which might, with him, result fatally." In the seventy-five days from the Port Huron speech to the end of the campaign, Thurman made only twenty-four speeches. He made many more short responses from his train's rear platform, but he confessed that "making these little speeches to crowds at the railway stations tires me as much as delivering two or three set addresses."[17]

Thurman did not carry the Democrats' speaking burden alone. He had help from such party luminaries as House Speaker John G. Carlisle and Congressman Roger Mills of Texas, and in the last few days even Secretary of State Thomas Bayard took to the stump. Although a younger and more vigorous vice presidential nominee might have done more good, it is not likely that many people voted against Cleveland because Thurman was on the ticket. On the other side, Levi Morton made virtually no speeches. No doubt he gave Harrison's chances a boost in his home state of New York, but many believed that party leaders had selected the wealthy banker primarily for the financial resources he and

The Republican magazine Judge *portrays Democratic vice presidential nominee Allen G. Thurman pulling the Cleveland machine plowing for votes, while campaign chairman Calvin S. Brice cracks the whip over the workhorse. (*Judge, *September 29, 1888)*

his friends could and did provide the cause. Thurman's speeches were well attended, and he larded them with self-deprecating humor that defused the age issue. Most important, he dealt with the tariff issue in a forceful way that the common folk among his listeners easily understood. Unlike the self-absorbed Blaine, Thurman had no illusions that the campaign of 1888 was in any way about him; rather, the fight was about the great economic issue that Cleveland had raised in his annual message.

THE MILLS BILL

While the two parties got their national campaigns under way, the contest over the tariff issue played out not only on the stump but also in the halls of Congress. After weeks of debate the House of Representatives passed the Mills bill on July 21 by a vote of 162 to 149. Only two Republicans voted for it, and only four Democrats, three from the president's own state, voted against it.[18] The most prominent Democratic opponent, Samuel J. Randall, was too ill to be present but sent word that he wanted it "announced and distinctly known that I am opposed to the passage of this bill."[19] After its passage the bill went to the Senate, where Republican leaders spent several weeks devising a response that would not only comport with the party's announced principles regarding the revenue question but also meet with maximum approval among the voters.

For their part, many Democrats were far from convinced that the Mills bill aided their electoral prospects. Protectionist Democrats who opposed the bill saw no essential change from the course Cleveland had set forth in his December message. They bridled at the notion, as one wrote to Randall, that in the campaign "all speakers are to endeavor to persuade democrats that the doctrine of the Message and the Mills Bill . . . is the settled doctrine of the party and that to vote with the party is to vote that doctrine." Those who supported the bill feared that the Republicans would cite it as further evidence that the Democrats favored free trade. On the day the House passed the bill, the *New York Herald* assured its readers that the legislation had been "drawn with the greatest care for the protection of workingmen," that it left forty-seven industries "absolutely untouched," and that in the "few industries affected," duties were only "slightly reduced." Thurman called the Mills bill "the most moderate reduction of the tariff duties that has ever been attempted in this country." He and other Democrats emphasized that the bill reduced the average duty levied on imports by only 7 percentage points, from 47 to 40 percent.[20]

Democrats' defensiveness about the bill was justified, for Republicans did not hesitate to attack it as destructive to the nation's economic well-being. As Harrison told a visiting delegation, "We would have more confidence in the protest of these reformers that they are not 'free-traders' if we could occasionally hear one of them say that he was a protectionist, or admit that our customs duties should adequately favor our domestic industries." Harrison scoffed at the Democrats' claim that the Mills bill wrought only a 7-point decline in duties. Such a decrease would certainly injure some American industries and reduce the wages of their workers. More important, Harrison said, "You may also fairly ask to see the free list, which does not figure in this 'average.'" It was a telling point, because Mills and his colleagues had placed numerous articles on the list of commodities that would enter American ports free of duty. Many were insignificant, but others such as lumber, hemp, flax, and especially wool represented important economic interests. With the expanded free list factored in, the overall reduction was substantially more than 7 percentage points. Again the Republicans raised the argument that the Democrats' revenue policy, as embodied in the Mills bill, undermined "the American system" and served foreign, particularly British, interests. "The British Parliament does not legislate with a view to advance the interests of the people of the United States," Harrison told a group of coal miners. "They—rightly—have in view the interest of that empire over which Victoria reigns. Should we not, also, as Americans, in our legislation, consider first the interests of our people?"[21]

These arguments hit home with Democratic campaign strategists. "We are fighting a defensive war on the tariff question," a Californian warned Cleveland, "*and defensive wars do not generally win in politics.*" An upstate New York newspaper editor told Lamont that there was "no use disguising the fact that two of our largest industries, salt and soda ash, are affected by the Mills bill and it is going to require a good deal of preaching through the Democratic press to hold men who are affected." After a visit to national party headquarters in New York, Massachusetts Congressman Patrick Collins recommended the immediate distribution of 10 million tariff documents. "If the working people once get 'free trade' into their heads," he warned Cleveland, "it will take a surgical operation to get it out." A leading Irish American Democrat,

A Republican poster portrays Harrison and Morton as defenders of American economic interests. (Library of Congress)

Collins bristled at the Republicans' allegation that Cleveland's policy favored Britain; to counteract it he even suggested that the president order the seizure of a former Confederate vessel flying the British flag. "Nine Blaine receptions would not have equal effect," he insisted. Cleveland ignored this absurd idea, but Collins was not alone in calling for some bold action against the British.[22]

TWISTING THE LION'S TAIL

Within the administration, Navy Secretary William C. Whitney took the lead in advocating some aggressive step to twist the British lion's tail for political benefit. Whitney and others saw their opportunity in a festering controversy with Great Britain over American fishing rights in Canadian waters. (In this era, Britain still conducted foreign affairs for the Dominion of Canada.) The rights of the two nations' fishermen in each other's waters had been defined by an 1871 treaty, which the United States abrogated in 1885 after concluding that the charges levied for fishing privileges in Canadian waters were too high. With those privileges now severely limited, the Canadians began seizing American fishing vessels found in dominion waters. Congress responded in March 1887 with a law that empowered the president, in the event of further seizures, to retaliate by barring Canadian vessels from U.S. waters and ports and by prohibiting the entry of fish or "any other product" of Canada into "any port or place of the United States." Cleveland signaled his willingness to enforce this law, but he also authorized Secretary of State Bayard to negotiate a new treaty with Britain, defining the fishing privileges. The president submitted the Bayard-Chamberlain Treaty to the Senate in February 1888, and after a rancorous debate the Senate rejected it by a vote of 27 to 30. Senate Republicans claimed that the treaty conceded too much to the Canadians, but in any event, they were hardly inclined to hand Cleveland a major diplomatic victory less than three months before the election.[23] The administration fully anticipated the rejection, and Cleveland was prepared to capitalize on it. Ten days before the vote, Whitney wrote, "I want him to take the aggressive on the fishing question and after they reject the treaty retaliate. I am sick of all this talk about an '*English*' party." Cleveland agreed, and two days after the Senate vote he sent Congress a sharply worded message designed less to elicit action than to make a statement for use by Democratic campaign orators. The president chided the Senate for rejecting the treaty without making any attempt to amend it. Denouncing Canadian officials for treating American fishermen "in a manner inexcusably harsh and oppressive," he asked for the authority to retaliate against Canada by suspending the transport of all goods across the territory of the United States to or from Canada, in effect cutting off all trade with the northern neighbor. His recommendations, he declared, "relate to the honor and dignity of our country and the protection and preservation of the rights and interests of all our people."[24]

The message was gratuitous on two counts. First, the 1887 retaliation act could easily be construed to authorize the measures Cleveland now requested. Second, during treaty negotiations, Bayard and his British counterpart had signed a modus vivendi that put the treaty's main provisions into effect without formal ratification and hence removed the likelihood of further ship seizures and the need for retaliation. Nonetheless, the Democratic House of Representatives threw together a retaliation measure, which, as expected, the Senate refused to pass.[25]

Cleveland's message to Congress had minimal impact on American relations with England and Canada, but for a time at least, it seemed to have the desired effect on the campaign. At the White House, Lamont leaked its contents in advance to reporters so that they could quickly round up favorable reactions, especially among Irish Americans. Thus, on the day the message appeared in the press, newspapers also printed statements such as one from James Mooney, former president of the Irish National League, who predicted that Cleveland's action would "have a good effect among all friends of Ireland and haters of England." The White House also released copies of the hundreds of laudatory telegrams that poured in after the message.[26] From New York, Brice exulted that the "wise and patriotic message" had earned Cleveland "the thanks of the nation regardless of party or nationality." Even Charles A. Dana's *New York Sun*, which seldom praised Cleveland, grudgingly labeled the message "good patriotism and good politics." A Democrat from Cleveland's hometown of Buffalo reported that everyone considered the message "vigorously American" and thought that it "repudiates the calumnies that your administration is in sympathy with England." A week later, Secretary of War William Endicott congratulated Whitney: "Your powder has exploded well, and you have much reason to be satisfied with the change in affairs, as the credit falls mainly to you."[27]

But how much had "affairs" in the campaign really changed? Cleveland's fisheries message may have dispelled some of the suspicion about the administration's relations with England, but it could not allay the anxiety many Americans felt over his position on the tariff, the economic issue that stood uppermost in their minds. This seemed clear from the Democrats' defeat in the Maine state elections two weeks after the message. In explaining his heavy loss, William Putnam, the Democratic candidate for governor, wrote to Bayard that once "the Fishery troubles were soon got out of the way," that issue had "rather strengthened" the party, especially in fishing towns. But "the Mills Bill," he added, "struck our State in so many different directions, that everybody seemed to be having sore shins." Only hard campaign work had kept the Maine defeat from being worse. On the Republican side, the Maine state chairman reported to Harrison, "Our largest gains were made in those counties that were most affected by the Mills bill, which argues well for the success of Republicans in the country at large."[28]

For weeks, worried Democrats had been urging Cleveland to use his formal letter of acceptance to clarify the party's position on the tariff. Concerned that Cleveland had alienated the Randall protectionist Democrats, New York party leader Smith Weed frankly told Lamont that "the Pres[iden]t—while I am sure he is not a free trader—has fallen into the habbit [sic] of using free trade words & sentences, and with the impression that now prevails, he has got to make a different impression on those people or he will lose their votes." It was vital, Weed argued, for Cleveland to distance himself from "the infernal Mills Bill." Four days after the fisheries message, J. H. MacDonald advised the president to "show clearly" in his letter that "the Democratic Party is contending only for a Scientific Tariff, not for the abolition of the Protective System." MacDonald defined a scientific tariff as one that would "give the UTMOST POSSIBLE PROTECTION and encouragement to Manufacturers, while at the same time it does the LEAST POSSIBLE HARM to Agriculture and Commerce."[29]

As he labored over his letter of acceptance, Cleveland took such advice into account, although he still intended to embrace the ideal of tariff reform. As he had with his proposed plank for the national platform, Cleveland aimed his appeal all along the low tariff–to–protectionist spectrum and once again left himself open to the accusation of straddling. In his letter, he opened the discussion of the tariff by playing on the ancient American aversion to taxes, condemning oppressive exactions from the people, and repeating the Democratic epigram, "Unnecessary taxation is unjust taxation." Excessive revenues led not only to waste and extravagance in expenditure; they also withdrew so much money from the private economy as to threaten depression. Cleveland repeated his arguments about lower prices for consumers and expanded trade opportunities for American manufacturers, but he also sought to allay fears that Democrats' ideas of tariff revision threatened domestic economic interests. He made no mention of the Mills bill by name and, indeed, extolled the "extreme moderation" of the House Democrats' attempt to reform the revenue system. "We have entered upon no crusade of free trade," he insisted. "The reform we seek to inaugurate is predicated upon the utmost care for established industries and enterprises, [and] a jealous regard for the interests of American labor." He specifically called for tariff rates that would "easily compensate for any difference that may exist between the standard of wages which should be paid to our laboring men and the rate allowed in other countries." Far from aiming to destroy the protective system, he said, Democrats believed that the "existence of such a system is entirely consistent with the regulation of the extent to which it should be applied and the correction of its abuses."[30]

The hybrid, if not to say equivocal, nature of Cleveland's treatment of the issue elicited a mix of responses. With a blend of hyperbole and murkiness perhaps appropriate for the national party chairman, Brice declared that "the President's bold, conservative, simple, Jacksonian programme will command the confidence of the business interests of the country, . . . and satisfy wage earners that in democratic success lies their best opportunity for successful individual exertion." Paralleling Cleveland's own ambivalence, the New York Times called the letter "a temperate and honest statement; it is not apologetic; on the contrary it is calmly but vigorously aggressive." The Democratic Indianapolis Sentinel chose to ignore the feint toward protectionism, focused on the tariff reduction portion of the letter, and hailed Cleveland's presentation as "masterly" and "incontrovertible." The New York Sun, in contrast, said that the letter offered "a distinctively protective program" and gave "distinct evidence of recent enlightenment on the part of the President." Two days later the New York Democratic state convention meeting at Buffalo declared that by abjuring "a crusade of free trade," Cleveland had "clearly presented the vital issues pending before the American people." On the Republican side, the New York Tribune dismissed the letter as a replay of Cleveland's December message "with a few bits of protection trimming." Less decorously, New Jersey Congressman John Kean told reporters, "He argues free trade and declares he is not a free trader. It is like a drunken man protesting that he is sober."[31]

The president's letter failed to satisfy many in the Democratic Party's protectionist wing. Former Ohio Congressman A. J. Warner complained to Randall that the argument sounded "the same as that put forward as the ground of the Mills Bill. . . . If the President had an intelligent comprehension of the subject, he would not have put side by side in the same document, his theory of a tariff and these declarations respecting the difference in the wages of labor." Cleveland's letter had by no means exorcised the free-trade incubus, and Randall came under enormous pressure to help rescue Cleveland. "Your position on all questions is so well known," pleaded Brice, "that an expression from you in favor of the Electoral ticket would have great weight." But Randall was virtually incapacitated by the rectal cancer that would claim his life two years later. He resisted Brice and others on the grounds that his doctors would not let him speak or even write letters. He merely referred the chairman to his acceptance of renomination to Congress by a district convention that endorsed the national ticket. "Of course you understand," he told Brice, "that I do not propose to take back any of my utterances, the result of conviction, on the tariff."[32]

Although Randall was sidelined, Democrats labored mightily to assuage the public's anxiety regarding the tariff issue. They distributed hundreds of thousands of printed speeches and pamphlets explaining the Mills bill and the party's tariff stance generally. Roger Mills himself told an Indiana audience that his bill was "no more free trade than was the reform made by a hard drinker to total abstinence when he reduced his drams from forty-seven a day to forty-two and a half." More important, Mills went on, Americans should understand that "the tariff cannot help the workingman. . . . The thing that will benefit workingmen is to have more work." And the key to more work was a reduction in the duties on raw materials in order to reduce the cost of America's products and thereby enlarge the demand for them in the markets of the world. In New York, Congressman Bourke Cockran told a mass meeting at Tammany Hall that the Democrats were free traders only in the sense that they were "bent upon giving freedom to labor." The Mills bill proposed to put wool on the free list, he said, "to give the American mechanic and laborer a better opportunity to drive his English competitor out of the market." Moreover, adverting to his party's classic doctrine of limited government, Cockran avowed that Democrats did "not believe that the American laborer depended upon an act of Congress for his prosperity." In the end, Democrats found the campaign of education to be an uphill struggle. "Had Cleveland let the tariff alone, he would have had a walkover," lamented one Democratic county chairman. "Now it takes the hardest kind of work to pull through."[33]

In contrast, Republicans generally felt much more comfortable defending their party's commitment to protectionism, as they had since the moment Cleveland submitted his message to Congress in December. Even so, GOP leaders found it necessary to adjust a few differences in order to present a united front to the Democratic foe. In the first place, not a few Republicans regarded the tariff plank that William McKinley had written at Chicago as extreme, especially its suggestion that Republicans were willing to raise import duties to prohibitive levels to reduce the surplus. Equally troubling was the passage that called for, in the event revenues still remained too high, the complete elimination of internal taxes rather than the surrender of any part of the protective system. Because alcohol was one of the chief commodities taxed internally, this plank opened the party to the charge of favoring "free whiskey," which especially irked Republicans who labored to stem losses to the Prohibition Party. In the weeks after the Republican convention, several party leaders, including many from Congress, urged Harrison to use his letter of acceptance to temper these provisions of the platform. Senator Preston Plumb of Kansas warned Harrison that the tariff plank was "too hide-bound in the direction of protection and is going to hurt us materially as the campaign goes on if it is not in some way qualified." Maine Senator Eugene Hale said it was a "blunder" to make the party appear to favor "letting whiskey go free of tax in order to raise revenue on sugar & other articles. . . . The practical & the religious sentiment of the country is against it." Similarly, the *Chicago Tribune*'s Joseph Medill told Harrison that he could still "combat the destructive effects of free trade" without endorsing the "recklessly expressed McKinley free whisky— no reduction—higher tariff plank." "You see," Medill wrote, "how even Cleveland seizes on it and rolls it as a sweet morsel under his tongue."[34]

If Harrison, like Cleveland, came under pressure to speak out of both sides of his mouth on the revenue issue, he seemed to do so more convincingly and with greater finesse than the president. Harrison had already begun this massaging of the tariff plank in his front porch speeches, telling one group that the Republican Party had shown "its capacity wisely to reduce our revenues and at the same time to preserve the American system." In his letter of acceptance, he addressed the Chicago revenue plank squarely: "The methods suggested by our convention will not need to be exhausted in order to effect the necessary reduction. We are not likely to be called upon, I think, to make a present choice between the surrender of the protective system and the entire repeal of the internal taxes. Such a contingency, in view of the present relation of expenditures to revenues, is remote." Most important, however, the point he wanted to drive home to Americans was that the tariff question was "not a contest between schedules, but between wide-apart principles." The Democrats, he insisted, waged an "open and defiant" assault on the protective system and would, "if supported by the country, place the tariff laws on a purely revenue basis. This is practical free trade—free trade in the English sense." A relieved Medill assured Harrison that his letter of acceptance was "all right and I am conducting the tariff fight from your—and not McKinley's—standpoint." A Minnesota Republican who had previously lamented the "bravado" of the tariff plank was pleased that "you have completely cured the defection resulting from the Chicago platform." That no doubt stretched the case, but surely Harrison had met his own aim of ensuring that his letter not "be an impediment in the campaign." From the campaign trail, Blaine told the nominee that he had covered "every point most admirably—not a word too many, not a word too few, not a word amiss."[35]

In addition to putting the best spin on the platform, Republicans wrestled with the question of how to deal with the Mills bill passed by the House. In the Senate many Republicans favored the preparation of a substitute bill that would clarify the GOP stance and, like Harrison's letter, soften the tariff plank. According to Wisconsin Senator John C. Spooner, "our remaining here during the sweltering heat of August, and during September, engaged in an honest, manly effort to reduce the revenues, and so revise the tariff upon protection principles as to take care of our American interests, would have a better effect upon the country than anything we could do individually upon the stump in the meantime." Senate Finance Committee member Frank Hiscock of New York wrote to Harrison that differing bills presented by the two chambers would "practically constitute the issues between the parties." Other Republicans disagreed, however. Whitelaw Reid warned Hiscock that a counterbill would bring "confusion," not clarity. "Between two bills, both changing the tariff, the issue will be less easily grasped than between free trade and its foes." John Sherman told Harrison, "Our bill, if framed by Angels or Divine power, would be open to such criticisms as could be made by Democratic politicians on the eve of an election." "It is better for us," Sherman believed, "that the contest take place on the principles of the Mills bill." But the Senate's failure to act, said Vermont Senator George F. Edmunds, would open the Republicans to charges of "incapacity, cowardice & trickery." It is "right to do right," Edmunds wrote to William B. Allison, "to keep the promise that we have repeatedly in our platforms & otherwise made, that we are capable of dealing & willing to deal with a revision of the tariff upon the broad lines of protection to American interests & that we are capable of reducing & willing to reduce any excess in the income of the government."[36]

The premise underlying all these arguments was that the American people were intensely interested in what the Senate planned to do about the tariff and internal revenue questions and that many voters would make their decisions accordingly. Indeed, despite the Populists' later characterization of the tariff issue as a "sham battle," Americans saw it as vitally important to their economic well-being. Major interests such as the American Iron and Steel Association certainly followed the Senate's deliberations closely, but smaller concerns and individuals did so as well. For instance, the superintendent of a Boston twine manufacturing company wrote to his senator, "We would earnestly urge you to use your best efforts to protect our industry, which is threatened with annihilation by the provisions of the Mills Bill. A reduction is proposed equivalent to about 8% on our raw material and 25% on our manufactured twines; this . . . means an entire transfer of our business to Great Britain and Ireland." The president of a Brooklyn company that made wool mats informed the Finance Committee that weavers in India received 10 to 15 cents per day, whereas he paid his workers $2 to $3 per day. A sufficient customs duty was thus essential "to equalize the *labor of India* with *our home labor.*" Consumers of manufactured goods, especially in the agricultural regions, took another view. As a local GOP official in Waterloo, Iowa, wrote to Allison, "It is useless to deny the fact that there are many Republicans in this county who are not radical protectionists and if they continue to vote and work for their party it will be somewhat under protest. They are looking with intense interest to the action of the Republican Senate in formulating a bill that will modify 'McKinleyism.'"[37]

The arguments in favor of proposing a bill prevailed. Even before the House had passed the Mills bill, a subcommittee of the Senate Finance Committee, headed by Allison, had begun drafting a potential substitute. The task involved multifarious, sometimes conflicting interests, and the committee spent weeks gathering testimony to shed light on the impact of the tariff on a wide variety of enterprises. The committee's study and deliberations dragged on for nearly three months. Particularly troublesome were schedules dealing with wool, woolens, lumber, and sugar. In the second week of September Allison reported to Harrison that "we are still struggling with percentages," and it looked as if the project for a Senate bill might collapse. Harrison thought it might be too late to frame a bill with "deliberation" and warned Allison against "a temptation towards the use of legislation for extreme party ends." Some Republican managers at headquarters in New York believed that not enough time remained before the election to shift voters' attention from the negatives of the Mills bill to the benefits of a Senate bill. Moreover, national party vice chairman James Clarkson told Allison, "All elements desiring protection indulge the hope and belief that the unborn bill will be as they want it to be, just as the father will indulge in the hope that the unborn child will be a boy. We cannot afford to disappoint anybody before the election."[38]

Nonetheless, Allison and his allies persevered and finally reported a bill to the Senate on October 3. They calculated that it would decrease revenues by more than $73 million, the principal reductions deriving from eliminating the internal tax on tobacco and cutting in half the customs duty on sugar. Additional remissions came from eliminating internal taxes on alcohol used in the industrial arts (not beverages), additions to the tariff-free list, and "other changes in the tariff schedules," which included both increases and decreases in rates. Some items, such as wool, salt, lumber, and tinplate, which the Mills bill had slated for the free list, would have protective duties restored under the Senate bill. The Finance Committee majority report, submitted by Nelson Aldrich of Rhode Island, declared that "reductions have been made whenever they have seemed desirable, and we have increased rates whenever it seemed necessary to preserve the workingmen engaged in any American industry requiring protection from ruinous or unequal competition." The Senate bill had no chance of passage, and Aldrich devoted only four pages to explaining it, whereas he filled forty-three pages eviscerating the House bill. Finance Committee chairman Justin Morrill of

Vermont had missed the committee's work because of illness, but he congratulated Aldrich on "the merciless logic with which the Mills Bill has been torn into pitiable fragments by your report."[39]

Aldrich's report, though overly long, served as a campaign document distributed by party committees and interest groups. Sherman came around to the conclusion that the bill "will do no harm and I now think [it] will strengthen us in the contest." The curmudgeonly Joseph Medill admitted to Allison that "the bill is not as bad as I feared." For their part, Democrats dealing with the bill on the stump argued that its promise of a reduced revenue represented a tacit endorsement of Cleveland's warnings about the surplus. The principal criticism they leveled was that the Republican measure increased taxes on necessities and reduced them on luxuries. "They take it off the rich," declared Indiana Senator David Turpie, "and put it on the poor." The *New York Herald* conceded that the Senate bill "makes reductions in the revenue which can for the most part be exactly calculated" but insisted that "the bill is framed from beginning to end to catch the votes of protected interests." Still, the bill's impact on the campaign is difficult to gauge. After a week, Medill optimistically concluded that "the Democratic papers have not been very successful as yet in their assaults upon the bill, and in fact have made no impression on the public mind." At the same time, however, a New York Democrat reported to Lamont at the White House that "the introduction of the Senate bill has taken all the sting out of the 'free-trade scare' in my county & has been of inestimable benefit to us." An upstate New York Republican assured Harrison that because the Republicans could argue that "the Senate Tariff bill is a better measure than the Mills Bill, thousands of Tariff Reform Democrats will refuse to follow Mr. Cleveland's leadership." That was no doubt an exaggeration, but in the equilibrium politics of 1888, any accretion to the party's cause, especially in a doubtful state like New York, could spell the difference between victory and defeat.[40]

SECTIONAL STRATEGIES

In the electoral college calculations that influenced the Republicans' embrace of the tariff issue, the party gave less weight to civil rights questions, which had been a key element in the party's stock-in-trade since its founding. If Harrison should win the normally Republican states of the North, with a total of 182 electoral votes, but lose New York (36 electoral votes) and Indiana (15), he would need to pick up 19 votes else-where to win the election; if he won Indiana, he would need 4 additional votes. The Republicans could perhaps gather the needed votes from the other two doubtful northern states, Connecticut (6) and New Jersey (9). But many party leaders argued that they had a better chance of closing the gap through some combination of border or upper South states, in-cluding Maryland (8), Virginia (12), West Virginia (6), Tennessee (12), North Carolina (11), and Missouri (16). Such a "southern strategy" called for Republicans to de-emphasize the sectional issues of the past and use the tariff arguments to appeal to states in the so-called New South that were experiencing the stirrings of industrialization or produced signifi-cant extractive commodities in need of protection. "Discourage the res-urrection of the bloody shirt," a Knoxville Republican advised Harrison shortly after his nomination. "Recognize the South, . . . encourage her iron, manufacturing, coal, and agricultural interests and you will win the gratitude of her people." "We can carry Virginia, West Virginia, Ten-nessee, and North Carolina on the tariff issue," Ohio Congressman Ben Butterworth told Harrison, "and one half the effort there that we usually put forth to carry Indiana and New York, will give us an overwhelming victory in those states."[41]

The national committee endorsed the emphasis on the tariff over sec-tional issues, although it had scant funds to underwrite a significant speaking campaign or organizational effort below the Mason-Dixon Line. Special-interest groups such as the American Iron and Steel As-sociation provided some help with the distribution of tariff literature. By October 1 the association had sent more than 50,000 protectionist pam-phlets into West Virginia alone, more than it had distributed in New York and New Jersey combined. But not all Republicans agreed that the party should sacrifice civil rights on the altar of a southern tariff strat-egy. Former Mississippi Congressman John R. Lynch, a leading black Republican, implored Harrison to treat the suppression of the ballot in the South as "one of the living vital issues of the day" and argued that, in comparison, "all others are secondary and subordinate." Wisconsin Sen-ator John C. Spooner thought that the national committee was wrong in its fear that a bolder campaign on the civil rights issue would deter "Democrats who are likely to come to us on the tariff question. . . . No party ever made anything yet by being cowardly, especially where the rights of citizenship (even the right to live) are involved."[42]

For his part, Harrison refused to sanction the complete abandonment of the issue of a free ballot and a fair count. "I would not be willing myself to purchase the Presidency by a compact of silence on this question," he told Whitelaw Reid. Although he devoted many more of his speeches to the tariff, he did not neglect the question of voting rights for the South's African Americans. Most important, he sought to combine the two issues. He told a campaign audience, "this great question of a free ballot, so much disturbed by race questions in the South, would be settled this year if the men of the South who believe with us upon the great question of the protection of American industries would throw off old prejudices and vote their convictions upon that question." Should they do so, he said, "the question of a free ballot, so far as it is a Southern question, will be settled forever, for they will have the power to insist that those who believe with them shall vote, and that their votes shall be counted." The question of pensions for Union veterans resonated with the broader sectional issue, and Harrison and other Republicans linked it to the tariff by arguing that surplus revenues ought to be applied to increase outlays to the men who had fought to preserve the Union and eradicate slavery. Continuing to criticize Cleveland for his niggling parsimony, Harrison told 2,000 visitors at Indianapolis, many of them old soldiers, "it is no time now to use an apothecary's scale to weigh the rewards of the men who saved the country."[43]

Cleveland and the Democrats naturally resisted the Republicans' attempts to make inroads in their party's southern base. They warned southerners not to be seduced by Republican promises of a tariff-born prosperity; Republicans' real aim, they claimed, was to fatten monopolistic interests in the North. Democrats applauded Cleveland for ushering in a new period of sectional rapprochement, with southerners once again welcomed in the national councils. Secretary of State Thomas Bayard, himself the scion of an aristocratic Delaware family, urged American voters never to place "in power a man or a party who would mark off his countrymen by their geographical place of residence." Yet when Democrats wrapped themselves in the mantle of sectional reconciliation, they were sending a coded signal that their party would allow dominant white southerners to continue to manage race relations in their states, unchecked by the federal government. At the same time, they encouraged the lingering deep resentment that most white southerners felt for the Republican Party by alleging that if the Republicans regained power, they would swiftly revive the horrors of Reconstruction. Indiana Senator Daniel Voorhees told an audience at Asheville, North Carolina, "I do not know a narrower, more bitter, unscrupulous, malignant hater of the South than this man Harrison." In his letter of acceptance, Cleveland called for "the guarantee to our colored citizens of all their rights of citizenship," and the Democrats subsidized a small pro-Cleveland movement among some northern black leaders who felt that the Republicans had taken them for granted. Nonetheless, white southerners knew that neither Cleveland nor the Democrats in Congress had any intention of taking significant steps to ensure blacks' right to vote or otherwise improve their lot. During the campaign the administration even took pains to insist that Cleveland had never invited Frederick Douglass to dinner at the White House. On the pension issue, Cleveland claimed to have "a generous regard and care for our surviving soldiers and sailors," but he could not resist adding that the system should be managed in such a way that the granting of pensions in any "improper cases may be prevented." In the end, Democrats, like Republicans, saw economic matters as paramount to the southern question in 1888. They too tried to connect the two issues, but in a way designed to arouse white southerners' fears. If the Republicans regained power, said the *New York Herald*, they would "revive the sectional policy of 'harrying the South'" by passing "new repressive legislation" that "would injure credit, disorganize industry and stop development all over the Southern States."[44]

THE LABOR QUESTION

While Democrats hoped that these attempts to frighten white voters would help them sustain their base in the Solid South, they spent a great deal more time and effort in trying to turn workers everywhere against the Republicans. The Gilded Age witnessed great labor unrest, and recent outbursts such as the Haymarket Affair in Chicago in 1886 fed the growing sense that workers were not receiving their fair share in the burgeoning American economy. In 1888 industrial labor and workers generally would have a powerful impact on the voting in the North, not least in the vital doubtful states, all of which had experienced substantial industrial development. Democrats recognized that the linchpin of the GOP's protectionist campaign was its promise of a decent living for American workers compared with the "pauper wages" of workers overseas. Republican orators and editors never tired of offering detailed statistical "proof" of workers' comparative prosperity derived from protective customs duties. And Democrats never tired of disputing these assertions. The high tariff, they insisted, increased the profits of the owners of factories and other enterprises, but those owners refused to share the benefits with their workers. Whatever advantages in remuneration American workers had over their foreign counterparts, Democrats said, derived less from the tariff than from greater productivity and the pressure of labor organizations. "Why," Thurman asked a campaign audience, "is there a necessity for all these extensive organizations if a high tariff gives high wages to the laborer?" Moreover, even though American workers might earn more than those in England, they found more money running out through their fingers in the form of customs duties or higher prices due to customs duties. "I would like to know how taxing a laboring man on everything from the crown of his head to the sole of his feet is going to enrich him," Thurman demanded.[45]

Beyond these general arguments, however, Democrats regarded Harrison as particularly vulnerable on the question of labor. The kid-gloved aristocrat, they said, had no true sympathy for the horny-handed workingman. Shortly after Harrison's nomination, the *Indianapolis Sentinel* published a highly colored account of his activity during the Great Railroad Strike of 1877, complete with a crude drawing of Harrison, rifle in hand, leading a military unit against the strikers. What the story lacked in accuracy, it made up for in sensation. Minimizing the fact that Harrison had also participated in arbitration efforts during the strike, the *Sentinel* insisted that the workers "conceived a hatred of the man eleven years ago and time has served to embitter that feeling rather than to wipe it out." Democrats on the stump and in print picked up the story and repeated it endlessly until the election. In its more virulent form, it included the allegation that Harrison had told the strikers that "a dollar a day was enough for any workingman" and that he "would shoot [them] down like dogs."[46]

Bombarded by labor groups and others with questions about these allegations, Harrison and the Republicans fought back. In his speeches on the tariff, the nominee repeatedly focused on protection's benefits to labor, which, he said, was "the beginning and the end of the tariff question." In addition, Harrison's official campaign biography, written by his friend Lew Wallace, the author of *Ben-Hur*, gave a benign account of Harrison's actions during the 1877 strike. The Republican organization also rushed out a pamphlet entitled *Gen. Harrison and Labor*, which featured his arguments in favor of legislation for the prompt payment of wages, safety regulations, and arbitration and against the importation of contract labor. Louis Michener touted the pamphlet as "a complete refutation to the 'dollar-a-day' lie." But two weeks before the election, Harrison's son wired from New York that party leaders at headquarters wanted him to "specifically deny [the] labor lies" in a speech. The next day the candidate told an assemblage of union leaders that the "malicious and scandalous stories" were "utterly false." He particularly insisted that the "dollar-a-day" tale, "with all its accompaniments and appendages, is not a perversion of anything I ever said—it is a false creation." The important thing to remember, he said, was that the Democrats' policy of "a revenue-only tariff or progressive free trade" would bring "a vast and sudden increase of importations," which in turn would mean "diminished work in our American shops." "If someone tells me that labor is not sufficiently rewarded here," Harrison concluded, "does he hope to have its rewards increased by striking down our protective duties and compelling our workmen to compete with the underpaid labor of Europe?" The next day Stephen Elkins wrote to Harrison that this was "the best of your many good speeches. The Republican party must get nearer the working people."[47]

THE POLITICS OF ETHNICITY

Closely akin to the Democrats' attacks on Harrison's labor record was their rekindling of the Chinese immigration issue that had plagued his nomination bid in the spring. Again claiming that, as a senator, Harrison had voted against imposing restrictions, Democrats argued that he had done so "because he was not in sympathy with the demand of American workingmen for protection against competition with the Asiatic hordes who have reduced the standard of wages on the Pacific slope to the pauper level." Although Democrats invoked these Chinese labor arguments throughout the country, they considered the issue most potent on the Pacific Coast. Party strategists figured that if they failed to capture the eastern doubtful states, they would need to pick up electoral votes from some normally Republican states. They saw grounds for hope in the West, especially California, where the Chinese question was most salient. The day after Harrison's nomination, a San Diego Democrat wrote to Cleveland that "the record of General Harrison on the Chinese question will lose him many votes on the Pacific Coast."[48]

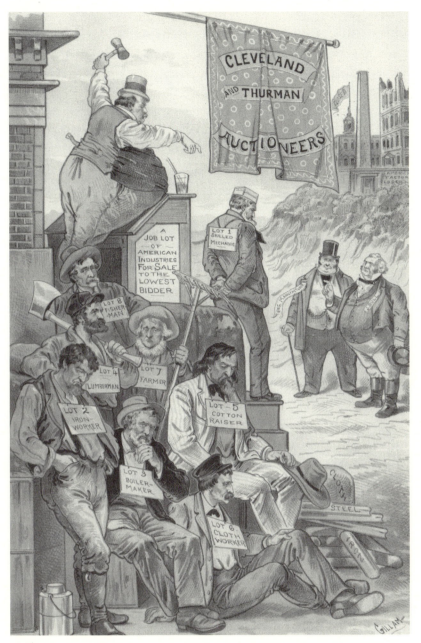

In Judge, *the red bandanna serves as a sign of Cleveland and Thurman selling out American industries and labor. (*Judge, *July 14, 1888)*

That prediction soon proved to be premature. In the early weeks of the campaign, California Democrats hammered away at the question. Panicky Republicans urged Harrison to respond directly to the charges in his letter of acceptance, which he agreed to do, but in the interim he left it to Republicans treating the issue locally in California to deny that he had ever favored Chinese immigration or, alternatively, to imply that if his Senate votes had seemed to condone it, he had since changed his mind. In mid-August he briefly mentioned the issue in one of his front-porch speeches, typically connecting it to the tariff question: "We should protect our people against competition with the products of underpaid labor abroad as well as against the coming to our shores of paupers, laborers under contract, and the Chinese labor. These two thoughts are twin thoughts." By the third week of August, California Republicans were reporting that because the state's voters found Harrison's position "entirely satisfactory," the issue was "cutting a very small figure in the campaign." Of greater concern was the threatened loss of tariff protection for such California commodities as raisins, wool, lumber, nuts, and fruits. "Cleveland's free-trade message and the Mills bill," a party worker wrote to Harrison, "have turned hundreds of Democrats in the state to your support." Other westerners thought that Cleveland's antipathy to silver coinage would also cost him support in the region. "The Chinese question is no longer a political issue," Nevada Senator William Stewart wrote to a San Francisco Republican, "but as to the silver question there can only be one choice as between Harrison and Cleveland."[49]

Another reason that the Chinese issue had lost some of its sting was that Californians and other Americans were awaiting the final outcome of the Cleveland administration's negotiations with China to limit immigration. In the spring Bayard had concluded a treaty to prohibit the migration of Chinese laborers to the United States for twenty years. After deliberating for several months, the Senate ratified the treaty and added amendments to restrict the return of laborers who had resided in the United States but had left the country. Months passed with no official response from Peking, and on September 1 American newspapers carried unofficial reports that China had rejected the amended treaty.[50]

California Democrats immediately saw a chance to resuscitate the political issue. The state committee chairman William English wired the White House that the Democrats in Congress should push a bill "forever excluding" Chinese who had departed from the United States. If the Democratic House passed such a measure, English said, "it will give

Cleveland and Thurman this coast." Cleveland seized the opportunity and entrusted the matter to his close ally, Pennsylvania Congressman William L. Scott, who the next day introduced and secured House passage of a bill embodying English's suggestion. Although Bayard considered these hasty proceedings "disgraceful," the Senate gave its approval four days later. Four days after that, Cleveland used his letter of acceptance to condemn "a servile immigration, which injuriously competes with our laboring men in the field of toil, and adds to our population an element ignorant of our institutions and laws, impossible of assimilation with our people, and dangerous to our peace and welfare." Still, Cleveland did not secure control of the issue. Not to be outdone, Harrison, in his letter of acceptance, promised to enforce applicable laws and to approve any additional legislation necessary "to stop further Chinese immigration." "The objections to Chinese immigration are distinctive and conclusive," Harrison declared, "and are now so generally accepted as such that the question has passed entirely beyond the stage of argument."[51]

Harrison's complete cave on the issue delighted Golden State Republicans. One party leader wrote that Harrison's letter met "the most hearty approval of the best thinking people here and elsewhere . . . and I shall not be surprised to see California poll an overwhelming Republican majority." This drift led a desperate Cleveland to make one last effort to reap political benefit from the issue. Although Bayard pleaded with the president that "the record of our party on the subject is perfectly clear— and needs no such reckless action as the 'Scott' bill proposes," Cleveland plowed ahead. Not only did he sign the Scott bill; on October 1 he also sent Congress an unusual special message announcing his approval. The president proclaimed his belief that "the experiment of blending the social habits and mutual race idiosyncrasies of the Chinese laboring classes with those of the great body of the people of the United States has been proved . . . to be in every sense unwise, impolitic, and injurious to both nations." California Democrats went wild, pouring into the streets "and greeting one another with the enthusiasm of school boys." "The Electoral Vote is yours sure," one of them wrote to Cleveland.[52]

But it was not to be. Although the state's Republicans were rattled by the message, they soon confidently reassured Harrison that the state would in fact be his, not Cleveland's. Two weeks before the election, a Republican newspaper editor wrote to Harrison that his "wise and apt reference to the Chinese Question" had been "just what we needed."

"California and the remaining Pacific Coast states are all right for republican success." In the end, Harrison had matched Cleveland in denouncing the immigration of Chinese labor and had succeeded in diminishing if not altogether neutralizing the question, thereby leaving the tariff as the paramount issue for California residents. Moreover, West Coast Republicans took heart from the influx of new residents and voters who had been moving from Republican regions in the East. Maine Congressman Thomas B. Reed, on a speaking tour in California at the end of the campaign, reported to Harrison that despite the Democrats' use of Cleveland's Scott bill message "for all it is worth," the "tariff question . . . is taking a strong hold and the [domestic] immigration into the State has been from the right quarter and these two things will pull us through."[53]

While the Chinese issue attenuated in the West, a different sort of ethnic politics burst forth in an episode involving the British minister to the United States, Sir Lionel Sackville-West. With one eye on the Irish American vote, Republicans had throughout the campaign branded Cleveland's tariff and other policies as pro-British, but the charge lost some of its force after Cleveland's fisheries message. Shortly after the message, a California Republican named George Osgoodby devised a scheme to breathe new life into the allegation. A Pomona fruit grower, Osgoodby had earlier urged Harrison to confront the Chinese issue. Now he meant to tap the hostility that the Irish and other Americans harbored for England. Posing as a British-born naturalized American citizen and using an assumed name (Charles F. Murchison), Osgoodby wrote to Sackville and explained that he wished to vote for the presidential candidate whose policies would be friendlier to the mother country. In light of Cleveland's fisheries message, he asked the minister, could he still assume that Cleveland was more favorable to Britain than Harrison was? Much to Osgoodby's surprise, the fatuous Sackville replied that Cleveland had designed his message merely to meet "the political situation" and that after his reelection he would still "manifest a spirit of conciliation" toward Britain. Osgoodby had acted on his own impulse, not at the behest of a party committee. But he showed the correspondence to his lawyers, who were Republicans, and they eventually convinced him to give it to the press, where it appeared two weeks before the election.[54]

Democrats were livid. John Boyle O'Reilly, a leading Irish Democrat and editor of the Irish American *Boston Pilot,* wired Cleveland that

Sackville had given "deep offence" and "his withdrawal ought to be the consequence." Sackville compounded his transgression by telling reporters that his correspondence with "Murchison" had been private and in no sense a breach of "international custom or courtesy." Beside himself with anger, Cleveland told Bayard that he feared Irish American leaders would cease "doing good work" for the campaign. This "stupid thing," he raged, would "greatly endanger or wreck our prospects" unless "this wretched marplot is recalled." After chastising Sackville for his indiscretion, Bayard ordered the American minister in London to inform the British government that the United States expected its "disapproval" of Sackville's action. When no response was immediately forthcoming, Democrats grew even angrier. "Don't, for God's sake, split hairs with this idiotic English 'Hoodoo,'" one wrote to Bayard. "Must a great party, championing a great economic question, one of vital importance to our people and our country, be sacrificed to diplomatic hair-splitting?" The British refused to recall the envoy, although the foreign minister informally suggested that the United States would be justified in demanding that he leave. This Cleveland did, much to the relief of Democratic orators and editors who heaped praise on the president for throwing Sackville out of the country. But the delay of nearly a week between the letter's first publication and the minister's dismissal robbed the president's act of some of its political impact. For their part, Republicans pushed the episode to the hilt. From New York, Blaine wrote to Harrison that Sackville's letter was "having a wonderful effect on the Irish here and proves more at the dash of a sentence than we could by argument during the whole campaign." Republicans distributed thousands of copies of the letter at a mass meeting of Irish protectionists at Madison Square Garden, citing it as one more piece of evidence that Cleveland was the stooge of British free traders.[55]

THE MUGWUMP DILEMMA

Such histrionics had slight impact on the Mugwumps and other self-styled reformers, many of whom watched the campaign with considerable discomfort. Unlike in the Cleveland-Blaine fight of 1884, when their united support, they believed, had placed Cleveland in the White House, these men found themselves unable to frame the contest of 1888 as a battle between virtue and vice. Cleveland's failure to fulfill his promise to end abuses in the civil service profoundly disappointed them, and the Democrats' weak platform plank on the subject provided no consolation. "The situation is unsatisfactory," George William Curtis wrote, "and our friends are in some degree divided as to the wiser course." Wayne MacVeagh, a leader in the Civil Service Reform Association, concluded that "the Association, *as such,* will do better to remain quiet during the present canvass." For civil service reformers who also espoused protectionism, the decision was relatively easy, for they could denounce not only Cleveland's recreancy on patronage but also his fostering, as Henry Lea put it, of "the flesh-pots of Free Trade." The Philadelphian was a leading voice among reformers who stood steadfastly against Cleveland for his betrayal on the civil service question. Shortly before the election, Lea published a searing article in the *Independent,* indicting the president for his treachery and declaring that his reelection would signify that "the people at large care nothing for reform" and "are satisfied to have political bosses foist their henchmen into office." The article, which Lea circulated widely, touched a nerve, and the outraged Cleveland thought that the "dirty mendacious" Lea "ought to be horsewhipped."[56]

But as a protectionist, Lea was in a minority among reformers. Most of the Mugwumps of 1884, some of whom had connections to importing interests, embraced "revenue reform" and took no offense at Cleveland's espousal of freer trade. Adherents of laissez-faire in general, most had warmly welcomed Cleveland's December tariff message. These men were more conflicted than protectionists like Lea, feeling compelled to wink at the president's patronage transgressions in order to endorse his reelection on the tariff issue. Cleveland sought to make their task easier by submerging the civil service question as much as possible, a move also aimed to appeal to Democratic Party regulars who had bridled at the president's reform efforts. Early in the campaign, when R. R. Bowker urged Cleveland to use a public letter to the New York Reform Club to endorse both revenue and civil service reform, Cleveland rejected the suggestion. He ignored civil service altogether in his letter and labeled tariff reduction "the reform which, of all others, at the present time is most needful." In formally accepting his nomination, Cleveland took only a portion of one sentence to refer to "a strict and steadfast adherence to the principles of civil service reform" as one of "numerous objects of domestic concern." Although Republicans such as Joseph Medill, who had served on the Civil Service Commission in the 1870s, called "what Cleveland says for civil service reform in the light of his performance

. . . laughable," many Mugwumps accommodated themselves to Cleveland's priorities. "In condemning the concessions to the spoils element in the Democratic party made by President Cleveland," declared Carl Schurz, "I go as far as his severest critic among the friends of reform." "But," said Schurz, "that is no reason why we should overlook or underestimate the merit of the other things he actually has done." Most notably by his tariff message, Schurz insisted, Cleveland had "identified himself and his candidacy with an economic policy which bids fair to correct existing evils . . . and to secure a steady development of the general prosperity."[57]

On the Republican side, Harrison did his best to attract wavering Mugwumps back to their old party allegiance. In framing his letter of acceptance, he twice met with fellow Hoosier Lucius B. Swift, a leader in the national civil service reform movement. In their conversations, Harrison was cautious, telling Swift that "he did not want to promise more than he could do" and "that not for the Presidency would he be in the position regarding his promises that Cleveland is in." What Swift and other reformers who advised Harrison most hoped for was a statement that he would not merely enforce the Pendleton Act but work to expand its provisions to cover more offices. Harrison complied. In his letter of acceptance he promised that he would "faithfully and rigorously" enforce existing law and also that he would approve "further legislation extending the reform to other branches of the service." "In appointments to every grade and department," he added, "fitness, and not party service, should be the essential and discriminating test, and fidelity and efficiency the only sure tenure of office. Only the interest of the public service should suggest removals from office."[58]

Harrison thus went far beyond Cleveland in highlighting civil service reform, but how effective he was in detaching Mugwumps from Cleveland's side is difficult to say. The treasurer of the Philadelphia Civil Service Reform Association assured Harrison that "with your letter before them I cannot see how any Civil Service Reformer who is a Republican can help supporting the ticket, which I trust will be successful in November." Many independents, however, thought that the Republican nominee was too much under the influence of the archvillain Blaine, and E. L. Godkin was convinced that the Republican campaign "has been going to pieces since Blaine came back" from Europe. Even so, Harrison showed no intention of distancing himself from the Plumed Knight. In the end, Cleveland could count on less help from the reformers in

1888 than he had enjoyed in 1884. A month before the election, the New Jersey Republican state chairman wrote to Harrison that "the Mugwump element has, so far as an organization is concerned, completely disappeared." "Quite a number of them" would still "vote for Cleveland because he is their representative free trader," but "in some counties there appear to be none left of this peculiar people." At the same time, an official of the Brooklyn Democratic Club warned the White House that "it is not an immoderate estimate to say, that in Brooklyn alone, one third of the independent Republicans who voted for Cleveland four years ago are inclined to withhold their support on account of the Civil Service Question." Once again, the loss of even a handful of votes in the key swing state of New York could result in defeat.[59]

CLEVELAND AND HILL

In New York, Governor David B. Hill's bid for reelection also fueled Mugwumps' hesitance in supporting the Democratic ticket. Hill's unvarnished partisanship, his open contempt for civil service reform, his implication in a scandal involving state contracts, and his close connection with the state's liquor interests all rendered him anathema to many of the reformist supporters Cleveland hoped to retain. Dealing with the Hill question proved maddening for the president and his aides. One independent warned the White House that the New York Mugwumps who had voted for Cleveland in 1884 "will not support Hill; and if he is nominated, it is easy to see how much it will weaken and embarrass their efforts to support and re-elect the President." Many of the "better element" among Democrats agreed. Former New York City Mayor W. R. Grace frankly told Cleveland, "I am by conviction thoroughly & deeply interested in your election but not sufficiently so to induce me to sacrifice my own conscientious convictions as to my duty to this state." More practical-minded Democrats, however, cautioned the administration that "we need Hill" because "he has much strength with an element that we cannot afford to ignore." Tammany boss Richard Croker told Lamont that despite the "bubblings" of a few opponents, Hill was popular among the state's Democrats, and it would be "a dangerous experiment" to block his renomination for governor.[60]

Recognizing the hazards on either side, Cleveland decided to "let the gubernatorial question alone," which he could safely do on the grounds that the national administration ought not to interfere in state party nominations. But once Hill's renomination was certain, Cleveland came under renewed pressure to publicly support his fellow Democrat's reelection. For his part, Hill had no newfound love for Cleveland, but he saw it as being in his own best interest to subdue his contempt and try to curry favor with the president. Two days before the Democratic state convention, in a rare direct communication, the governor wrote to Cleveland to commend his letter of acceptance for its "good judgment, sound sense, and plain statements" expressing the "soundest Democratic doctrine." At the convention Hill saw to it that an ardent Cleveland supporter served as chairman and that his own name was placed in nomination by the same man who had nominated Cleveland for mayor of Buffalo, for governor in 1882, and for president in 1884. After his nomination, Hill told a crowd of well-wishers that it was his "sincere wish and desire that . . . every friend of mine shall vote for Cleveland and Thurman," because "success in the nation is of paramount importance." All these overtures were for naught. Grace and others continued to argue that lending support to Hill would be "absolutely suicidal" for Cleveland and "more than the Presidency is worth." Despite warnings that unless he gave his endorsement, Hill's backers would "knife" the national ticket, Cleveland refused to write a letter on the governor's behalf.[61]

Hill's enemies made no secret of their own intention to knife the governor. They formed a Committee of Democrats and Independents and appealed to Democrats to vote for the president and against the governor on the grounds that Cleveland "has steadily elevated his party," while Hill "has done all in his power to debase and degrade it." Cleveland's failure to restrain this group naturally led Hill to retaliate. He cleverly devised a strategy whereby he professed his support for the national ticket but gave relatively little aid to Cleveland in New York. With presidential ambitions of his own, Hill reasoned that if he could secure his own reelection while Cleveland lost New York, he would hold the upper hand four years hence. In agreeing to fulfill speaking engagements for the national committee in October, Hill proposed to concentrate on Indiana, New Jersey, and Connecticut, where Cleveland victories attributable in part to Hill's work would be a plus for his own political future. On his tour, the governor spoke enthusiastically for the president, but in his speeches in New York he gave more attention to state issues. And when a worried Cleveland agreed to review a mass parade in New York City in late October, Hill refused to attend. To Democrats who wrote to inquire whether he really supported the national ticket, Hill

The breach-of-promise theme in Judge's depiction of the Cleveland-Hill
enmity conveys a not-so-subtle parody of Cleveland's "woman scrape" and
also reminds temperance voters that liquor interests support the Democrats.
(Judge, October 20, 1888)

and his secretary merely referred them to his speech on the night of his renomination.[62]

As the election approached, Hill and his advisers spurred their allies in New York to greater efforts but, by implication, counseled relaxation with regard to the national ticket because, they said, "Indiana, New Jersey, and Connecticut seem to be sure for Cleveland and Thurman." Most telling of all was the governor's private encouragement of ticket splitting, the very knifing advisers had warned Cleveland about. In this era of paper ballots distributed by the parties, if a voter wished to split his ticket, he did so by placing a "paster" bearing the name of the candidate he preferred over the name of the candidate printed on the ballot. In mid-October Hill's secretary ordered 200,000 extra pasters "for the Governor's personal use." Hill himself joined in the distribution of these pasters, asking local Democrats to "do some special work for me." For the Cleveland camp, turnabout was fair play. When Roger Mills and Thomas Bayard took to the stump in New York late in the campaign, they both made speeches for the president that omitted any mention of Hill, though supposedly inadvertently. And a week before the election, Lamont at the White House ordered a thousand New York presidential ticket pasters for distribution in the president's home state.[63]

In New York City Cleveland faced a microcosm of the statewide troubles. Throughout his administration, the two local Democratic factions, Tammany Hall and the County Democracy, had battled each other for federal patronage. Neither was fully satisfied, and each decided in 1888 to concentrate on local offices and field its own municipal ticket. Tammany nominated Sheriff Hugh Grant for mayor, while the County Democracy backed the incumbent Abram S. Hewitt. Neither faction had much affection for the president, and it soon became clear that both were willing to sacrifice Cleveland in exchange for Republican votes for their local tickets. National party leaders were frantic; Lamont and Navy Secretary Whitney rushed to New York to effect a reconciliation behind one slate of candidates, but they failed to do so. Republicans, of course, took great delight in the Democratic melodrama in New York. "The awkwardness of the situation between Hill and Cleveland is most helpful," Reid wrote to Harrison. And from New York City, Clarkson reported that the Republicans' "harmony and activity" posed a wonderful contrast to the Democrats' "angry and greedy factions."[64]

Evidence of Republican harmony in New York showed clearly in the campaign of former Senator Warner Miller, who ran against Hill for governor. Miller's nomination grew out of the accommodation that he, Platt, and other party leaders had reached at the national convention when they agreed to unite on Harrison and to back Levi P. Morton for vice president. A temperance advocate, Miller focused his campaign on the liquor issue. In 1884 Cleveland had surpassed Blaine by slightly more than a thousand votes in New York, while the Prohibition Party had polled more than twenty times that number in the state. In 1888 Republican leaders fully appreciated the need to stem desertions to the drys. The Republican convention that nominated Miller condemned Hill's veto of legislation to limit the liquor traffic, and on the stump Miller attacked Hill on the issue, telling audiences that he would rather have the churches behind him than the saloons. Miller and other Republican leaders had no great confidence that he could defeat the governor, who enjoyed solid backing by liquor interests as well as by Democrats who recoiled at sumptuary legislation. But Miller was willing to make the sacrifice to achieve the larger goal. "The position I have taken has stopped the defection of temperance Republicans which otherwise would have been large this year," he reported to Harrison. "We all feel confident of carrying the National ticket through by a safe majority."[65]

THIRD PARTIES: POTENTIAL SPOILERS

As was typical of the Gilded Age in general, third parties were not real contenders for the presidency in 1888, but instead were vehicles for voter protest. Their significance turned on their ability to disturb the calculations of the major party strategists, especially in the doubtful states. The Union Labor Party, an amalgamation of labor and farmer organizations, nominated A. J. Streeter for president and called for government ownership of the means of transportation and communication, free coinage of silver, and the elimination of banks from the creation of the money supply. The United Labor Party, an outgrowth of Henry George's single-tax movement, nominated Robert Cowdrey and advocated a single tax on land, as well as other policies similar to those the Union Laborites pushed. Both Republican and Democratic strategists believed, correctly, that few voters would warm to these radical ideas, but they nonetheless sought to limit defections. To curb the labor protest vote, each major party portrayed its tariff policy as designed primarily in the interest of workers and cast the other party's approach as fundamentally destructive of labor's well-being. Most American workers, in fact, stayed

The Union Labor ticket in 1888. (Library of Congress)

with one or the other of the major parties and accepted their framing of the contest as one of protection for labor versus relief for the working class from high taxes and prices.[66]

The prohibition question was more complicated. The Prohibition Party ticket headed by presidential nominee Clinton B. Fisk, a well-known philanthropist, had no chance of carrying any state in 1888. The American people generally rejected the party's call for a complete ban on the manufacture, importation, and sale of all alcoholic beverages. Still, as Miller's campaign in New York showed, the GOP labored mightily to curtail losses to the Prohibitionists. Yet the Republicans did not want to go so far toward embracing temperance measures as to repulse Democrats who might come over to their side on the tariff and other issues. For their part, Democrats historically had opposed sumptuary legislation. They generally stood by that position in 1888 and often depicted the Republicans as favoring undue interference with individuals' private decisions. At the same time, however, Democrats hoped that significant numbers of Republican temperance supporters would abandon the GOP for the Prohibitionists, and behind the scenes, Democrats took steps to bolster the third party. "From my stand point," William L. Scott wrote to Lamont from New York, "the most important thing for us to do is to work the prohibition movement in this state for all there is in it." Thanks to Democratic largesse, the drys had ample funds. Scott placed great importance on financing speakers in "the tent system" of temperance meetings in New York and Indiana. He and other Democrats hoped that men who attended such meetings and took the temperance pledge would also be inclined to abandon the Republicans and vote the Prohibition ticket.[67]

In combating these efforts by the Democrats, the Republicans enlisted the aid of J. Ellen Foster, a prominent voice in the women's temperance movement. Aided by Clarkson, Foster founded and became the first president of the Woman's National Republican Association, which served to support women's activities in behalf of the Republican ticket. Financed by the national committee, Foster made a series of speeches in which she not only touted the virtues of the protective tariff but also stressed the importance of protecting the American home from the evil effects of drink. She insisted that the Prohibition Party was an ineffective vehicle for curtailing the liquor traffic and that only the Republicans could achieve the necessary reforms. The national committee also supported campaign speeches by the well-known lecturer Anna Dickinson.

Principles of the Prohibition Party. (Library of Congress)

But Dickinson tended to concentrate on southern civil rights questions, tangential to the central thrust of the committee's emphasis, and it eventually withdrew its support.[68]

On the Democratic side, Cleveland's most effective female supporter was his twenty-four-year-old wife, Frances. She made no speeches nor advocated any particular policy, but she was immensely popular and helped soften Cleveland's image. When scurrilous rumors arose that he mistreated her, she described her husband as "kind, attentive, considerate, and affectionate." Capitalizing on her youthful good looks, the Democrats reproduced her image widely—on banners, buttons, and campaign posters. During a campaign swing through Indiana two weeks before the election, Thurman's son "saw not less than twenty 'Frankie Cleveland Clubs,' all dressed in red bandanas," marching "right in the procession through the mud and rain . . . like the boys." After "a most successful trip" through the Hoosier State, young Thurman reported to Lamont, "if enthusiasm and noise will carry the State, we certainly will win."[69]

GETTING OUT THE VOTE

However widespread such enthusiasm might be, it could not mask the deep anxiety that strategists in both major parties felt about the outcome in Indiana and New York. The electoral college math was such that the presidency itself was riding on those key doubtful states. To win, a party must poll a full vote among its own adherents and attract as many as possible from the opposing camp and from among the relatively small numbers of voters who wavered between the two. Through most of the campaign of 1888, the quest for support focused on the issues, most notably the tariff, with both parties using hundreds of speakers and mountains of literature to broadcast their appeals, as well as mass rallies and parades to spark citizens' enthusiasm. In the final days and on election day itself, each party's organization would face the ultimate challenge of getting out its maximum vote. In that effort, money inevitably played a role.

On October 8 the *Indianapolis Journal,* the Hoosier State's principal Republican newspaper, printed what was purported to be a circular letter from a Democratic county chairman to party precinct workers, asking them to supply lists of their precincts' voters and to "mark every one who has to have money as a 'float.' Those who have to be bought

First Lady Frances Cleveland, a favorite of the Democrats, flanked by the nominees. (Library of Congress)

are not 'doubtful' but are 'floats.' Look closely after every one. Let no one escape." Allegations of activity of this sort were not unusual in a campaign, but Harrison took the threat seriously enough to mention it in a letter to Reid. "My belief," Harrison wrote, "is that the Dem[ocratic] managers are counting wholly for success upon the free use of money late in the campaign. They are making a careful list of what they call 'floats,' which one of their circulars explains as meaning purchasable voters." Hoosier Republicans, the nominee implied, were in no position to match the Democrats on this front. Harrison's managers at the Chicago convention had promised eastern party leaders that Indiana Republicans would supply their own finances in the campaign, and Quay intended to concentrate the national committee's last-minute outlays in New York. Harrison felt a strong sense of personal pride at stake in Indiana, but a dearth of big donors in the state made fund-raising difficult. The national committee had recently sent the Indiana party $6,000, but, Harrison told Reid, "we are still sailing very close to the wind." Believing that the party "must run no risk in Indiana," Reid and other party leaders responded. The editor himself personally carried $10,000 in cash to Indianapolis. Murat Halstead of the *Cincinnati Commercial Gazette* ran a subscription and raised a fund for Indiana amounting to $1 per precinct. In New York Blaine took time out from speechmaking to hold a conference with party benefactors in his hotel room to impress upon them "the necessity of every aid to Indiana." And in the last week of the campaign, Walter Gresham wrote to a friend that Harrison's son Russell had come to Chicago to raise money and that Abraham Lincoln's son Robert Todd Lincoln had told him that he was "in favor of chipping in . . . because the democrats were using money the same way."[70]

Clearly, Republicans saw a need to place themselves on an equal footing with the Democrats in Indiana. On October 31 the *Indianapolis Sentinel* printed a facsimile of what purported to be a circular letter from the treasurer of the Republican National Committee, Harrison's Hoosier friend William Dudley, to Republican county chairmen in the state. The letter urged the local party officials to "divide the floaters into blocks of five, and put a trusted man with necessary funds in charge of these five, and make him responsible that none get away and that all vote our ticket." Publication of the letter created a much greater sensation than had the similarly worded Democratic circular a few weeks earlier, in large part because the GOP document supposedly emanated from a national party official. Harrison and other party leaders disavowed any knowledge of such a scheme, and state GOP managers denied that Dudley had any role in the Indiana campaign. Dudley admitted that he had written a letter discussing party organization, but he denounced the printed version as a forgery and sued several Democratic newspapers for libel. Not long before the date of the letter, Dudley had suffered a lengthy bout of a typhoid-like fever, with his temperature ranging as high as 103 and "a dangerous pulse." One may speculate as to how much this illness may have affected his discretion, if not his judgment. In any event, Harrison refused to make a public statement exonerating Dudley, and their friendship ended. After the election the Cleveland administration's Justice Department moved to prosecute Dudley, but a Republican federal judge quashed the indictment.[71]

Louis Michener, Harrison's political alter ego, years later wrote that Dudley's letter, as he had written it, contained nothing "illegal or immoral" and that this sort of get-out-the-vote instruction was not unusual. Indeed, shortly before Dudley's letter was written, Wilson Bissell, Cleveland's closest friend from Buffalo, reminded Lamont that he had written "the Pres[iden]t the other day asking that you send me a list of trusty men, one in each county [in New York]. This should be done promptly if at all as it's getting late." At the same time, Lamont heard from a Syracuse Democrat that "if we can take care of the floating or commercial vote of our city (which we are preparing to do) the republican majority of our county will not exceed that of four years ago." Similarly, two weeks before the election, a state senator from Rochester urged Lamont to write to party workers, "placing special stress upon the importance of having some kind of an organization for the express purpose of getting voters to the polls on the day of election, and getting them there *early*. The old managers need not be told very much about what they ought to do."[72]

Through the years, the presidential election of 1888 has borne the reputation as one of the most corrupt in history, largely because of the Dudley letter. But regardless of whether Dudley wrote the letter as published, it bespoke a practice common to both parties in the doubtful states in this era of equilibrium politics. The notion that one party "stole" the election in the doubtful states seems meaningless when one recognizes that the parties' tactics were essentially identical and that the result was so close that it could easily have turned out in the reverse. Nor were underhanded tactics particularly reliable. In one hotly contested town in Indiana, a party worker reported after the election that the opponents "had lots of two dollar bills & so did we. We used ours. They froze to theirs." Nefarious methods tainted both parties in Indiana and New York, and they may well have canceled each other out. Moreover, the evidence suggests that the allegations of contemplated fraud put officials from both parties on high alert to prevent trickery at the polls. In New York City the chief federal election supervisor, John I. Davenport, hired hundreds of temporary assistants to check fraudulent registrations and to man the voting places on election day. One-third of the federal Justice Department's entire expenditure for election supervisors went to New York State, and Quay further underwrote Davenport's operation with national committee funds. As a result, according to one scholar, the city "had an unusually honest election." In the absence of large federal outlays for supervisors in Indiana, civic-minded citizens manned the polls; in South Bend, Mrs. Clement Studebaker, wife of the great wagon maker, "arranged to give workers sandwiches & coffee" in two precincts. One historian has concluded that the Dudley letter episode had so aroused the vigilance of reporters and politicians that the "election was the cleanest in Indiana in years." And a study of voting and election practices generally in the period asserts, "Most of those who did receive money on election day were paid to vote for their own party. 'Floaters'—men who cast a ticket for the highest bidder—formed a distinct minority of the paid vote." "The majority of voters," this study concluded, "were not bribed but, rather, voted for their party out of deep and longstanding loyalty."[73]

Most important, the last-minute scramble for votes in the doubtful states should not overshadow the much greater importance of the preceding months-long campaign and its focus on matters of public policy. This was no sham battle. Party leaders acted on the assumption that their efforts to convince voters of the correctness of their views stood central to the campaign and that the result of the election would determine which set of wide-apart principles would guide the nation. Thus, it was not for nothing that Grover Cleveland agonized about the tariff plank in the Democratic platform, or that Benjamin Harrison persevered in the daily grind of speechmaking and handshaking at Indianapolis, or that James G. Blaine campaigned nearly nonstop from his return to America until election day, or that Allen Thurman literally tempted death by his arduous speaking tour, or that the American Iron and Steel Association distributed more than 1.3 million tariff pamphlets, or that thousands of Republicans and Democrats labored day after day to "educate" the electorate about the issues they confronted. The politicians and citizens of 1888 did not perform all this work with the thought that in the end it would all be meaningless and that the fate of the nation and the direction of its economic policy would turn simply on the discreet disbursement of two-dollar bills by "trusted" or "trusty" men in Indiana and New York.

The real travesty in the election of 1888 was not the Dudley letter or Hill's sneaky use of pasters in New York against Cleveland. It was, rather, the suppression of the African American vote by incorrigible white Democrats throughout much of the South. Outright violence had waned since earlier days, but an effective residue of intimidation still hung about southern polling places, compounded by complex voting procedures designed to baffle the uninitiated and by outright fraud in the counting of votes. "The niggers can vote if they want to," declared one Mississippi Democrat, but "we *count* the votes, and you can just bet your bottom dollar that the white men are going to stay on top." This despotic system cost the Republicans untold tens of thousands of popular votes and a potentially conclusive number of electoral votes. As the election outcome would show, had the ballot been free and all the votes counted in the South, Benjamin Harrison and the Republicans could have enjoyed a much different electoral dynamic, one that would have greatly reduced the significance of the northern doubtful states.[74]

But that was not the case, and on election morning Grover Cleveland and Benjamin Harrison each woke up with good reason to believe that he would be taking the oath of office on the fourth of March next. Each had received confident reports of impending success. Shortly after ten o'clock in the morning Harrison walked with his son from his house on Delaware Street to his polling place at a nearby livery stable. He voted, then chatted briefly with bystanders before heading back home, where telegraph linemen were stringing wires to his house. Emblematic of his performance generally in the campaign, Cleveland did not bother to return to his home in New York to vote. On election day he attended to routine matters, paid a few personal bills, and wrote some letters. To a friend he wrote, "You know how I feel in the matter and how great will be the *personal* compensations of defeat. I am very sure that any desire I may have for success rests upon the conviction that the triumph of my party at this time means the good and the prosperity of the country. You see I am in a good mood to receive the returns whatever they may be."[75]

5 A MINORITY AND A MANDATE

As the polls were closing across the nation on November 6, President Cleveland settled with friends and advisers in the White House library, where the election returns arrived in brief, sometimes cryptic telegraphic messages. A similar scene unfolded at the Harrison house on North Delaware Street in Indianapolis. From GOP headquarters in New York, national treasurer William Dudley wired bulletins with returns from around the country, which Russell Harrison conveyed to his father and his guests. By midnight both camps knew that Harrison had taken New York and the election.[1]

When the counting was done, Harrison had amassed 5,443,892 popular votes and 233 electoral votes from 20 states. Cleveland won 18 states for a total of 5,534,488 popular votes and 168 electoral votes. Harrison's margin over Cleveland in New York amounted to just 14,373, or 1.1 percent of the total vote. The Prohibitionist Clinton Fisk posted a nationwide total of a quarter of a million votes; Union Labor candidate A. J. Streeter received nearly 150,000; and Robert Cowdrey of the United Labor Party and other minor-party candidates amassed fewer than 10,000. Fisk won 30,231 votes in the Empire State, or 2.3 percent, but he received nearly 12,000 fewer votes than his party had won there in 1887. David Hill won reelection as governor by a margin of more than 19,000 votes. Although Warner Miller lost to Hill, his temperance campaign had paid off for the national ticket in New York. The only state besides New York to switch from Cleveland's column in 1884 to the Republicans' in 1888 was Indiana, which Harrison carried by

2,376 votes out of half a million, or just 0.4 percent. Cleveland managed to win the other two northern doubtful states: New Jersey by 2.4 percent and Connecticut by just 336 votes, or 0.2 percent. In Indiana, New York, and New Jersey, turnout exceeded 90 percent, and in Connecticut it was 85.5 percent. In the end, the Chinese immigration issue did little damage to Harrison. He carried California, Oregon, and Nevada, the latter two by greater margins than James G. Blaine had scored in 1884.[2]

Cleveland's nationwide plurality of 90,596 made Harrison a "minority" president, but that result masked the sectional character of the two parties' support. Cleveland carried only two states outside the old domain of slavery, Connecticut and New Jersey; Harrison won none of the former slave states. Cleveland's overall plurality in the South stood at 563,869, while in the rest of the nation Harrison surpassed Cleveland by 473,273 votes. Cleveland's overall plurality and Harrison's minority status clearly rested on the Democrats' suppression of the African American vote in several southern states, a vote that would have been overwhelmingly Republican. Soon after Cleveland's nomination, a Charleston editor had assured him that South Carolina Democrats would "see what we can do in the way of piling up a big majority." That they did. Cleveland carried the Palmetto State by a margin of 52,088, or 65.1 percent, in a state where blacks constituted nearly 60 percent of the population. In the two previous decades the black population of South Carolina had grown by more than 60 percent, but between 1872 and 1888, the number of Republican votes for president in the state had declined by more than 80 percent. Turnout in South Carolina in 1888 was 35 percent, the lowest in the nation. Other Deep South states showed similar election results, most notably the other two states with black-majority populations, Louisiana and Mississippi. Cleveland carried Louisiana by 54,372 and Mississippi by 55,356. These margins, added to that in South Carolina, totaled 161,816. Thus, Cleveland's plurality in these three repressive states amounted to substantially more than his margin over Harrison nationwide.

Because congressional representation and electoral votes were based on population, the disfranchisement of blacks in the South tended to swell the political power of southern whites relative to that of northern voters. The total vote counted in Louisiana, Mississippi, and South Carolina in 1888 was 311,674, and those three states combined had 26 electoral votes. The inequity showed clearly in comparisons with the vote numbers from several northern Republican states. In Illinois, for instance, voters cast a total of 747,813 popular votes, but the state had just 22 electoral votes, and Ohioans cast 839,357 votes to choose 23 electors. In addition, Iowa, Kansas, Massachusetts, Michigan, and Wisconsin each posted more popular votes and had substantially fewer electoral votes than the three black-majority southern states combined. Most significantly for 1888, if elections had been open and fair in Louisiana, Mississippi, and South Carolina, and Harrison had won their 26 electoral votes with sufficient black votes as part of the popular tally, he could have lost both Indiana and New York and still won the presidency by an electoral vote of 208 to 193. It is little wonder, then, that when the Republicans took power, they made election reform in the South a high priority.[3]

But even though Republicans found themselves falling further behind in the Deep South, their strategy of emphasizing the tariff issue nearly paid off in the upper South, where "New South" economic ambitions stirred many voters. Harrison lost Virginia by just 1,605 votes; he garnered 49.5 percent of the vote in the Old Dominion, a higher proportion than he won in either New York or Indiana. He polled 49 percent of the vote in West Virginia and lost that state by only 506 votes. His total surpassed 47 percent in both Maryland and North Carolina, and he received nearly 46 percent of the vote in Tennessee. Republicans would remember these results when they mapped strategy in future campaigns.[4]

Equally important, twenty-five southern Republicans won seats in the House of Representatives, nine more than in the previous election. Nearly all of them represented upper South or border state constituencies. Three of them were African Americans. These victories helped the GOP take control of the House with a small but effective majority under the resolute leadership of Speaker Thomas Brackett Reed of Maine. In addition, the Republicans retained control of the Senate, where their majority grew after the admission to the Union of several new Republican states in the West (Montana, Washington, and the Dakotas in 1889, and Idaho and Wyoming in 1890). For the first time in more than a decade, the Republicans would control the White House and clear majorities in both houses of Congress. This victory across the board, James G. Blaine wrote to President-elect Harrison, "gives you . . . the amplest power for a useful, strong and impressive Administration."[5]

The result in the presidential election was so close and the variables so numerous that it is impossible to explain Harrison's victory with precision or assurance. Democrats' election practices in the South and the consequent tainted character of Cleveland's national plurality left Democrats no moral grounds on which to complain that the "winner" of the popular vote was being denied the presidency unfairly. Some Democrats, however, did claim that the Republicans had cheated the president out of reelection by the use of fraud and corruption in the doubtful states. Free-trader David Wells took "comfort in the fact that we have pushed the cause of tariff reform forward," but he concluded that "after all, the influence that overcame us was primarily the unprecedented use of money." New York's Tammany Hall boss Richard Croker assured Cleveland that "in this city we left nothing undone that could secure a vote for the National ticket," and with no apparent sense of irony he blamed the Democrats' loss on "the extravagant use of money in this State by our opponents." Similarly, William L. Scott, who had secretly subsidized the Prohibitionist Party to undermine the Republicans, told Cleveland that the GOP's "corrupt use of money alone finally decided the contest; and against this, it was impossible to protect ourselves." No one expressed greater indignation than Secretary of State Thomas Bayard, who wrote to his son after the election, "Mr. Harrison is an honest man personally, but a bitter partisan, and [he] is surrounded by a very corrupt set." Bayard concluded that "debauchery by bribery" had been "a shocking and *sickening* cause" of the Democrats' defeat.[6]

But Democrats also cited other reasons for their defeat. Some alleged that the supporters of Governor Hill and the New York mayoral candidates deliberately "traded" Cleveland for their own ends, thereby boosting Harrison's plurality in the decisive Empire State. Others blamed the administration's patronage policies, which managed to offend both Democratic spoilsmen and civil service reformers. Still others thought that, as one Pension Bureau officer put it, Cleveland's vetoes "embittered the old veterans," and the national committee aggravated that feeling by assigning too many southern brigadiers to speak in the North. Many decried a lack of organization or outright mismanagement by those running the campaign. Even Calvin Brice, the Democrats' campaign chairman, admitted to Cleveland, "The party organization, it seems to me, was neglected somewhat until the campaign was fully on, and it was then too late." Others blamed Cleveland's own apparent languor and political ineptitude. Joseph Pulitzer argued that "Cleveland sacrificed party and the Presidency by his stupidity," while the *New York Sun* concluded that the lesson taught by the "campaign of education" was that "the President of the United States has to be a politician." Conversely, some Democrats thought that the Republicans had simply run a much better canvass. In the words of veteran New York Congressman Samuel S. Cox, "The truth is, Harrison's campaign was well managed. He did not hurt it by his talks to or about soldiers, about protection or otherwise. He pleased his party and reconciled it. He won fairly."[7]

Publicly at least, Cleveland did not join in accusing the Republicans of fraud, nor did he engage in recriminations against his fellow Democrats. Perhaps with his fingers crossed, he told reporters that he harbored "not the slightest doubt of Governor Hill's absolute good faith and honesty in the campaign." The ever-tactful Lamont wrote to Hill, "Your triumph does much to break the force of the blow that we all feel in the loss of the National ticket which but for the aid of your remarkable campaign would have been much more staggering." Cleveland, who in past victorious campaigns had made much of the character issue by presenting himself as a righteous tribune of the people, this time insisted that the outcome was "not a personal matter." "It is not proper," he declared, "to speak of it as my victory or as my defeat. It was a contest between two great parties battling for the supremacy of certain well defined principles." He admitted no second thoughts about focusing on the tariff issue. "The time had come when the issue between the two parties had to be made and the democrats made it. I don't regret it."[8]

But Cleveland's attempts during the campaign to moderate his party's tariff stance had not clarified the issue to his advantage. He had failed to dispel popular anxieties aroused by Republican warnings against free trade. Most Democrats, whether or not they approved of how Cleveland handled the tariff issue, agreed with him that this question, more than anything else, determined the election's outcome. Even the *Indianapolis Sentinel,* which had first printed the Dudley letter, admitted that Harrison's victory "must be accepted as a popular verdict against tariff reform and in favor of the extreme protective policy advocated in the Chicago platform." Democrats who opposed Cleveland's policy lost no time in laying the party's defeat at the president's door. From San Francisco, former Senator James G. Fair groused to Bayard, "It was the people[']s idea here that the president was alone in his free trade ideas & that none of his advisers agreed with him in these ideas and fearing a free trade policy they were compelled for their own protection to vote for his enemies. . . . It is so hard to think that the wrong ideas of one man should destroy the will & wish of more than half of the American people." New

York Democratic leader Smith Weed, who thought that Cleveland's embrace of tariff reform had been "foolish," reported to Lamont that three out of four "of our own party men hesitated & doubted on that issue, and we had to use all sorts of arguments & persuasions to get them to vote." Democratic national chairman William H. Barnum confessed to Samuel Randall that he shared Randall's protectionist opinions and believed that Cleveland had placed "an unnecessary burden" on the party. "The people were not in the state to accept the tariff question as set forth in the President's message, and I had many fears as to the result of the election during the entire campaign."9

Among Democrats who subscribed to the president's low-tariff views, many applauded his campaign but doubted that the moment had been right to present those views as the key issue. "There was time enough to arouse against you the storm of ignorance, prejudice and passion," wrote the eminent constitutional lawyer James C. Carter, "but not time enough to dispel it by the gathering strength of reflection and reason." Samuel Tilden's old ally John Bigelow agreed that the time to educate voters "has proved a little too short." "To your bold and patriotic attempt to reform our revenue system we no doubt owe our defeat," Bigelow wrote to the president, "but who would not rather be the Hector of the greatest of Epics than its Agamemnon?" Of course, this invocation of martyrdom appealed to Cleveland's own conception of his selfless political persona. "We were defeated, it is true," he told reporters, "but the principle of tariff reform will surely win in the end." Four days after the election, Frances Cleveland wrote to Bayard, "the little saying each American is taught in his youth has been running in my head . . . that 'It's better to be right than to be President.' As a Democrat I am not a bit downcast or discouraged, and as my husband's wife I am extremely happy."10

The Republicans were happy, too, as they gleefully assigned credit rather than blame for the outcome. Harrison received high praise for what Wisconsin Senator John Spooner called "your long series of perfect speeches," which contributed much to "the glorious victory." In turn, the president-elect thanked chairman Matthew Quay for his "brilliant work" during the campaign and showed his gratitude to Blaine by inviting him to head his cabinet as secretary of state. Republicans did not overlook particular circumstances such as Miller's sacrificial campaign in New York, but overall, like the Democrats, they saw the tariff issue as the overriding influence in the outcome. They had gladly welcomed Cleveland's December tariff message as framing the issue for 1888, and they made the most of it. "American markets for the American Producer and the American Workingman was the watchword which brought us the victory," a Wisconsin Republican wrote to William Allison, "one which may perhaps influence our prosperity for a century, because if we keep our Home Markets, our Home Markets will keep us." As the *New York Tribune* put it, the Republican Party had "not only won its victory by gains due to the tariff issue"; it now would have "the power to make far greater gains in the future by making its protective policy more complete and effective wherever experience has shown that it is inadequate." For longtime Republicans such as Joseph Medill, Harrison's victory had a redemptive character. "The defeat of our grand and patriotic party four years ago by the Confederates of the South and their slum allies around New York bay filled me with bitterness and mortification," the editor wrote to Harrison. "But that grave mistake is corrected in your election."[11]

As Medill's comment suggested, despite the general acceptance of the primacy of the tariff issue in determining the result, an undercurrent of sectionalism ran through election postmortems. A New Jersey Republican congratulated Harrison not only on the "grand victory" of "American protection over British free trade" but also on "the triumph of the Blue over the Gray." Even within Cleveland's own party, northern protectionists condemned the president for having framed his tariff stance on the advice of "'Southern Brigadiers,' who knew no more about the business interests of our country than a boot black." Southern Democrats shuddered at the prospect that a Republican president and Congress would take action to disturb their dominance of the region's social and racial structure. After the election, no less a figure than Secretary of State Bayard confessed "to a sinking of the heart when I think of the renewal of Negro domination." "The band of political brigands and foul birds who come forth now to rule and direct contains the mercenary Negroes whom I had fondly hoped would never again venture into the public eye!" For their part, southern African Americans greeted Harrison's election as a new political emancipation, offering the prospect, as a Knoxville editor wrote, that "the colored voters of [the] South are at last free." And northern Republicans such as Murat Halstead hoped the victory would "aid us in finally fracturing and demolishing the political menace in our country, the solid South."[12]

Certainly, Republicans did not let the sectional character of the popular vote or Harrison's "minority" status disturb their conviction that their victory represented a mandate to govern. Harrison had a deep sense of "the large and generous expectations which are in the minds of the people." A month after the election he wrote to a friend, "I have often seen tears in the eyes of some of the good people who called to see me during the campaign, as they talked of the dangers that were to be avoided and the good to be reached for our country by Republican success this year." The election of 1888 broke the stalemate of divided party control in Washington that had characterized much of the late nineteenth century, and the Republicans proceeded to govern with vigor. Drawing on the party's platform and his own campaign pronouncements, Harrison larded his inaugural address not merely with the standard encomiums to the nation's greatness but also with a long list of specific proposals for action.[13]

The Fifty-first Congress responded energetically. Under Speaker Reed's direction, the Republicans passed a host of landmark laws. To preserve protection yet cut the surplus they designed the McKinley Tariff Act of 1890 largely along lines they had set forth during 1888. With the Dependent Pension Act they put aside the apothecary's scale for weighing the nation's obligations to veterans and their dependents. They took an important step against trusts with the Sherman Anti-Trust Act and crafted a delicate compromise on the coinage question with the Sherman Silver Purchase Act. Reciprocity agreements authorized by the McKinley Act, the Meat Inspection Act, and subsidies for steamship companies were all aimed at expanding American trade overseas. Forest reserve legislation empowered Harrison to set aside vast sections of public land as national forests, thereby launching an important conservation effort in advance of the Progressive Era. The Republicans increased spending on internal improvements and on defense, especially the navy, all of which helped diminish the surplus. Harrison and the Fifty-first Congress elected in 1888 set a record for peacetime legislative accomplishment, enacting 531 public laws, a number unequaled until Theodore Roosevelt's second term.[14]

Instituting new techniques of executive leadership, Harrison was a hands-on president. He pushed his agenda in Congress not only by his regular and special messages but also by informal private persuasion. One Republican recalled that during the McKinley Act deliberations,

The inauguration of Benjamin Harrison, twenty-third president of the United States, March 4, 1889. (Library of Congress)

"the President made little dinner parties, in order to bring the leading Republicans together for conference and discussion, with a view of bringing about an agreement between the contending parties and securing tariff legislation." Harrison also carried forward the spirit of his front-porch campaign by speaking frequently before public audiences. Using these occasions to tout specific elements of the Republican program or to espouse more general ideals such as equality and economic development, the twenty-third president anticipated Theodore Roosevelt's use of the "bully pulpit" to build support for his party and its agenda. In addition, Harrison and Blaine pursued a spirited foreign policy that broke the century-old pattern of reactive diplomacy. They ushered in what historians have called a "new paradigm," which signified a more activist quest for influence around the world, especially in markets and investment opportunities. Harrison successfully steered the nation through a series of midsized crises, particularly with Great Britain and Chile, which earned the United States enhanced respect from the world's powers both great and small.[15]

The administration's most significant failure came in the narrow defeat of the Lodge federal elections bill, designed to restore blacks' right to vote in the South. The measure had the potential to remake the political landscape in the South and, consequently, in the nation at large. For that reason Democrats strained to the utmost against it and, with the help of a handful of pro-silver western Republican senators, secured its defeat. The Lodge bill represented the last serious attempt at civil rights legislation until the mid-twentieth century. At last bowing to the southern whites' implacable intransigence and northerners' growing indifference, Republicans forbore further attempts to protect blacks' rights. Instead, they began to give greater stress to sectional harmony, building on the southern strategy of 1888, using economic issues such as the tariff to appeal to voters in the New South.[16]

Harrison's personal quarrels with party bosses over patronage, discontent in various economic sectors in the country, and Americans' conservative suspicion of the Republicans' activism cost the GOP control of the House in the 1890 midterm elections, and in 1892 Grover Cleveland and a Democratic congressional majority swept back into power. But the Democrats' revival proved short-lived. Soon after Cleveland replaced Harrison in the White House, a financial panic devastated the nation's economy, and the Democrats' concept of limited government proved unavailing to reverse the downward spiral or to alleviate its calamitous effects. In his second inaugural address Cleveland lectured his fellow citizens that "while the people should patriotically and cheerfully support their government its functions do not include the support of the people." However much such notions might fit with the nation's Jeffersonian ideals, these hollow maxims were utterly inadequate to meet the new requirements of an industrializing economy.[17]

No one understood these changes better than William McKinley, the author of the Republicans' platform in 1888 and chairman of the House Ways and Means Committee during the Fifty-first Congress. In the 1896 presidential race, some Republicans thought of turning again to Harrison, but he had no interest in running, and the party nominated McKinley. In his campaign McKinley showed how much he had learned from his Republican predecessor. Under Mark Hanna's direction, his campaign was well-heeled and well managed. Like Harrison, McKinley conducted an effective front porch campaign, and even more than Harrison, he sought to bury sectional animosities, stress the harmony of North and South, and appeal to southerners to accept Republican views on the way to prosperity, especially the protective tariff. As a result, McKinley carried the upper South states of Kentucky, West Virginia, Maryland, and Delaware. He was the first Republican in twenty years to win any southern state, and his appeal in the upper South set a pattern that lasted for a generation. In the White House, McKinley again borrowed heavily from Harrison, employing many of his new techniques of leadership, though he did so with greater finesse and personal warmth and, consequently, greater success.[18]

Seen in the light of what followed in the 1890s and after, the contest of 1888 was, if not quite a turning point, then a clear harbinger of what was to develop in presidential elections. It marked an important phase in the devolution of what historians term the third American party system, the decades-long competition between Republicans and Democrats dominated by a fierce sectional antagonism originating in the 1850s and 1860s. Both major parties in 1888 put economic appeals at the center of their campaign efforts and conducted a canvass aimed at voters' pocketbooks. Those emphases would continue in presidential elections, and the bloody shirt was at last laid aside in national politics. In the South, however, white Democrats nursed racial and political bitterness until well into the twentieth century, when Republicans such as Richard Nixon and Ronald Reagan tapped those feelings to make the GOP, once the champion of blacks' rights, the party of resentment. The

election of 1888 did not break the national equilibrium between the major parties, but the performance by Harrison and the Republicans suggested the strategies that would spur the major shift to the GOP in the
mid-1890s: an emphasis on federal policies in the interest of economic
development, personal participation by the presidential candidate, a
well-financed organization, and coordination with beneficiaries of the
party's agenda, especially its economic policies.

The campaign of 1888 was also significant as the first national debate
regarding American trade policy. Although Cleveland couched the tariff
issue primarily as a taxation and revenue question, he also argued that
lower duties on imported raw materials would give American manufacturers an advantage in foreign trade. Harrison and the Republicans cautioned against the lowering of trade barriers with nations where labor
endured conditions far below American standards. Once in power, the
Republicans maintained protectionism and employed targeted reciprocity agreements to expand trade with individual nations. These contrasting approaches reflected the two parties' differing notions regarding
federal government activism in general. True to Democratic Party traditions, Cleveland clung to localism and limited government. In his last
annual message delivered after his loss to Harrison, he cited myriad
problems in the nation but insisted that "extravagant appropriations
of public money, with all their demoralizing consequences, should not
be tolerated," and he urged Americans to resist the encroachment of
"Federal legislation into the domain of State and local jurisdiction upon
the plea of subserving the public welfare." Republicans, in contrast, saw
possibilities for good in an energetic national government. Americans,
Harrison told a campaign audience, ought "not to be frightened by the
use of that ugly word 'subsidy.'" As president, he spoke of the "minister-
ing care" of "a liberal and united Government" and argued that it was
time "to reach forward to grander conceptions than have entered the
minds of some of our statesmen in the past." These contrasting notions
about the purposes of government continued in the ensuing decades,
but eventually the position of the two parties would be substantially
reversed.[19]

Finally, the administration launched by the election of 1888 foreshad-
owed emphases and methods of leadership that characterize the modern presidency. Both openly and behind the scenes Harrison intervened
in the deliberations of Congress and proved to be an effective legislative
president. He struck a blow for presidential independence by resisting

the dictation of party bosses in matters of patronage. He traveled widely, spoke often, and carried the presidency to the people. He took a central role in foreign affairs, sometimes acting as the nation's chief diplomat. Cleveland's second term, by contrast, turned out to be a disaster, demonstrated most clearly by his near-complete alienation from his party in Congress, but also resulting from Cleveland's pinched sense of what the government could and should do. Benjamin Harrison was not a mere caretaker between the two terms of Grover Cleveland. William McKinley, viewed by many scholars as a transformational leader in the White House, rejected the negative lessons of the Cleveland presidency and instead picked up where Harrison had left off. Thus, it was Harrison, much more than Cleveland, who set the stage for the creation of the modern presidency. That achievement formed a significant and enduring legacy of the presidential election of 1888.

APPENDIX A
BALLOT TOTALS: REPUBLICAN NATIONAL CONVENTION, 1888

Candidate	Ballot							
	1st	2nd	3rd	4th	5th	6th	7th	8th
Russell Alger	84	116	122	135	143	137	120	100
William B. Allison	72	75	88	88	99	73	76	
James G. Blaine	35	33	35	42	48	40	15	5
Chauncey M. Depew	99	99	91					
Frederick Douglass				1				
Edwin H. Fitler	24							
Joseph B. Foraker				1		1	1	
Frederick Dent Grant						1		
Walter Q. Gresham	107	108	123	98	87	91	91	59
Benjamin Harrison	85	91	94	216	212	231	279	544
William R. Hawley	13							
Creed Haymond							1	
John J. Ingalls	28	16						
Robert T. Lincoln	3	2	2	1			2	
William McKinley	2	3	8	11	14	12	16	4
Samuel F. Miller			2					
William Walter Phelps	25	18	5					
Jeremiah Rusk	25	20	16					
John Sherman	229	249	244	235	224	244	230	118
Totals	831	830	830	828	827	830	831	830

Source: *Official Proceedings of the Republican National Convention Held at Chicago, June 19, 20, 21, 22, 23, 25, 1888* (Minneapolis: Charles W. Johnson, 1903), 159–199.

APPENDIX B
1888 GENERAL ELECTION RESULTS

State	Harrison (Republican)	Cleveland (Democrat)	Popular Vote (%) Fisk (Prohibition)	Streeter (Union Labor)	Other	Electoral Vote BH	GC
Alabama	57,177 (32.7)	117,314 (67.0)	594 (0.3)	—	—		10
Arkansas	59,752 (38.0)	86,062 (54.8)	614 (0.4)	10,630 (6.8)	—		7
California	124,816 (49.7)	117,729 (46.8)	5,761 (2.3)	—	3,033 (1.2)	8	
Colorado	50,772 (55.2)	37,549 (40.8)	2,182 (2.4)	1,266 (1.4)	177 (0.2)	3	
Connecticut	74,584 (48.4)	74,920 (48.7)	4,234 (2.7)	240 (0.2)	—		6
Delaware	12,950 (43.5)	16,414 (55.1)	399 (1.3)	—	1		3
Florida	26,529 (39.9)	39,557 (59.5)	414 (0.6)	—	—		4
Georgia	40,499 (28.3)	100,493 (70.3)	1,808 (1.3)	136 (0.1)	—		12
Illinois	370,475 (49.5)	348,351 (46.6)	21,703 (2.9)	7,134 (1.0)	150	22	
Indiana	263,366 (49.0)	260,990 (48.6)	9,939 (1.9)	2,693 (0.5)	—	15	
Iowa	211,607 (52.3)	179,876 (44.4)	3,550 (0.9)	9,105 (2.2)	556 (0.1)	13	
Kansas	182,845 (55.2)	102,739 (31.0)	6,774 (2.0)	37,838 (11.4)	937 (0.3)	9	
Kentucky	155,138 (45.0)	183,830 (53.3)	5,223 (1.5)	677 (0.2)	—		13
Louisiana	30,660 (26.5)	85,032 (73.4)	160 (0.1)	39	—		8
Maine	73,730 (57.5)	50,472 (39.4)	2,691 (2.1)	1,344 (1.0)	16	6	
Maryland	99,986 (47.4)	106,188 (50.3)	4,767 (2.3)	—	—		8
Massachusetts	183,892 (53.4)	151,590 (44.0)	8,701 (2.5)	—	60	14	
Michigan	236,387 (49.7)	213,469 (44.9)	20,945 (4.4)	4,555 (1.0)	—	13	
Minnesota	142,492 (54.1)	104,372 (39.7)	15,201 (5.8)	1,097 (0.4)	—	7	

State							
Mississippi	30,095 (26.0)	85,451 (73.8)	240 (0.2)	—	—		9
Missouri	236,252 (45.3)	261,943 (50.2)	4,539 (0.9)	18,625 (3.6)	—		16
Nebraska	108,417 (53.5)	80,552 (39.8)	9,435 (4.7)	4,226 (2.1)	—	5	
Nevada	7,229 (57.5)	5,303 (42.2)	41 (0.3)	—	—	3	
New Hampshire	45,734 (50.4)	43,382 (47.8)	1,596 (1.8)	—	58 (0.1)	4	
New Jersey	144,347 (47.5)	151,493 (49.9)	7,794 (2.6)	—	—		9
New York	650,338 (49.3)	635,965 (48.2)	30,231 (2.3)	627	2,587 (0.2)	36	
North Carolina	134,784 (47.2)	147,902 (51.8)	2,840 (1.0)	—	37		11
Ohio	416,054 (49.6)	395,456 (47.1)	24,356 (2.9)	3,491 (0.4)	—	23	
Oregon	33,291 (53.8)	26,518 (42.8)	1,676 (2.7)	—	404 (0.7)	3	
Pennsylvania	526,091 (52.7)	446,633 (44.8)	20,947 (2.1)	3,873 (0.4)	24	30	
Rhode Island	21,969 (53.9)	17,530 (43.0)	1,251 (3.1)	18	7	4	
South Carolina	13,736 (17.2)	65,824 (82.3)	—	48	437 (0.5)		9
Tennessee	138,978 (45.8)	158,699 (52.3)	5,969 (2.0)	—	—		12
Texas	88,604 (25.0)	232,189 (65.5)	4,739 (1.3)	28,880 (8.1)	—		13
Vermont	45,193 (71.2)	16,788 (26.4)	1,460 (2.3)	—	35 (0.1)	4	
Virginia	150,399 (49.5)	152,004 (50.0)	1,684 (0.6)	—	—		12
West Virginia	78,171 (49.0)	78,677 (49.3)	1,084 (0.7)	1,508 (0.9)	—		6
Wisconsin	176,553 (49.8)	155,232 (43.8)	14,277 (4.0)	8,552 (2.4)	—	11	
Totals	5,443,892 (47.8)	5,534,488 (48.6)	249,819 (2.2)	146,602 (1.3)	8,519 (0.1)	233	168

Source: *Congressional Quarterly's Guide to U.S. Elections* (Washington, D.C.: Congressional Quarterly, 1994), 384, 442.

BENJAMIN HARRISON'S
INAUGURAL ADDRESS, MARCH 4, 1889

Fellow-Citizens:

There is no constitutional or legal requirement that the President shall take the oath of office in the presence of the people, but there is so manifest an appropriateness in the public induction to office of the chief executive officer of the nation that from the beginning of the Government the people, to whose service the official oath consecrates the officer, have been called to witness the solemn ceremonial. The oath taken in the presence of the people becomes a mutual covenant. The officer covenants to serve the whole body of the people by a faithful execution of the laws, so that they may be the unfailing defense and security of those who respect and observe them, and that neither wealth, station, nor the power of combinations shall be able to evade their just penalties or to wrest them from a beneficent public purpose to serve the ends of cruelty or selfishness.

My promise is spoken; yours unspoken, but not the less real and solemn. The people of every State have here their representatives. Surely I do not misinterpret the spirit of the occasion when I assume that the whole body of the people covenant with me and with each other to-day to support and defend the Constitution and the Union of the States, to yield willing obedience to all the laws and each to every other citizen his equal civil and political rights. Entering thus solemnly into covenant with each other, we may reverently invoke and confidently expect the favor and help of Almighty God—that He will give to me wisdom, strength, and fidelity, and to our people a spirit of fraternity and a love of righteousness and peace. . . .

I will not attempt to note the marvelous and in great part happy contrasts between our country as it steps over the threshold into its second century of organized existence under the Constitution and that weak but wisely ordered young nation that looked undauntedly down the first century, when all its years stretched out before it.

Our people will not fail at this time to recall the incidents which accompanied the institution of government under the Constitution, or to find inspiration and guidance in the teachings and example of Washington and his great associates, and hope and courage in the contrast which thirty-eight populous and prosperous States offer to the thirteen States, weak in everything except courage and the love of liberty, that then fringed our Atlantic seaboard.

The Territory of Dakota has now a population greater than any of the original States (except Virginia) and greater than the aggregate of five of the smaller States in 1790. The center of population when our national capital was located was east of Baltimore, and it was argued by many well-informed persons that it would move eastward rather than westward; yet in 1880 it was found to be near Cincinnati, and the new census about to be taken will show another stride to the westward. That which was the body has come to be only the rich fringe of the nation's robe. But our growth has not been limited to territory, population, and aggregate wealth, marvelous as it has been in each of those directions. The masses of our people are better fed, clothed, and housed than their fathers were. The facilities for popular education have been vastly enlarged and more generally diffused.

The virtues of courage and patriotism have given recent proof of their continued presence and increasing power in the hearts and over the lives of our people. The influences of religion have been multiplied and strengthened. The sweet offices of charity have greatly increased. The virtue of temperance is held in higher estimation. We have not attained an ideal condition. Not all of our people are happy and prosperous; not all of them are virtuous and law-abiding. But on the whole the opportunities offered to the individual to secure the comforts of life are better than are found elsewhere and largely better than they were here one hundred years ago.

The surrender of a large measure of sovereignty to the General Government, effected by the adoption of the Constitution, was not accomplished until the suggestions of reason were strongly reenforced by the more imperative voice of experience. The divergent interests of peace speedily demanded a "more perfect union." The merchant, the shipmaster, and the manufacturer discovered and disclosed to our statesmen and to the people that commercial emancipation must be added to the political freedom which had been so bravely won. The commercial policy of the mother country had not relaxed any of its hard and oppressive features. To hold in check the development of our commercial marine, to prevent or retard the establishment and growth of manufactures in the States, and so to secure the American market for their shops and the carrying trade for their ships, was the policy of European statesmen, and was pursued with the most selfish vigor.

Petitions poured in upon Congress urging the imposition of discriminating duties that should encourage the production of needed things at home. The patriotism of the people, which no longer found a field of exercise in war, was energetically directed to the duty of equipping the young Republic for the defense of its independence by making its people self-dependent. Societies for the promotion of home manufactures and for encouraging the use of domestics in the dress of the people were organized in many of the States. The revival at the end of the century of the same patriotic interest in the preservation and development of domestic industries and the defense of our working people against injurious foreign competition is an incident worthy of attention. It is not a departure but a return that we have witnessed. The protective policy had then its opponents. The argument was made, as now, that its benefits inured to particular classes or sections.

If the question became in any sense or at any time sectional, it was only because slavery existed in some of the States. But for this there was no reason why the cotton-producing States should not have led or walked abreast with the New England States in the production of cotton fabrics. There was this reason only why the States that divide with Pennsylvania the mineral treasures of the great southeastern and central mountain ranges should have been so tardy in bringing to the smelting furnace and to the mill the coal and iron from their near opposing hillsides. Mill fires were lighted at the funeral pile of slavery. The emancipation proclamation was heard in the depths of the earth as well as in the sky; men were made free, and material things became our better servants.

The sectional element has happily been eliminated from the tariff discussion. We have no longer States that are necessarily only planting States. None are excluded from achieving that diversification of pursuits among the people which brings wealth and contentment. The cotton plantation will not be less valuable when the product is spun in the country town by operatives whose necessities call for diversified crops and create a home demand for garden and agricultural products. Every new mine, furnace, and factory is an extension of the productive capacity of the State more real and valuable than added territory.

Shall the prejudices and paralysis of slavery continue to hang upon the skirts of progress? How long will those who rejoice that slavery no longer exists cherish or tolerate the incapacities it put upon their communities? I look hopefully to the continuance of our protective system and to the consequent development of manufacturing and mining enterprises in the States hitherto wholly given to agriculture as a potent influence in the perfect unification of our people. The men who have invested their capital in these enterprises, the farmers who have felt the benefit of their neighborhood, and the men who work in shop or field will not fail to find and to defend a community of interest.

Is it not quite possible that the farmers and the promoters of the great mining and manufacturing enterprises which have recently been established in the South may yet find that the free ballot of the workingman, without distinction of race, is needed for their defense as well as for his own? I do not doubt that if those men in the South who now accept the tariff views of Clay and the constitutional expositions of Webster would courageously avow and defend their real convictions they would not find it difficult, by friendly instruction and cooperation, to make the black man their efficient and safe ally, not only in establishing correct principles in our national administration, but in preserving for their local communities the benefits of social order and economical and honest government. At least until the good offices of kindness and education have been fairly tried the contrary conclusion can not be plausibly urged.

I have altogether rejected the suggestion of a special Executive policy for any section of our country. It is the duty of the Executive to administer and enforce in the methods and by the instrumentalities pointed out and provided by the Constitution all the laws enacted by Congress. These laws are general and their administration should be uniform and equal. As a citizen may not elect what laws he will obey, neither may the Executive elect which he will enforce. The duty to obey and to execute embraces the Constitution in its entirety and the whole code of laws enacted under it. The evil example of permitting individuals, corporations, or communities to nullify the laws because they cross some selfish or local interest or prejudices is full of danger, not only to the nation at large, but much more to those who use this pernicious expedient to escape their just obligations or to obtain an unjust advantage over others. They will presently themselves be compelled to appeal to the law for protection, and those who would use the law as a defense must not deny that use of it to others.

If our great corporations would more scrupulously observe their legal limitations and duties, they would have less cause to complain of the unlawful limitations of their rights or of violent interference with their operations. The community that by concert, open or secret, among its citizens denies to a portion of its members their plain rights under the law has severed the only safe bond of social order and prosperity. The evil works from a bad center both ways. It demoralizes those who practice it and destroys the faith of those who suffer by it in the efficiency of the law as a safe protector. The man in whose breast that faith has been darkened is naturally the subject of dangerous and uncanny suggestions. Those who use unlawful methods, if moved by no higher motive than the selfishness that prompted them, may well stop and inquire what is to be the end of this.

An unlawful expedient can not become a permanent condition of government. If the educated and influential classes in a community either practice or connive at the systematic violation of laws that seem to them to cross their convenience, what can they expect when the lesson that convenience or a supposed class interest is a sufficient cause for lawlessness has been well learned by the ignorant classes? A community where law is the rule of conduct and where courts, not mobs, execute its penalties is the only attractive field for business investments and honest labor.

Our naturalization laws should be so amended as to make the inquiry into the character and good disposition of persons applying for citizenship more careful and searching. Our existing laws have been in their administration an unimpressive and often an unintelligible form. We accept the man as a citizen without any knowledge of his fitness, and he assumes the duties of citizenship without any knowledge as to what they are. The privileges of American citizenship are so great and its duties so grave that we may well insist upon a good knowledge of every person applying for citizenship and a good knowledge by him of our institutions. We should not cease to be hospitable to immigration, but we should cease to be careless as to the character of it. There are men of all races, even the best, whose coming is necessarily a burden upon our public revenues or a threat to social order. These should be identified and excluded.

We have happily maintained a policy of avoiding all interference with European affairs. We have been only interested spectators of their contentions in diplomacy and in war, ready to use our friendly offices to promote peace, but never obtruding our advice and never attempting unfairly to coin the distresses of other powers into commercial advantage to ourselves. We have a just right to expect that our European policy will be the American policy of European courts.

It is so manifestly incompatible with those precautions for our peace and safety which all the great powers habitually observe and enforce in matters affecting them that a shorter waterway between our eastern and western seaboards should be dominated by any European Government that we may confidently expect that such a purpose will not be entertained by any friendly power.

We shall in the future, as in the past, use every endeavor to maintain and enlarge our friendly relations with all the great powers, but they will not expect us to look kindly upon any project that would leave us subject to the dangers of a hostile observation or environment. We have not sought to dominate or to absorb any of our weaker neighbors, but rather to aid and encourage them to establish free and stable governments resting upon the consent of their own people. We have a clear right to expect, therefore, that no European Government will seek to establish colonial dependencies upon the territory of these independent American States. That which a sense of justice restrains us from seeking they may be reasonably expected willingly to forego.

It must not be assumed, however, that our interests are so exclusively American that our entire inattention to any events that may transpire elsewhere can be taken for granted. Our citizens domiciled for purposes of trade in all countries and in many of the islands of the sea demand and will have our adequate care in their personal and commercial rights. The necessities of our Navy require convenient coaling stations and dock and harbor privileges. These and other trading privileges we will feel free to obtain only by means that do not in any degree partake of coercion, however feeble the government from which we ask such concessions. But having fairly obtained them by methods and for purposes entirely consistent with the most friendly disposition toward all other powers, our consent will be necessary to any modification or impairment of the concession.

We shall neither fail to respect the flag of any friendly nation or the just rights of its citizens, nor to exact the like treatment for our own. Calmness, justice, and consideration should characterize our diplomacy. The offices of an intelligent diplomacy or of friendly arbitration in proper cases should be adequate to the peaceful adjustment of all international difficulties. By such methods we will make our contribution to the world's peace, which no nation values more highly, and avoid the opprobrium which must fall upon the nation that ruthlessly breaks it.

The duty devolved by law upon the President to nominate and, by and with the advice and consent of the Senate, to appoint all public officers whose appointment is not otherwise provided for in the Constitution or by act of Congress has become very burdensome and its wise and efficient discharge full of difficulty. The civil list is so large that a personal knowledge of any large number of the applicants is impossible. The President must rely upon the representations of others, and these are often made inconsiderately and without any just sense of responsibility. I have a right, I think, to insist that those who volunteer or are invited to give advice as to appointments shall exercise consideration and fidelity. A high sense of duty and an ambition to improve the service should characterize all public officers.

There are many ways in which the convenience and comfort of those who have business with our public offices may be promoted by a thoughtful and obliging officer, and I shall expect those whom I may appoint to justify their selection by a conspicuous efficiency in the discharge of their duties. Honorable party service will certainly not be esteemed by me a disqualification for public office, but it will in no case be allowed to serve as a shield of official negligence, incompetency, or delinquency. It is entirely creditable to seek public office by proper methods and with proper motives, and all applicants will be treated with consideration; but I shall need, and the heads of Departments will need, time for inquiry and deliberation. Persistent importunity will not, therefore, be the best support of an application for office. Heads of Departments, bureaus, and all other public officers having any duty connected therewith will be expected to enforce the civil-service law fully and without evasion. Beyond this obvious duty I hope to do something more to advance the reform of the civil service. The ideal, or even my own ideal, I shall probably not attain. Retrospect will be a safer basis of judgment than promises. We shall not, however, I am sure, be able to put our civil service upon a nonpartisan basis until we have secured an incumbency that fair-minded men of the opposition will approve for impartiality and integrity. As the number of such in the civil list is increased removals from office will diminish.

While a Treasury surplus is not the greatest evil, it is a serious evil. Our revenue should be ample to meet the ordinary annual demands upon our Treasury, with a sufficient margin for those extraordinary but scarcely less imperative demands which arise now and then. Expenditure should always be made with economy and only upon public necessity. Wastefulness, profligacy, or favoritism in public expenditures is criminal. But there is nothing in the condition of our country or of our people to suggest that anything presently necessary to the public prosperity, security, or honor should be unduly postponed.

It will be the duty of Congress wisely to forecast and estimate these extraordinary demands, and, having added them to our ordinary expenditures, to so adjust our revenue laws that no considerable annual surplus will remain. We will fortunately be able to apply to the redemption of the public debt any small and unforeseen excess of revenue. This is better than to reduce our income below our necessary expenditures, with the resulting choice between another change of our revenue laws and an increase of the public debt. It is quite possible, I am sure, to effect the necessary reduction in our revenues without breaking down our protective tariff or seriously injuring any domestic industry.

The construction of a sufficient number of modern war ships and of their necessary armament should progress as rapidly as is consistent with care and perfection in plans and workmanship. The spirit, courage, and skill of our naval officers and seamen have many times in our history given to weak ships and inefficient guns a rating greatly beyond that of the naval list. That they will again do so upon occasion I do not doubt; but they ought not, by premeditation or neglect, to be left to the risks and exigencies of an unequal combat. We should encourage the establishment of American steamship lines. The exchanges of commerce demand stated, reliable, and rapid means of communication, and until these are provided the development of our trade with the States lying south of us is impossible.

Our pension laws should give more adequate and discriminating relief to the Union soldiers and sailors and to their widows and orphans. Such occasions as this should remind us that we owe everything to their valor and sacrifice.

It is a subject of congratulation that there is a near prospect of the admission into the Union of the Dakotas and Montana and Washington Territories. This act of justice has been unreasonably delayed in the case of some of them. The people who have settled these Territories are intelligent, enterprising, and patriotic, and the accession of these new States will add strength to the nation. It is due to the settlers in the Territories who have availed themselves of the invitations of our land laws to make homes upon the public domain that their titles should be speedily adjusted and their honest entries confirmed by patent.

It is very gratifying to observe the general interest now being manifested in the reform of our election laws. Those who have been for years calling attention to the pressing necessity of throwing about the ballot box and about the elector further safeguards, in order that our elections might not only be free and pure, but might clearly appear to be so, will welcome the accession of any who did not so soon discover the need of reform. The National Congress has not as yet taken control of elections in that case over which the Constitution gives it jurisdiction, but has accepted and adopted the election laws of the several States, provided penalties for their violation and a method of supervision. Only the inefficiency of the State laws or an unfair partisan administration of them could suggest a departure from this policy.

It was clearly, however, in the contemplation of the framers of the Constitution that such an exigency might arise, and provision was wisely made for it. The freedom of the ballot is a condition of our national life, and no power vested in Congress or in the Executive to secure or perpetuate it should remain unused upon occasion. The people of all the Congressional districts have an equal interest that the election in each shall truly express the views and wishes of a majority of the qualified electors residing within it. The results of such elections are not local, and the insistence of electors residing in other districts that they shall be pure and free does not savor at all of impertinence.

If in any of the States the public security is thought to be threatened by ignorance among the electors, the obvious remedy is education. The sympathy and help of our people will not be withheld from any community struggling with special embarrassments or difficulties connected with the suffrage if the remedies proposed proceed upon lawful lines and are promoted by just and honorable methods. How shall those who practice election frauds recover that respect for the sanctity of the ballot which is the first condition and obligation of good citizenship? The man who has come to regard the ballot box as a juggler's hat has renounced his allegiance.

Let us exalt patriotism and moderate our party contentions. Let those who would die for the flag on the field of battle give a better proof of their patriotism and a higher glory to their country by promoting fraternity and justice. A party success that is achieved by unfair methods or by practices that partake of revolution is hurtful and evanescent even from a party standpoint. We should hold our differing opinions in mutual respect, and, having submitted them to the arbitrament of the ballot, should accept an adverse judgment with the same respect that we would have demanded of our opponents if the decision had been in our favor.

No other people have a government more worthy of their respect and love or a land so magnificent in extent, so pleasant to look upon, and so full of generous suggestion to enterprise and labor. God has placed upon our head a diadem and has laid at our feet power and wealth beyond definition or calculation. But we must not forget that we take these gifts upon the condition that justice and mercy shall hold the reins of power and that the upward avenues of hope shall be free to all the people.

I do not mistrust the future. Dangers have been in frequent ambush along our path, but we have uncovered and vanquished them all. Passion has swept some of our communities, but only to give us a new demonstration that the great body of our people are stable, patriotic, and law-abiding. No political party can long pursue advantage at the expense of public honor or by rude and indecent methods without protest and fatal disaffection in its own body. The peaceful agencies of commerce are more fully revealing the necessary unity of all our communities, and the increasing intercourse of our people is promoting mutual respect. We shall find unalloyed pleasure in the revelation which our next census will make of the swift development of the great resources of some of the States. Each State will bring its generous contribution to the great aggregate of the nation's increase. And when the harvests from the fields, the cattle from the hills, and the ores of the earth shall have been weighed, counted, and valued, we will turn from them all to crown with the highest honor the State that has most promoted education, virtue, justice, and patriotism among its people.

For the full text of Harrison's address, see James D. Richardson, *A Compilation of the Messages and Papers of the Presidents, 1789–1902* (Washington, D.C.: Bureau of National Literature and Art, 1903), 9:5–14.

NOTES

ABBREVIATIONS

ANB	*American National Biography,* 24 vols., ed. John A. Garraty and Mark C. Carnes (New York: Oxford University Press, 1999)
BH	Benjamin Harrison
BH-Home	Benjamin Harrison Papers, Benjamin Harrison Home, Indianapolis
BH-IHSL	Benjamin Harrison Papers, Indiana Historical Society Library
BH-LC	Benjamin Harrison Papers, Library of Congress
CE	*Cincinnati Enquirer*
CI-O	*Chicago Inter-Ocean*
CR	*Congressional Record*
CSB	Calvin S. Brice
CT	*Chicago Tribune*
CWF	Charles W. Fairbanks
CWF-LL	Charles W. Fairbanks Papers, Lilly Library, Indiana University
DBH	David B. Hill
DBH-NYSL	David B. Hill Papers, New York State Library
DSL	Daniel S. Lamont
DSL-LC	Daniel S. Lamont Papers, Library of Congress
EGH	Eugene Gano Hay
EGH-LC	Eugene Gano Hay Papers, Library of Congress
GC	Grover Cleveland
GC-LC	Grover Cleveland Papers, Library of Congress
GFH	George F. Hoar
GFH-MHS	George F. Hoar Papers, Massachusetts Historical Society
HCL	Henry C. Lea
HCL-HSP	Henry C. Lea Papers, Historical Society of Pennsylvania
HSP	Historical Society of Pennsylvania
IJ	*Indianapolis Journal*
IS	*Indianapolis Sentinel*
ISL	Indiana State Library
JCS	John C. Spooner
JCS-LC	John C. Spooner Papers, Library of Congress
JGB	James G. Blaine
JGB-LC	James G. Blaine Papers, Library of Congress
JS	John Sherman
JS-LC	John Sherman Papers, Library of Congress
JSC	James S. Clarkson
JW	John Wanamaker

JW-HSP	John Wanamaker Papers, Historical Society of Pennsylvania
JWF	John W. Foster
LBS	Lucius B. Swift
LBS-ISL	Lucius B. Swift Papers, Indiana State Library
LC	Library of Congress
LPM	Levi P. Morton
LPM-NYPL	Levi P. Morton Papers, New York Public Library
LTM	Louis T. Michener
LTM-LC	Louis T. Michener Papers, Library of Congress
MM	Manton Marble
MM-LC	Manton Marble Papers, Library of Congress
MSQ	Matthew S. Quay
MSQ-LC	Matthew S. Quay Papers, Library of Congress
NCB	Noble C. Butler
NCB-IHSL	Noble C. Butler Papers, Indiana Historical Society Library
NWA	Nelson W. Aldrich
NWA-LC	Nelson W. Aldrich Papers, Library of Congress
NYEP	*New York Evening Post*
NYH	*New York Herald*
NYS	*New York Sun*
NYT	*New York Times*
NYTr	*New York Tribune*
NYW	*New York World*
RBH	Russell B. Harrison
SBE	Stephen B. Elkins
SBE-WVU	Stephen B. Elkins Papers, West Virginia University Library
SBT	*South Bend Tribune*
SFE	*San Francisco Examiner*
SJR	Samuel J. Randall
SJR-HSP	Samuel J. Randall Papers, Historical Society of Pennsylvania
SR	*Springfield Republican*
TCP	Thomas Collier Platt
TFB	Thomas F. Bayard
TFB-LC	Thomas F. Bayard Papers, Library of Congress
WB	Wharton Barker
WB-LC	Wharton Barker Papers, Library of Congress
WBA	William B. Allison
WBA-SHSI	William B. Allison Papers, State Historical Society of Iowa
WCW	William C. Whitney
WCW-LC	William C. Whitney Papers, Library of Congress
WGR	William G. Rice
WGR-NYSL	William G. Rice Papers, New York State Library
WHS	William Henry Smith
WHS-IHSL	William Henry Smith Papers, Indiana Historical Society Library

WMS	William M. Stewart
WMS-NHS	William M. Stewart Papers, Nevada Historical Society
WP	*Washington Post*
WQG	Walter Q. Gresham
WQG-IHSL	Walter Q. Gresham Papers, Indiana Historical Society Library
WQG-LC	Walter Q. Gresham Papers, Library of Congress
WR	Whitelaw Reid
WR-LC	Reid Family Papers, Library of Congress
WSB	Wilson S. Bissell

INTRODUCTION

1 Allen W. Thurman to GC, October 23, 1888, GC-LC.
2 *Statistical History of the United States from Colonial Times to the Present* (New York: Basic Books, 1976), 1072.

CHAPTER 1. THE POLITICAL UNIVERSE OF THE 1880S

1 *Statistical History of the United States from Colonial Times to the Present* (New York: Basic Books, 1976), 8, 105–108, 139, 684, 694, 731, 788.
2 *Providence Journal*, February 11, 1887.
3 JGB to WR, January 26, 1888, WR-LC; "Nat'l Campaign—1888 Subscriptions," and "Disbursements of the Republican National Committee, 1888," MSQ-LC.
4 BH to LTM, January 13, 1885, LTM-LC.

CHAPTER 2. "GROVER, GROVER, FOUR MORE YEARS!"

1 Grover Cleveland, *The Writings and Speeches of Grover Cleveland*, ed. George F. Parker (New York: Casell, 1892), 187; Robert Kelley, *The Transatlantic Persuasion: The Liberal Democratic Mind in the Age of Gladstone* (New York: Alfred A. Knopf, 1969), 307.
2 Allan Nevins, *Grover Cleveland: A Study in Courage* (New York: Dodd, Mead, 1932), 28–59.
3 Nevins, *Cleveland*, 57–64, 162–169; *NYT*, August 12, 1884.
4 Nevins, *Cleveland*, 74, 167; David F. Day to M. M. Fisher, July 29, 1884, privately held, photocopy in my possession; *NYT*, August 12, 1884.
5 Nevins, *Cleveland*, 79–83.
6 Nevins, *Cleveland*, 84–91.
7 Nevins, *Cleveland*, 94–104; George F. Parker, *Recollections of Grover Cleveland* (New York: Century, 1909), 52–53; Geoffrey Blodgett, "The Emergence of Grover Cleveland: A Fresh Appraisal," *New York History* 73 (April 1992): 141–142.
8 *NYTr*, September 23, 1882, quoted in Mark D. Hirsch, *William C. Whitney: Modern Warwick* (New York: Dodd, Mead, 1948), 188; Blodgett, "Emergence of Cleveland," 142; *Appletons' Annual Cyclopaedia and Register of Important Events of the Year 1882* (New York: D. Appleton, 1883), 608–609.

9 Congressional Quarterly's Guide to U.S. Elections (Washington, D.C.: Congressional Quarterly, 1994), 440, 697; Cleveland, Writings and Speeches, 242; GC to William N. Cleveland, November 7, 1882, in Letters of Grover Cleveland, ed. Allan Nevins (Boston: Houghton Mifflin, 1933), 18.

10 Nevins, Cleveland, 107–118; NYT, March 3, 4, 6, 8, 11, 1883.

11 Nevins, Cleveland, 115, 120–123; Thomas F. Grady to GC, May 4, 1883, GC-LC; NYT, May 5, 6, 7, 1883.

12 Appletons' Annual Cyclopaedia and Register of Important Events of the Year 1883 (New York: D. Appleton, 1884), 572; GC to John Kelly, October 20, 1883, in Cleveland, Letters, 28; Irving Katz, August Belmont: A Political Biography (New York: Columbia University Press, 1968), 265–266; NYT, November 12, 1883.

13 H. Wayne Morgan, From Hayes to McKinley: National Party Politics, 1877–1896 (Syracuse, N.Y.: Syracuse University Press, 1969), 186–191, 197–200; Nevins, Cleveland, 145–148; NYT, March 10, June 13, 1884.

14 Official Proceedings of the National Democratic Convention, Held in Chicago, Ill., July 8th, 9th, 10th, and 11th, 1884 (New York: Douglas Taylor, 1884), 12–15, 123–130, 176–178.

15 Buffalo Evening Telegraph, July 21, 1884; Nevins, Cleveland, 162–167; David F. Day to M. M. Fisher, July 29, 1884, privately held, photocopy in my possession; NYT, August 12, October 28, 1884; Brooks Adams to GC, October 23, 28, 1884, GC-LC.

16 Mark Wahlgren Summers, Rum, Romanism, and Rebellion: The Making of a President, 1884 (Chapel Hill: University of North Carolina Press, 2000), 184–189; T. B. Boyd, comp., The Blaine and Logan Campaign of 1884 (Chicago: J. L. Reagan, 1884), 46–213; Cleveland, Writings and Speeches, 11, 284, 301, 302.

17 Summers, Rum, Romanism, and Rebellion, 275–303; Guide to U.S. Elections, 441; Morgan, From Hayes to McKinley, 232–235; NYT, September 13, 1884; Kenneth C. Martis, The Atlas of Political Parties in the United States Congress, 1789–1989 (New York: Macmillan, 1989), 136–139.

18 Blodgett, "Emergence of Cleveland," 167–168; GC to WSB, November 13, December 25, 1884, in Cleveland, Letters, 48, 51.

19 Horace White to Carl Schurz, January 24, 1885, in Speeches, Correspondence and Political Papers of Carl Schurz, ed. Frederic Bancroft (New York: G. P. Putnam's Sons, 1913), 4:351; Charles Nordhoff to David Wells, February 21, 1885, quoted in Blodgett, "Emergence of Cleveland," 168.

20 Schurz to GC, December 10, 1884, in Schurz, Speeches, Correspondence and Political Papers, 4:299.

21 NYT, December 30, 1884.

22 Nevins, Cleveland, 193–198; E. L. Godkin to GC, February 26, 1885, in The Gilded Age Letters of E. L. Godkin, ed. William M. Armstrong (Albany: State University of New York Press, 1974), 321; Schurz to L. Q. C. Lamar, March 2, 1885, in Schurz, Speeches, Correspondence and Political Papers, 4:356.

23 *Orations and Addresses of George William Curtis,* ed. Charles Eliot Norton (New York: Harper & Brothers, 1894), 2:284–285.

24 Justus Doenecke, "Grover Cleveland and the Enforcement of the Civil Service Act," *Hayes Historical Journal* 4 (Spring 1984): 48; Samuel J. Tilden to Daniel Manning, June 9, 1885, in *Letters and Memorials of Samuel J. Tilden,* ed. John Bigelow (New York: Harper & Brothers, 1908), 2:687.

25 GC to WSB, June 25, 1885, GC to Daniel Manning, June 20, 1885, in Cleveland, *Letters,* 65, 64; Doenecke, "Cleveland and the Enforcement of the Civil Service Act," 53.

26 Louis Fisher, "Grover Cleveland against the Senate," *Capitol Studies* 7 (Spring 1979): 11–25; Schurz to Wayne McVeagh, March 30, 1886, in Schurz, *Speeches, Correspondence and Political Papers,* 4:435–436.

27 HCL to LBS, May 19, 1888, LBS-ISL; GC to WSB, March 21, 1888, in Cleveland, *Letters,* 177; F. G. Babcock to Charles S. Cary, April 27, 1888, GC-LC.

28 *CR,* 49th Cong., 1st sess., 2790–2797; BH to D. S. Alexander, April 23, 1886, BH-LC; BH to LTM, March 27, April 2, 1886, LTM-LC.

29 Leonard D. White, *The Republican Era: A Study in Administrative History, 1869–1901* (New York: Free Press, 1965), 209; Nevins, *Cleveland,* 327; James D. Richardson, *A Compilation of the Messages and Papers of the Presidents, 1789–1902* (Washington, D.C.: Bureau of National Literature and Art, 1903), 8:360, 438.

30 Richard E. Welch Jr., *The Presidencies of Grover Cleveland* (Lawrence: University Press of Kansas, 1988), 62–63; William H. Glasson, *Federal Military Pensions in the United States* (New York: Oxford University Press, 1918), 277–280; Richardson, *Messages,* 439, 441, 702.

31 Richardson, *Messages,* 8:525, 549–557; Edward McPherson, *A Hand-Book of Politics for 1888* (Washington, D.C.: James J. Chapman, 1888), 17–18.

32 Horace White to GC, February 12, 1887, O. O. Stealey to DSL, February 20, 1887, GC-LC.

33 McPherson, *Hand-Book of Politics for 1888,* 18, 22–29; A. Denny to JS, February 11, 1887, JS-LC.

34 Nevins, *Cleveland,* 333; McPherson, *Hand-Book of Politics for 1888,* 100–101; Mary R. Dearing, *Veterans in Politics: The Story of the G.A.R.* (Baton Rouge: Louisiana State University Press, 1952), 348; *NYTr,* June 17, 1887.

35 John C. Black to DSL, June 16, 1887, "Many Democrats" to GC, June 17, 1887, GC-LC; *NYTr,* June 17, 1887; Robert McElroy, *Grover Cleveland: The Man and the Statesman* (New York: Harper & Brothers, 1923), 1:217; GC to John W. Frazier, June 24, 1887, in Cleveland, *Letters,* 143.

36 J. B. Foraker to GC, telegram, June 15, 1887, Wm. Larrabee to GC, telegram, June 15, 1887, GC-LC; Foraker to JS, June 21, 1887, JS-LC; J. B. Foraker, "The Return of the Republican Party," *Forum* 3 (August 1887): 557–558.

37 Foraker, "Return of the Republican Party," 544, 545, 548; Richardson, *Messages,* 8:302; Robert M. Goldman, *"A Free Ballot and a Fair Count": The Department of Justice and the Enforcement of Voting Rights in the South, 1877–1893*

(New York: Fordham University Press, 2001), 134–140; John F. Gowey to JS, June 24, 1887, JS-LC.

38 *NYTr,* January 10, 1888; Charles W. Calhoun, *Conceiving a New Republic: The Republican Party and the Southern Question, 1869–1900* (Lawrence: University Press of Kansas, 2006), 216–217.

39 *Guide to U.S. Elections,* 441.

40 Heather Cox Richardson, *The Greatest Nation of the Earth: Republican Economic Policies during the Civil War* (Cambridge, Mass.: Harvard University Press, 1997), 78, 90–91; Irwin Unger, *The Greenback Era: A Social and Political History of American Finance, 1865–1879* (Princeton, N.J.: Princeton University Press, 1964), 68–91.

41 Unger, *Greenback Era,* 250–263, 289–291, 311–312, 353–355; Allen Weinstein, *Prelude to Populism: Origins of the Silver Issue, 1867–1878* (New Haven, Conn.: Yale University Press, 1970).

42 Donald Bruce Johnson and Kirk H. Porter, comps., *National Party Platforms, 1840–1972* (Urbana: University of Illinois Press, 1975), 66, 73.

43 *Annual Report of the Secretary of the Treasury on the State of the Finances for the Year 1884* (Washington, D.C.: Government Printing Office, 1884), xxix–xxxiii; Nevins, *Cleveland,* 201–204; A. J. Warner and others to GC, February 11, 1885, GC-LC; GC to Warner and others, February 28, 1885, in *Cleveland, Letters,* 56–57; *CR,* 48th Cong., 2nd sess., 2209–2211; BH to LTM, March 1, 1885, BH-LC.

44 Richardson, *Messages,* 8:302, 341–346, 512–513; *CR,* 49th Cong., 1st sess., 165, 212, 384, 423, 481, 486, 487, 533, 3300–3301; Edward McPherson, *A Hand-Book of Politics for 1886* (Washington, D.C.: James J. Chapman, 1886), 100; *Commercial and Financial Chronicle* quoted in Richard Franklin Bensel, *The Political Economy of American Industrialization, 1877–1900* (Cambridge: Cambridge University Press, 2000), 398.

45 Welch, *Presidencies of Grover Cleveland,* 52, 72–73, 157–162, 164–165, 178–179.

46 *The Statistical History of the United States from Colonial Times to the Present* (New York: Basic Books, 1976), 1104.

47 Richardson, *Messages,* 8:301–302, 341, 508–511; Nevins, *Cleveland,* 286–298; McPherson, *Hand-Book of Politics for 1886,* 149–156; McPherson, *Hand-Book of Politics for 1888,* 51–52.

48 Richardson, *Messages,* 8:509; *Appletons' Annual Cyclopaedia and Register of Important Events of the Year 1887* (New York: D. Appleton, 1888), 266–267, 780; *Annual Report of the Secretary of the Treasury on the State of the Finances for the Year 1887* (Washington, D.C.: Government Printing Office, 1887), xxvi–xxviii.

49 J. G. Carlisle to GC, August 9, 1887, W. L. Scott to GC, September 16, 1887, GC-LC; Nevins, *Cleveland,* 289–290, 371–375.

50 *Appletons' Annual Cyclopaedia . . . 1887,* 550–552; *NYT,* October 6, 1887.

51 *NYT,* September 22, October 2, 4–8, 11–14, 16–21, 23, 1887; Nevins, *Cleveland,* 315–320.

52 J. R. Fellows to DSL, November 1, 1887, O. O. Stealey to DSL, November 1, 1887, Th. E. Benedict to DSL, November 9, 1887, John E. Bazley to DSL, November 10, 1887, GC-LC; GC to Edward Cooper, November 2, 1887, in *NYT*, November 5, 1887; Schurz to Abram S. Hewitt, November 5, 1887, in Schurz, *Speeches, Correspondence and Political Papers*, 4:489; *Appletons' Annual Cyclopaedia . . . 1887*, 552–555.

53 WCW to GC, November 9, 1887, Henry Stowell to DSL, November 12, 1887, GC-LC; Wm. H. English to the Editor of the *World*, November 10, 1887, in *NYW*, November 11, 1887; *NYT*, November 11, 1887.

54 GC to WCW, November 11, 1887, WCW-LC; *NYH*, November 18, 1887; John P. Townsend to GC, November 18, 1887, GC-LC.

55 George Hoadly to GC, November 22, 25, 1887, T. E. Powell to GC, November 12, 1887, GC-LC; *The Tribune Almanac and Political Register for 1888*, ed. Edward McPherson (New York: Tribune Association, 1888), 25–26, 28; *Appletons' Annual Cyclopaedia . . . 1887*, 643.

56 A. K. McClure to DSL, November 22, [1887], McClure to GC, November 25, [1887], GC-LC; *NYS*, November 25, 1887; James M. Swank to SJR, November 19, 1887, SJR-HSP.

57 Richardson, *Messages*, 8:580–591.

58 Henry Watterson to GC, December 9, 1887, Henry George to GC, December 7, 1887, R. R. Bowker to GC, December 6, 1887, C. R. Breckinridge to GC, December 6, 1887, WCW to GC, December 11, 1887, GC-LC; *Nation*, December 8, 1887.

59 JGB, draft "interview," [December 7, 1887], JGB-LC; *NYTr*, December 8, 1887; *Appletons' Annual Cyclopaedia . . . 1887*, 552.

60 John Hay to WR, December 8, 1887, WR-LC; *NYTr*, December 8, 1887; *Iowa State Register*, December 10, 1887.

61 *NYTr*, December 7, 1887; *NYH*, December 7, 1887; JCS to S. L. Lord, December 9, 1887, JCS-LC.

62 J. W. Cooper to SJR, December 8, 1887, SJR-HSP; *NYH*, December 7, 1887; *NYS*, December 7, 11, 1887.

63 One draft of the interview is in GC-LC and the other in DSL-LC. Both are dated December 12, 1887.

64 *NYH*, December 16, 1887; *NYT*, December 16, 1887; *NYS*, December 15, 1887.

65 GC to TFB, December 18, 1887, TFB-LC.

66 James A. Barnes, *John G. Carlisle: Financial Statesman* (New York: Dodd, Mead, 1931), 128–132.

67 George L. Converse to SJR, December 12, 1887, SJR-HSP; *NYH*, January 15, 19, May 24, 1888; *NYS*, January 19, 22, 23, March 12, May 19, 22, 24, 1888; William Foyle to DSL, May 10, 1888, GC-LC.

68 GC to WSB, August 12, 1886, GC-LC; Herbert J. Bass, *"I Am a Democrat": The Political Career of David Bennett Hill* (Syracuse, N.Y.: Syracuse University Press, 1961), 76–85.

69 Bass, *"I Am a Democrat,"* 85–89; GC to WSB, January 13, 1888, GC to Daniel Magone, February 20, 1888, in Cleveland, *Letters*, 170–171, 174; Magone to

DSL, January 27, 1888, W. R. Grace to DSL, February 20, 24, 1888, GC-LC; *NYT,* January 27, 1888.

70 *NYS,* February 6, 10, 1888.

71 GC to James Shanahan, March 7, 1888, in Cleveland, *Letters,* 175; Shanahan to GC, February 5, 1888, O. U. Kellogg to DSL, February 15, 1888, R. A. Maxwell to DSL, February 15, 1888, WSB to GC, February 16, 28, 1888, W. R. Grace to DSL, March 2, 1888, J. W. Hinkley to DSL, March 22, 1888, GC-LC.

72 *NYT,* April 6, May 16, 1888; DBH to Smith Weed, March 28, 1888, Gould Collection, Center for American History, University of Texas; Charles Davis to DSL, April 15, 1888, Smith Weed to DSL, April 5, 6, 7, 1888, Weed to DBH, April 7, 1888, Nathaniel C. Mack to DSL, April 29, 1888, D. Cady Herrick to DSL, May 18, 1888, GC-LC; Bass, *"I Am a Democrat,"* 90–91.

73 *NYT,* May 16, 1888; *NYS,* May 17, 1888; *NYTr,* May 16, 1888.

74 Smith Weed to DSL, January 30, February 10, March 21, 1888, John W. Davis to GC, April 6, 1888, GC-LC; DSL to Weed, February ? 1888, Gould Collection; *Appletons' Annual Cyclopaedia and Register of Important Events of the Year 1888* (New York: D. Appleton, 1889), 715–716.

75 R. R. Bowker to Roger Q. Mills, March 14, 1888, GC-LC; Festus P. Summers, *William L. Wilson and Tariff Reform* (New Brunswick, N.J.: Rutgers University Press, 1953), 80–82.

76 *CR,* 50th Cong., 1st sess., 3057–3064; House Report No. 1496, 50th Cong., 1st sess.; *Tariff Rates: The Tariff Act of 1890, Compared with the Tariff Act of 1883 and the Mills Bill* (Washington, D.C.: Government Printing Office, 1891); *What the Mills Bill Is: A Comparative Table Showing the Rate of Duty Now Paid, with an Estimate of the Rate to Be Collected under the Proposed Bill* (New York: n.p., 1888); Joanne Reitano, *The Tariff Question in the Gilded Age: The Great Debate of 1888* (University Park: Pennsylvania State University Press, 1994), 20–21; Nevins, *Cleveland,* 389; Morgan, *From Hayes to McKinley,* 280.

77 James M. Swank to SJR, March 1, 1888, SJR-HSP; *CR,* 50th Cong., 1st sess., 3065, 3307, 4400; *NYTr,* March 2, 1888.

78 Ellis H. Potter to GC, April 7, 1888, Weed to DSL, March 21, 1888, GC-LC; GC to TFB, April 9, 1888, TFB-LC; GC to Fitzhugh Lee, April 15, 1888, in Cleveland, *Letters,* 181.

79 GC to TFB, April 9, 1888, TFB-LC; *IS,* April 27, 1888; *NYH,* May 3, 4, 1888; Johnson and Porter, *National Party Platforms,* 65–66.

80 GC, draft of 1888 New York Democratic platform, GC-LC; *NYH,* May 16, 1888; *NYS,* May 16, 1888; *NYT,* May 17, 1888.

81 WCW to MM, May 27, 1888, MM to WCW, May 27, 1888, MM, "Draft for Platform of Natl Dem. Convention St. Louis 1888," MM-LC; Charles J. M. Guinn to DSL, May 21, 1888, Edward Cooper to DSL, May 31, 1888, GC, draft of platform, dated (in another's hand) May 31, 1888, John P. Irish to GC, April 8, 1888, GC-LC; Nevins, *Cleveland,* 401; *Appletons' Annual Cyclopaedia . . . 1888,* 673.

82 *NYH,* June 6, 7, 1888; *NYS,* June 6, 7, 1888; *IS,* June 6, 7, 8, 10, 1888; GC, draft of platform, dated (in another's hand) May 31, 1888, W. L. Scott to DSL, June 6, 1888, DSL, draft telegram to Scott, [June 6, 1888], GC-LC.

83 GC, draft of platform, dated (in another's hand) May 31, 1888, W. L. Scott to DSL, June 7, 1888, GC-LC; *NYH*, June 7, 8, 1888; *NYS*, June 7, 8, 1888; *IS*, June 7, 8, 1888; *Official Proceedings of the National Democratic Convention Held in St. Louis, Mo., June 5th, 6th and 7th, 1888* (St. Louis: Woodward & Tiernan, 1888), 94–101; A. P. Gorman to MM, June 12, 1888, MM-LC; *NYT*, June 7, 1888.

84 MM to Gorman, Tuesday [June 5, 1888], MM to Henry Watterson, n.d. (telegram), MM-LC; GC, draft of platform, dated (in another's hand) May 31, 1888, GC-LC; *Official Proceedings of the National Democratic Convention . . . 1888*, 95–96.

85 *Official Proceedings of the National Democratic Convention . . . 1888*, 99–100; *IS*, June 8, 1888; *WP*, June 7, 1888; *SR*, June 8, 1888; *NYS*, June 8, 1888; *NYTr*, June 8, 1888; A. J. Warner to SJR, June 27, 1888, SJR-HSP.

86 Daniel Magone to DSL, May 28, 1888, WSB to DSL, May 31, June 4, 1888, Daniel Dougherty to DSL, June 1, 1888, Richard Croker to DSL, June 2, 4, 1888, GC-LC; Croker to DSL, June 5, 1888, DSL-LC; *NYS*, June 3, 6, 7, 1888; *Official Proceedings of the National Democratic Convention . . . 1888*, 76–85.

87 *IS*, April 25, 1888; William H. English to GC, April 28, 1888, GC-LC.

88 *NYH*, June 1–3, 1888; Allen G. Thurman to GC, February 7, 1887, GC-LC.

89 *NYH*, June 1–5, 1888.

90 D. McConville to DSL, June 2, 1888, Edward Murphy to DSL, June 2, 1888, Richard Croker to DSL, June 4, 1888, George Hoadly and W. P. Thompson to DSL, June 1, 1888, GC-LC; Croker to DSL, June 5, 1888, DSL-LC; *NYH*, June 1–5, 1888; *NYS*, June 4, 5, 1888; *IS*, June 5–7, 1888; *Official Proceedings of the National Democratic Convention . . . 1888*, 103–127.

91 *NYH*, June 1, 1888; *NYS*, June 8, 1888; *Official Proceedings of the National Democratic Convention . . . 1888*, 128–131.

92 *NYH*, June 8, 1888; Thomas S. Morgan to DSL, June 15, 1888, GC-LC.

CHAPTER 3. THE REPUBLICAN CHALLENGER: IF NOT BLAINE, WHO?

1 JCS to S. L. Lord, December 9, 1887, JCS-LC.

2 For a discussion of this struggle within the Republican Party in the 1880s, see Charles W. Calhoun, *Conceiving a New Republic: The Republican Party and the Southern Question, 1869–1900* (Lawrence: University Press of Kansas, 2006), chaps. 7–9.

3 The incident, probably apocryphal, is recounted in William C. Hudson, *Random Recollections of an Old Political Reporter* (New York: Cuples & Long, 1911), 112.

4 T. B. Boyd, comp., *The Blaine and Logan Campaign of 1884* (Chicago: J. L. Reagan, 1884), 57, 75.

5 JSC to SBE, May 18, 1888, SBE-WVU; Julia B. Foraker, *I Would Live It Again: Memories of a Vivid Life* (New York: Harper & Brothers, 1932), 132. On Blaine, see Edward P. Crapol, *James G. Blaine: Architect of Empire* (Wilmington, Del.: SR Books, 2000), and David Saville Muzzey, *James G. Blaine: A Political Idol of Other Days* (New York: Dodd, Mead, 1934).

6 Muzzey, *Political Idol*, 73–224.

7 James G. Blaine, *Twenty Years of Congress* (Norwich, Conn.: Henry Bill, 1884, 1886); W. Dean Burnham, *Presidential Ballots, 1836–1892* (Baltimore: Johns Hopkins University Press, 1955), 640–641.

8 James G. Blaine, *Political Discussions: Legislative, Diplomatic, and Popular, 1856–1886* (Norwich, Conn.: Henry Bill, 1887).

9 JGB to WR, October 11, November 25 (with draft editorial), 1887, WR-LC.

10 WR to JGB, December 23, 1887, January 2, 1888, WR-LC.

11 JGB to WR, January 12, 18, 26, 1888, WR-LC; JGB to Patrick Ford, January 1888, in Gail Hamilton, *Biography of James G. Blaine* (Norwich, Conn.: Henry Bill, 1895), 604.

12 *NYTr*, February 13, 1888.

13 *Letters of Mrs. James G. Blaine*, ed. Harriet S. Blaine Beale (New York: Duffield, 1908), 2:172; M. A. Dodge to SBE, January 24, 1888, SBE-WVU; SBE to WR, February 11, 1888, WR-LC.

14 *IJ*, February 14, 1888; *NYH*, February 14, 1888.

15 William Walter Phelps to WR, February 15, 1888, WR to Felix Angus, February 16, 1888, WR to Cassius M. Clay, March 7, 1888, WR to L. M. Brown, March 9, 1888, WR-LC.

16 *NYH*, December 24, 1887; JGB to WR, October 11, 1887, WR-LC.

17 *Reply to the President's Message: Speech of Hon. John Sherman, of Ohio, Delivered in the Senate of the United States, January 4, 1888* (Washington, D.C.: n.p., 1888); J. J. Landram to JS, April 23, 1888, Frederick Douglass to JS, April 25, 1888, JS-LC; John Hay to WR, March 16, 1888, WR-LC. In the absence of a modern biography of Sherman, the most comprehensive account of his career remains his memoir, *Recollections of Forty Years in the House, Senate and Cabinet* (Chicago: Werner, 1895).

18 Sherman, *Recollections*, 2:727–728; H. Wayne Morgan, *From Hayes to McKinley: National Party Politics, 1877–1896* (Syracuse, N.Y.: Syracuse University Press, 1969), 284–285; Robert D. Marcus, *Grand Old Party: Political Structure in the Gilded Age, 1880–1896* (New York: Oxford University Press, 1971), 110–111; WR to Phelps, March 20, 1888, WR-LC.

19 Leland L. Sage, *William Boyd Allison: A Study in Practical Politics* (Iowa City: State Historical Society of Iowa, 1956), 204–216; George F. Hoar, *Autobiography of Seventy Years* (New York: Scribner's, 1903), 1:239; Marcus, *Grand Old Party*, 108–109; JSC to SBE, May 18, 1888, SBE-WVU.

20 WR to C. F. Crocker, April 23, 1888, WR-LC; Jake Covert to BH, February 26, 1888, James N. Tyner to BH, February 20, 1888, BH-LC. For Gresham's career, see Charles W. Calhoun, *Gilded Age Cato: The Life of Walter Q. Gresham* (Lexington: University Press of Kentucky, 1988).

21 *ANB*, 10:351–352.

22 *ANB*, 1:288–289; *Official Proceedings of the Republican National Convention Held at Chicago, June 19, 20, 21, 22, 23 and 25, 1888* (Minneapolis: Charles W. Johnson, 1903), 133–139; Morgan, *From Hayes to McKinley*, 285.

23 *ANB*, 8:45–46; 19:83–85.

24 *ANB* 6:459–460; WR to Frank Hiscock, February 20, 1888, Hiscock to WR, February 25, 1888, WR to Henry S. Chubb, March 27, 1888, WR-LC.

25 *ANB*, 17:434–435.

26 Lew Wallace, *Life of Gen. Ben Harrison* (Philadelphia: Hubbard Brothers, 1888), 61. The biographical details in this and succeeding paragraphs are derived from Charles W. Calhoun, *Benjamin Harrison* (New York: Times Books–Henry Holt, 2005).

27 BH to John Anderson, October 10, 1853, BH-LC.

28 *IJ*, October 2, 1876; Harry J. Sievers, *Benjamin Harrison: Hoosier Statesman* (New York: University Publishers, 1959), 127.

29 *IJ*, August 24, 1884.

30 BH to LTM, June 11, 1884, LTM-LC.

31 BH to John F. Williams, December 18, 1885, BH to Uriah Coulson, December 11, 1885, BH-LC; BH to William Dudley Foulke, December 31, 1885, William Dudley Foulke Papers, LC; *IJ*, n.d. [November 1887], clipping, Scrapbook No. 2, BH-LC.

32 BH to Theron P. Keator, February 19, 1885, SBE to BH, November 13, 1886, Preston B. Plumb to BH, November 10, 1886, BH-LC.

33 BH to Margaret W. Peltz, November 12, 1886, SBE to BH, February 11, 14, 1888, WB to BH, August 27, 1887, P. B. Plumb to BH, October 1, 1887, BH-LC; BH to SBE, February 18, 1888, SBE-WVU; newspaper clipping, n.d., Scrapbook No. 2, BH-LC.

34 D. S. Alexander to BH, November 13, 1887, S. B. Benson to BH, November 9, 1887, BH-LC.

35 BH to SBE, January 30, 1888, J. W. Study to BH, February 1, 1888 (with Harrison's draft reply), BH to Charles Scranton, December 10, 1887, W. W. Dudley to BH, December 19, 1887, BH-LC; BH to SBE, January 7, 1888, SBE-WVU; BH to WB, January 3, 1888, WB-LC; LTM, "The Harrison Campaign for the Nomination in 1888," typescript, LTM-LC.

36 *IJ*, February 14, 1888; *Speeches of Benjamin Harrison*, comp. Charles Hedges (New York: United States Book Company, 1892), 9–24.

37 Marcus, *Grand Old Party*, 109–110; *NYH*, June 9, 1888; Green B. Raum to JS, April 20, 1888, Warner Miller to JS, June 11, 1888, JS-LC.

38 Sage, *Allison*, 212–214, 216, 219; WR to C. F. Crocker, April 23, 1888, WR-LC.

39 *NYH*, May 9, June 4, 1888; Morgan, *From Hayes to McKinley*, 285.

40 Calhoun, *Gilded Age Cato*, 91–95.

41 *SBT*, February 14, 1888.

42 SBE to BH, February 14, 1888, BH-LC; BH to SBE, February 18, 1888, SBE-WVU.

43 JGB to SBE, March 1, 1888, SBE-WVU.

44 JGB to SBE, March 1, 1888, LTM to SBE, February 27, 1888, SBE-WVU; SBE to LTM, March 3, 21, 26, 1888, LTM-LC; SBE to BH, February 27, March 15, 16, 18, 1888, BH-LC; SBE to WR, March 23, 26, 1888, WR-LC.

45 SBE to BH February 27, 1888, BH-LC.

46 BH, "Private Memoranda," in *The Correspondence between Benjamin Harrison and James G. Blaine*, ed. Albert T. Volwiler (Philadelphia: American Philosophical Society, 1940), 296–297.

47 SBE to BH, March 3, 15, 1888, John H. Mitchell to BH, March 17, 1888, BH-LC; SBE to LTM, March 3, 21, 1888, LTM-LC; *NYH*, February 22, 1888; JWF to CWF, February 22, 1888, CWF-LL; LTM to SBE, March 9, 1888, BH to SBE, March 12, 1888, SBE-WVU; *NYTr*, March 15, 1888.

48 SBE to BH, February 27, 1888, WB to BH, February 5, 1888, BH-LC.

49 JWF to WQG, February 14, 1888, WQG-LC; *SBT*, February 17, 1888.

50 JWF to CWF, February 22, 1888, CWF-LL; *CT*, February 28, 1888; *Indianapolis News*, February 29, 1888; Jake Covert to BH, February 26, 1888, BH-LC.

51 WHS to CWF, February 27, 1888, CWF to WQG, February 29, 1888, WQG to CWF, April 3, 11, 1888, Morris McDonald to CWF, April 6, 1888, Eugene Bundy to CWF, March 15, 1888, CWF-LL; JWF to WQG, March 16, 26, 1888, WQG-LC; LTM to EGH, March 15, 1888, EGH-LC.

52 *IJ*, April 20, May 4, 1888; *CT*, April 21, 1888; LTM to EGH, April 28, 1888, EGH-LC; LTM to E. F. Tibbott, October 1, 1895, C. S. Harrison to RBH, May 7, 9, 1888, BH-LC.

53 JWF to WQG, May 11, 1888, WQG-LC; *IJ*, May 28, June 9, 1888; E. W. Halford to CWF, June 11, 1888, CWF-LL; LTM to Halford, May 25, 1888, BH-LC; *NYW*, June 2, 1888.

54 LTM to WB, March 3, 1888, WB to WQG, May 25, 1888, WB-LC; WQG to Alexander. P. Brown, June 10, 1888, WQG-IHSL; *CI-O*, March 16, 1888; *CT*, June 7, 1888; WB to Robert S. Taylor, June 11, 1888, Robert S. Taylor Papers, ISL; WB to BH, April 26, 1888, BH-LC.

55 LTM to SBE, April 10, 20, 1888, SBE-WVU; SBE to LTM, April 7, May 8, 1888, LTM-LC; SBE to BH, April 6, 16, 1888, BH-LC.

56 BH to WB, May 12, 1888, LTM to WB, April 28, May 10, 1888, WB-LC; WB to BH, May 7, 1888, C. S. Harrison to RBH, May 7, 9, 1888, BH-LC.

57 JGB to SBE, April 8, 1888, SBE-WVU; J. M. Scovel to JS, April 18, 1888, JS-LC; SBE to WR, May 8, 17, 1888, WR-LC.

58 WR to C. F. Crocker, April 23, 1888, WR to W. W. Clapp, May 2, 1888, WR-LC.

59 *NYH*, May 16, 17, 1888; WR to F. N. Downer, May 11, 1888, WR to Phelps, May 14, 1888, WR-LC.

60 JSC to SBE, May 18, 1888, SBE-WVU; SBE to JSC, May 6, 1888, quoted in Sievers, *Hoosier Statesman*, 327; Elkins recounted his conversation with Foster in SBE to WR, May 12, 1888, WR-LC.

61 LTM to WB May 10, 1888, WB-LC; JGB to WR, May 14 (two letters), 17, 1888, WR-LC; *NYTr*, May 30, 1888.

62 SBE to WR, June 8, 1888, TCP to WR, May 29, 1888, WR to SBE, June 1, 1888, WR to Cuthbert Bullitt, June 4, 1888, WR-LC; *NYH*, June 9, 1888; John Hay to JS, June 14, 1888, JS-LC.

63 SBE to WR, June 8, 1888, WR to M. H. De Young, June 2, 1888, WR to Cuthbert Bullitt, June 4, 1888, WR to Ellis H. Roberts, June 12, 1888, WR-LC.

64 SBE to LTM, June 7, 10, 1888, W. H. H. Miller to LTM, June 15, 1888, LTM-LC; Phelps to WR, June 10, 1888, WR-LC; LTM to SBE, June 8, 1888, SBE-WVU; SBE to BH, June 10, 13, 1888, BH-LC.

65 Harrison recounted their conversation in BH to SBE, February 2, 1889, SBE-WVU. See also LTM, "Published in the Star of March 10, 1910," typescript, LTM-LC.

66 LTM, "Published in the Star of March 10, 1910," typescript, LTM-LC; LTM and John B. Elam to BH, June 17, 1888, with draft of [BH] to Thos. M. Bayne, BH-LC.

67 Robert McKee to Mary McKee, June 13, 16, 17, 18, 1888, BH-Home; *NYH*, June 19, 1888.

68 *NYTr*, June 19, 1888; A. E. Bateman to JS, June 18, 21, 1888, JS-LC; Robert McKee to Mary McKee, June 17, 18, 19, 1888, BH-Home.

69 *Proceedings of the Republican National Convention . . . 1888*, 9, 13–14, 22.

70 *Proceedings of the Republican National Convention . . . 1888*, 39–42, 64–88; *NYH*, June 19, 21, 23, 1888; *NYS*, June 21, 1888; *IS*, June 20, 1888; John Hay to WR, June 22, 1888, WR-LC.

71 *Proceedings of the Republican National Convention . . . 1888*, 108–113.

72 *NYTr*, June 22, 1888; Joseph Medill to Charles Farwell, June 22, 1888, Charles B. Farwell Papers, Chicago Historical Society; Calhoun, *Gilded Age Cato*, 99; *IS*, June 22, 1888; *NYH*, June 22, 1888.

73 *Proceedings of the Republican National Convention . . . 1888*, 114–151; *IS*, June 22, 1888.

74 LTM, "The National Convention of 1888," typescript, LTM-LC; W. W. Dudley to BH, December 19, 1887, BH-LC.

75 A. E. Bateman to JS, June 21, 1888, A. M. Jones to JS, June 21, 1888, JS-LC; *IS*, June 22, 1888; BH, "Private Memoranda," in Volwiler, *Correspondence between Harrison and Blaine*, 296.

76 John Hay to WR, June 22, 1888, WR-LC; *Proceedings of the Republican National Convention . . . 1888*, 153–167.

77 Chauncey Depew to Cyrenus Cole, September 22, 1922, Chauncey Depew Papers, Yale University Library; A. E. Bateman to JS, June 22, 1888, Mark Hanna to JS, June 22, 1888, A. M. Jones to JS, June 22, 1888, Green B. Raum to JS, June 22, 1888 (telegram at 9:55 P.M., misdated June 23), JS-LC; *IS*, June 23, 1888; *NYH*, June 23, 1888; *NYT*, June 23, 1888; *Proceedings of the Republican National Convention . . . 1888*, 168–171.

78 *Proceedings of the Republican National Convention . . . 1888*, 172–182; J. M. Rusk to LTM, November 10, 1888, LTM-LC; JCS to JS, June 24, 1888, JS-LC; Walker Blaine to Mrs. JGB, July 5, 1888, JGB-LC.

79 *NYT*, June 24, 1888; *NYH*, June 24, 1888; *NYS*, June 24, 1888; *IS*, June 24, 1888; JS to Mark Hanna, June 23, 1888 (three draft telegrams), JS to Charles Foster, June 23, 1888, JS-LC; WHS to WR, [June 23, 1888], WR to WHS, June 23, 1888, WHS-IHSL; W. H. H. Miller to LTM, June 22, 1888, LTM-LC; *Proceedings of the Republican National Convention . . . 1888*, 182–184.

80 WB to JS, June 23, 1888, JS to Mark Hanna, June 24, 1888, JS to Benjamin Butterworth and Charles Foster, June 24, 1888, JS-LC; WB to BH, June 30, 1888, BH-LC; *NYH,* June 24, 1888; *NYS,* June 25, 1888.

81 JS to Warner Miller, June 24, 1888, A. E. Bateman to JS, June 24, 1888, Mark Hanna to JS, June 24, 1888, Frank Hiscock and TCP to JS, June 24, 1888, JS to Hanna, June 24, 1888, JS-LC.

82 LTM to WB, June 24, 1888, Devoy, Breslin, and Carroll to WB, June 24, 1888, WB-LC; Henry L. Stoddard, *As I Knew Them: Presidents and Politics from Grant to Coolidge* (New York: Harper & Brothers, 1927), 160; Sievers, *Hoosier Statesman,* 348; *IS,* June 25, 1888; *NYH,* June 25, 1888; M. Halstead to JS, June 24, 1888, A. E. Bateman to JS, June 24, 1888, JS-LC. Platt later asserted that the promise of the treasury post came immediately after Harrison's nomination. Thomas Collier Platt, *The Autobiography of Thomas Collier Platt* (New York: B. W. Dodge, 1910), 206–207. In another version of the story, Platt placed the promise from Elkins on Sunday. *Washington Evening Star,* March 8, 1910. Elkins's denial is in *Washington Evening Star,* March 9, 1910. Michener denied that Harrison ever countenanced such a promise. LTM, "Published in the Star of March 10, 1910," typescript, LTM-LC.

83 *IS,* June 25, 1888; *NYH,* June 26, 1888; LTM, "The National Convention of 1888," typescript, and "Published in the Star of March 10, 1910," typescript, LTM-LC.

84 LTM, "Published in the Star of March 10, 1910," typescript, LTM-LC; Charles Foster to JS, June 25, 1888, Mark Hanna to JS, June 25, 1888, A. E. Bateman to JS, June 25, 1888, JS-LC; *NYH,* June 26, 1888.

85 *Proceedings of the Republican National Convention . . . 1888,* 186–190; LTM, "The National Convention of 1888," typescript, LTM-LC.

86 JSC to LTM, May 19, 1915, LTM, "The National Convention of 1888," typescript, and "Published in the Star of March 10, 1910," typescript, LTM-LC; *Proceedings of the Republican National Convention . . . 1888,* 191–207; LTM to BH, June 25, 1888, BH-LC.

87 Andrew Carnegie, *Autobiography of Andrew Carnegie* (Boston: Houghton Mifflin, 1920), 344–345; *NYT,* June 25, 1888; Charles Foster to JS, June 27, 1888, JS to Alfred M. Hoyt, June 26, 1888, JS-LC; Phelps to WR, June 28, 1888, WR-LC; *Proceedings of the Republican National Convention . . . 1888,* 207–234.

88 Sievers, *Hoosier Statesman,* 353–354; Harrison, *Speeches,* 25–27.

89 WQG to NCB, July 5, 1888, NCB-IHSL; *IJ,* October 25, 1888.

90 JS to John Fehrenbatch, June 28, 1888, John Hay to JS, June 25, 1888, JS-LC; JS to BH, June 30, 1888, BH-LC; Sherman, *Recollections,* 1029–1030.

91 JGB to WR, July 6, 1888, WR-LC; Richard Smith quoted in WHS to JS, June 25, 1888, JS-LC; BH, "Private Memoranda," in Volwiler, *Correspondence between Harrison and Blaine,* 296.

92 JGB to WR, July 6, 1888, WR-LC; JGB to BH, June 26, 1888, BH to JGB, June 30, 1888, in Volwiler, *Correspondence between Harrison and Blaine,* 28, 30.

93 *NYTr,* June 28, 1888.

1 GC to Chauncey F. Black, September 14, 1888, in *Letters of Grover Cleveland*, ed. Allan Nevins (Boston: Houghton Mifflin, 1933), 189.

2 JS to BH, July 13, 1888, JSC to BH, July 25, 1888, BH-LC; LTM, "Organization of National Committee in 1888," typescript, LTM-LC; *NYH*, July 12, 1888.

3 *Nation*, July 26, 1888; *NYEP*, October 30, 1888; Matthew Josephson, *The Politicos, 1865–1896* (New York: Harcourt, Brace, 1938), 424–425; Allan Nevins, *Grover Cleveland: A Study in Courage* (New York: Dodd, Mead, 1932), 418; Robert D. Marcus, *Grand Old Party: Political Structure in the Gilded Age, 1880–1896* (New York: Oxford University Press, 1971), 129, 137.

4 MSQ to JW, July 24, 1888, JSC to JW, November 13, 1888, JW-HSP; Charles Emory Smith to LTM, June 29, August 2, 6, November 10, December 15, 1888, LTM, "Organization of National Committee in 1888," typescript, LTM-LC; "Nat'l Campaign—*1888* Subscriptions," and "Disbursements of the Republican National Committee, 1888," MSQ-LC. Nearly twenty years later, Clarkson wrote to President Theodore Roosevelt's secretary, William Loeb Jr., that the Republicans had raised $3.3 million in 1888. Although many historians have cited this figure, it was undoubtedly an exaggeration. Clarkson was writing to push his pet idea that Republican clubs should be at the forefront of campaigns. He argued that their work was relatively inexpensive, and overstating the expense of financing regular kinds of campaigns was key to his argument. Moreover, Clarkson's claim is contradicted by the close accounts of national committee revenue and expenditures that Quay kept. JSC to William Loeb Jr., August 19, 1906, Theodore Roosevelt Papers, LC; H. Wayne Morgan, *From Hayes to McKinley: National Party Politics, 1877–1896* (Syracuse, N.Y.: Syracuse University Press, 1969), 306, 584n119.

5 BH to WB, October 17, 1888, WB-LC.

6 GC to WSB, June 17, 1888, in Cleveland, *Letters*, 184; *Official Proceedings of the National Democratic Convention, Held in St. Louis, Mo., June 5th, 6th and 7th, 1888* (St. Louis: Woodward & Tiernan, 1888), 155; W. L. Scott to DSL, July 9, 1888, GC-LC; WCW to Mrs. WCW, July 17, 1888, WCW-LC; *NYH*, July 15, 18, 1888; *NYS*, July 18, 1888.

7 *NYS*, July 18, August 13, 14, 1888; *CE*, August 10, 1888; *NYH*, September 2, 1888; WSB to DSL, October 3, 1888, John H. Reagan to CSB, August 19, 1888, GC-LC.

8 *NYS*, September 3, 23, 28, 1888; *NYT*, October 27, 1889; CSB to DSL, September 11, 1888, William L. Scott to DSL, September 14, October 2, 1888, GC-LC.

9 *NYH*, June 27, 1888.

10 BH to WR, October 9, 1888, WR-LC; Allan Peskin, *Garfield* (Kent, Ohio: Kent State University Press, 1999), 499–500.

11 LTM, "Harrison's Speeches in 1888," typescript, LTM-LC; William Hazen to BH, July 10, 1888, BH-LC; *Speeches of Benjamin Harrison*, comp. Charles Hedges (New York: United States Book Company, 1892), 73–76.

12 LTM, "Harrison's Speeches in 1888," typescript, James N. Tyner to LTM, September 21, 1888, LTM-LC; Harrison, *Speeches*, 25–108, 115–187; *Reception Speeches by Gen. Benj. Harrison* (Indianapolis: Indiana Republican State Central Committee, 1888); BH to LPM, October 29, 1888, LPM-NYPL; Charles F. Manderson to BH, October 11, 1888, BH-LC; Mary Scott Dimmick to Elizabeth Lord, "Monday Morning" [August 20, 1888], BH to Dimmick, February 28, 1895, BH-Home.

13 NYH, August 11, 1888; JS to BH, August 4, 1888, BH-LC; William W. Ivins to DSL, August 10, 1888, GC-LC.

14 *The Welcome Home and Campaign Speeches of James G. Blaine* (New York: J. S. Ogilvie, 1888), 61, 89; Hans B. Thorelli, *The Federal Antitrust Policy* (Baltimore: Johns Hopkins University Press, 1955), 166–169; *Public Opinion*, August 25, 1888; Edward McPherson, *A Hand-Book of Politics for 1890* (Washington, D.C.: James J. Chapman, 1890), 29, 33.

15 NYH, September 1, October 26, 1888; William W. Ivins to DSL, August 22, 1888, GC-LC; Charles Marseilles to BH, August 4, September 11, 1888, JSC to BH, October 1, 1888, Patrick Ford to BH, October 25, 1888, JGB to BH, November 3, 1888, BH-LC; JGB to BH, October 7, 9, 20, 1888, in *The Correspondence between Benjamin Harrison and James G. Blaine*, ed. Albert T. Volwiler (Philadelphia: American Philosophical Society, 1940), 34–38; IJ, October 12, 1888.

16 IS, August 23, 1888; *Speech of Hon. Allen G. Thurman, Democratic Candidate for Vice-President, Delivered at Port Huron, Michigan, August 22, 1888* (n.p., 1888); NYH, August 24, 1888.

17 NYH, August 25, 26, September 2, 7, 1888; NYS, September 9, October 6, 1888; IS, November 4, 1888; Allen W. Thurman to DSL, October 23, 1888, GC-LC.

18 Edward McPherson, *A Hand-Book of Politics for 1888* (Washington, D.C.: James J. Chapman, 1888), 166. New Yorker Ashbel P. Fitch, who voted for the bill, had been elected as a Republican but was running for reelection as a Democrat.

19 Joanne Reitano, *The Tariff Question in the Gilded Age: The Great Debate of 1888* (University Park: Pennsylvania State University Press, 1994), 104. Reitano offers an extended account of the Mills bill debate.

20 A. J. Warner to SJR, September 3, 1888, SJR-HSP; NYH, July 21, 1888; IS, August 23, 1888.

21 Harrison, *Speeches*, 62, 66, 85.

22 H. C. Kinne to GC, August 11, 1888, S. L. Lapham to DSL, August 7, 1888, P. A. Collins to GC, August 2, 1888, GC-LC.

23 WCW to Mrs. WCW, August 11, 1888, WCW-LC; Charles S. Campbell, *The Transformation of American Foreign Relations* (New York: Harper & Row, 1976), 122–123, 126–128; *Supplement to the Revised Statutes of the United States . . . 1874–1891* (Washington, D.C.: Government Printing Office, 1891), 555–556; McPherson, *Hand-Book of Politics for 1888*, 38–42, 114–122.

24 WCW to Mrs. WCW, August 11, 1888, WCW-LC; James D. Richardson, *A Compilation of the Messages and Papers of the Presidents, 1789–1902* (Washington, D.C.: Bureau of National Literature and Art, 1903), 8:620–627.

25 Campbell, *Transformation of American Foreign Relations*, 127–128; Nevins, *Cleveland*, 413.

26 Ballard Smith to *World* (telegram), August 23, 1888, DSL-LC; *NYH*, August 24, 25, 1888; *NYT*, August 25, 1888.

27 CSB to GC, August 24, 1888, Norman Emack to GC, August 25, 1888, GC-LC; *NYS*, August 24, 1888; Wm. C. Endicott to WCW, August 30, 1888, WCW-LC.

28 Wm. L. Putnam to TFB, September 10 (telegram misfiled under September 18), September 11 (telegram and letter), 1888, TFB-LC; J. H. Manley to BH, September 19, 1888, BH-LC.

29 H. G. Woodruff to GC, June 28, 1888, Smith Weed to DSL, July 6, 20, 1888, J. H. MacDonald to GC, August 27, 1888, GC-LC.

30 McPherson, *Hand-Book of Politics for 1890*, 30–34.

31 *NYH*, September 11, 13, 1888; *NYT*, September 10, 1888; *IS*, September 10, 1888; *NYS*, September 10, 1888; *NYTr*, September 10, 1888.

32 A. J. Warner to SJR, September 12, 1888, CSB to SJR, October 6, 1888, SJR to CSB, October 10, 1888, E. W. Greenman to SJR, October 5, 1888, SJR-HSP; SJR to William Foyle, September 13, 1888, Foyle to DSL, September 15, 1888, GC-LC.

33 *IS*, September 21, 1888; *NYH*, October 20, 1888; William Foyle to SJR, November 2, 1888, SJR-HSP.

34 Preston Plumb to BH, July 3, 1888, Eugene Hale to BH, July 8, 1888, Joseph Medill to BH, September 11, 1888, BH-LC.

35 Harrison, *Speeches*, 66, 109–111; Joseph Medill to BH, September 16, 1888, EGH to BH, August 10, September 20, 1888, BH-LC; BH to WBA, September 14, 1888, WBA-SHSI; JGB to BH, September 12, 1888, in Volwiler, *Correspondence between Harrison and Blaine*, 33.

36 JCS to Horace Rublee, July 27, 1888, JCS-LC; Frank Hiscock to BH, July 12, 1888, JS to BH, September 12, 1888, BH-LC; WR to Hiscock, July 23, 1888, WR-LC; George F. Edmunds to WBA, September 14, 1888, WBA-SHSI.

37 James M. Swank to WBA, September 26, 1888, J. C. Gates to WBA, September 7, 1888, WBA-SHSI; John H. Ross to GFH, July 19, 1888, GFH-MHS; D. D. Cohen to Justin Morrill, July 14, 1888, JS-LC.

38 WBA to BH, August 4, September 12, 1888, BH-LC; BH to WBA, September 14, 1888, JSC to WBA, September 24, 1888, WBA-SHSI.

39 *The Tariff Bill of 1888. Report of N. W. Aldrich of Rhode Island, from the Committee on Finance, to the Senate of the United States, October 4, 1888* (Washington, D.C.: Government Printing Office, 1888), quotations from 47, 49; Justin Morrill to NWA, October 6, 1888, NWA-LC.

40 WBA to BH, October 13, 1888, JS to BH, October 1, 1888, William J. Fowler to BH, October 10, 1888, BH-LC; Joseph Medill to WBA, October 12, 1888,

WBA-SHSI; *NYH,* October 4, 12, 1888; *IS,* October 18, 1888; George S. Weed to DSL, October 11, 1888, GC-LC.

41 J. A. Gilbert to BH, June 28, 1888, Ben Butterworth to BH, July 13, 1888, BH-LC.

42 American Iron and Steel Association, "1,239,258 Tariff Tracts Distributed!" flyer, October 1, 1888, John R. Lynch to BH, July 2, 1888, BH-LC; JCS to J. V. Quarles, October 10, 1888, JCS-LC.

43 BH to WR, September 27, 1888, WR-LC; Harrison, *Speeches,* 71, 162–163.

44 *NYS,* November 2, 1888; John W. Plummer to BH, August 21, 1888, with news clipping, BH-LC; McPherson, *Hand-Book of Politics for 1890,* 31; draft letter to "My dear Sir," September 19, 1888, GC-LC; *NYH,* July 24, 25, 26, 27, October 28, 1888; Lawrence Grossman, *The Democratic Party and the Negro: Northern and National Politics, 1868–92* (Urbana: University of Illinois Press, 1976), 143–145.

45 Thurman, *Speech . . . at Port Huron,* 8, 9.

46 *IS,* June 28, 1888; *NYH,* July 27, 1888; *NYS,* August 30, 1888; notarized affidavit of William S. Elliot enclosed in J. C. Wheat to BH, October 8, 1888, BH-LC.

47 Harrison, *Speeches,* 179, 183–184; Lew Wallace, *Life of Gen. Ben Harrison* (Philadelphia: Hubbard Brothers, 1888), 321–332; *Gen. Harrison and Labor* ([Indianapolis]: Republican State Central Committee of Indiana, 1888); LTM to M. H. De Young, October 12, 1888, RBH to BH, October 24, 1888, SBE to BH, October 26, 1888, BH-LC.

48 *IS,* June 28, 1888; W. H. H. Russell to GC, June 26, 1888, GC-LC.

49 M. H. De Young to BH, June 27, 1888, M. M. Estee to BH, July 17, 1888, BH to George Osgoodby, July 14, 1888, J. P. Jackson to BH, July 24, 1888, Frank Kimball to BH, August 18, 1888, Symmes Hunt to BH, August 18, 1888, BH-LC; *San Francisco Wasp,* July 21, 1888; *SFE,* July 14, 1888; R. Hal Williams, *The Democratic Party and California Politics, 1880–1896* (Stanford, Calif.: Stanford University Press, 1973), 125; WMS to Charles Aiken, June 28, 1888, WMS-NHS.

50 McPherson, *Hand-Book of Politics for 1888,* 193–194; Williams, *Democratic Party and California Politics,* 121.

51 William D. English to DSL, September 2, 1888, GC-LC; McPherson, *Hand-Book of Politics for 1890,* 13, 28, 31; TFB to John Russell Young, September 14, 1888, TFB-LC.

52 M. M. Estee to BH, September 12, 1888, BH-LC; TFB to GC, September 15, 1888, TFB-LC; Richardson, *Messages,* 8:630–635; M. F. Tarkey to DSL, October 3, 1888, Thomas Wilkinson to GC, October 1, 1888, GC-LC.

53 J. P. Jackson to BH, October 23, 1888, T. B. Reed to BH, October 26, 1888, BH-LC.

54 George Osgoodby to BH, June 28, 1888, BH to Osgoodby, July 14, 1888, BH-LC; T. C. Hinckley, "George Osgoodby and the Murchison Letter," *Pacific Historical Review* 27 (November 1958): 359–368.

55 John Boyle O'Reilly to GC, October 25, 1888, Patrick J. Meehan to GC, October 30, GC-LC; GC to TFB, October 26, 1888, TFB to E. J. Phelps, October 25, 1888, Samuel D. Darling to TFB, October 26, 1888, Phelps to TFB, October 28, 1888, TFB to Lord Sackville, October 30, 1888, TFB-LC; *NYTr,* October 24, 1888; JGB to BH, October 25, 1888, in Volwiler, *Correspondence between Harrison and Blaine,* 38; RBH to BH, October 26, 1888, BH-LC.

56 George William Curtis to LBS, July 7, 1888, HCL to LBS, May 19, 1888, LBS-ISL; HCL to Wayne MacVeagh, July 7, 1888, MacVeagh Family Papers, HSP; Wayne MacVeagh to HCL, July 12, 1888, William J. Sewell to HCL, October 24, 1888, HCL-HSP; *Independent,* October 18, 1888; Ari Hoogenboom, *Outlawing the Spoils: A History of the Civil Service Reform Movement, 1865–1883* (Urbana: University of Illinois Press, 1968), 261–262.

57 R. R. Bowker to DSL, June 11, 1888, GC to [Reform Club], June 14, 1888, GC-LC; McPherson, *Hand-Book of Politics for 1890,* 31; Joseph Medill to BH, September 11, 1888, BH-LC; Carl Schurz to Thaddeus C. Pound, September 15, 1888, in *Speeches, Correspondence and Political Papers of Carl Schurz,* ed. Frederic Bancroft (New York: G. P. Putnam's Sons, 1913), 4:511, 527–528.

58 LBS, diary entry for August 21, 1888, LBS-ISL; H. W. Chaplin to BH, July 19, 1888, Roger Wolcott to BH, July 19, 1888, BH-LC; McPherson, *Hand-Book of Politics for 1890,* 29.

59 Edward S. Sayres to BH, September 18, 1888, Charles Marseilles to BH, August 4, 1888, Garret A. Hobart to BH, October 13, 1888, BH-LC; E. L. Godkin to Frederick Sheldon, September 10, 1888, in *The Gilded Age Letters of E. L. Godkin,* ed. William M. Armstrong (Albany: State University of New York Press, 1974), 369; Harrington Putnam, "Memorandum to Mr. Shepard," October 4, 1888, GC-LC.

60 Herbert J. Bass, *"I Am a Democrat": The Political Career of David Bennett Hill* (Syracuse, N.Y.: Syracuse University Press, 1961), 102–107; D. H. Chamberlain to DSL, June 11, 1888, W. R. Grace to GC, July 13, 1888, W. L. Brown to DSL, June 11, 1888, Richard Croker to DSL, September 7, 1888, GC-LC.

61 GC to W. R. Grace, July 14, 1888, GC to WSB, July 17, 1888, in Cleveland, *Letters,* 185–186; *NYT,* September 12, 1888; *NYS,* September 14, 1888; DBH to GC, September 10, 1888, Grace to GC, September 20, 1888, Samuel R. Honey to GC, October 5, 1888, Daniel W. McCanley to GC, October 1, 1888, GC-LC.

62 Circular, Committee of Democrats and Independents to Dear Sir, September 21, 1888, GC-LC; *NYT,* September 19, 1888; *NYS,* October 9, 20, 28, 1888; WGR to Albert Moore, October 22, 1888, DBH to Peter J. Leonard, October 23, 1888, WGR to DBH, October 24, 1888, DBH-NYSL.

63 WGR to William Murtha, October 12, 1888, WGR to William Sheehan, October 22, 23, 1888, DBH to John Foley, October 22, 1888, DBH to John Banfield, November 2, 1888, DBH to D. H. Rice, November 3, 1888, WGR to John Franey, October 29, 1888, DBH-NYSL; DSL to WGR, November 3, 1888, WGR-NYSL; DSL to Chas. R. De Freest, October 30, 1888, DSL-LC.

64 D. A. Black to DSL, October 18, 1888, GC-LC; W. H. Winton to BH, October 11, 1888, W. Scott O'Connor to BH, October 24, 1888, WR to BH, October 6, 1888, JSC to BH, November 2, 1888, BH-LC; Allan Nevins, *Abram S. Hewitt, With Some Account of Peter Cooper* (New York: Harper & Brothers, 1935), 521–527.

65 Gerrit H. Smith to BH, September 6, 1888, Warner Miller to BH, October 1, 1888, Charles A. Ray to BH, October 13, 1888, BH-LC; *NYT*, August 28, 29, September 18, 1888; *Congressional Quarterly's Guide to U.S. Elections* (Washington, D.C.: Congressional Quarterly, 1994), 441.

66 *Appletons' Annual Cyclopaedia and Register of Important Events of the Year 1888* (New York: D. Appleton, 1889), 778–779.

67 *Appletons' Annual Cyclopaedia . . . 1888*, 777–778; W. L. Scott to DSL, September 14, 1888, GC-LC; J. R. Burton to BH, August 6, 1888, BH-LC.

68 Melanie Susan Gustafson, *Women and the Republican Party, 1854–1924* (Urbana: University of Illinois Press, 2001), 71–76; "Disbursements of the Republican National Committee, 1888," MSQ-LC.

69 Rebecca Edwards, *Angels in the Machinery: Gender in American Party Politics from the Civil War to the Progressive Era* (New York: Oxford University Press, 1997), 63–65; *NYT*, June 7, 1888; Allen W. Thurman to DSL, October 23, 1888, GC-LC.

70 *IJ*, October 8, 1888; BH to WR, September 27, October 9, 1888, WR to BH, October 16 (copy with note), 1888, WR-LC; M. Halstead to BH, October 23, November 1, 1888, JGB to BH, October 25, 1888, BH-LC; WQG to NCB, October 30, 1888, NCB-IHSL.

71 *IS*, October 31, 1888; LTM, "The Dudley Letter," typescript, LTM-LC; JSC to BH, October 15, 1888, BH-LC; Harry J. Sievers, *Benjamin Harrison: Hoosier Statesman* (New York: University Publishers, 1959), 417–421; Charles W. Calhoun, *Gilded Age Cato: The Life of Walter Q. Gresham* (Lexington: University Press of Kentucky, 1988), 104.

72 LTM, "The Dudley Letter," typescript, LTM-LC; WSB to DSL, October 15, 1888, H. J. Morris to DSL, October 16, 1888, Geo. F. Spinney to DSL, October 23, 1888, GC-LC.

73 [J.] Graham to EGH, November 9, 1888, EGH-LC; *Annual Report of the Attorney-General of the United States for 1889* (Washington, D.C.: Government Printing Office, 1889), 184; "Disbursements of the Republican National Committee, 1888," MSQ-LC; Charles H. Heustis, *The Great Conspiracy of Four Years Ago* (Philadelphia: Allen, Lane & Scott, 1892); Mark Wahlgren Summers, *Party Games: Getting, Keeping, and Using Power in Gilded Age Politics* (Chapel Hill: University of North Carolina Press, 2004), 10; Clement Studebaker to BH, November 6, 1888, BH-LC; Richard J. Jensen, *The Winning of the Midwest: Social and Political Conflict, 1888–1896* (Chicago: University of Chicago Press, 1971), 29; John F. Reynolds and Richard L. McCormick, "Outlawing 'Treachery': Split Tickets and Ballot Laws in New York and New Jersey, 1880–1910," *Journal of American History* 72 (March 1986), 850. See also James L. Baumgardner, "The 1888 Presidential Election: How Corrupt?" *Presidential Studies Quarterly* 14 (Summer 1984): 416–427.

74 Summers, *Party Games*, 11–13.
75 *IS*, November 7, 1888; GC to S. B. Ward, November 6, 1888, in Cleveland, *Letters*, 191.

CHAPTER 5. A MINORITY AND A MANDATE

1 Allan Nevins, *Grover Cleveland: A Study in Courage* (New York: Dodd, Mead, 1932), 439; J. R. McKee to Bernard Batty, December 12, 1938, BH-Home. Dudley's telegrams are in Series 4, BH-LC.
2 *Congressional Quarterly's Guide to U.S. Elections* (Washington, D.C.: Congressional Quarterly, 1994), 441, 442, 470, 697; *Appletons' Annual Cyclopaedia and Register of Important Events of the Year 1887* (New York: D. Appleton, 1888), 552; *Statistical History of the United States from Colonial Times to the Present* (New York: Basic Books, 1976), 1072.
3 Octavus Cohen to GC, June 12, 1888, GC-LC; *Guide to U.S. Elections*, 438, 442; *Statistical History of the United States*, 1072.
4 *Guide to U.S. Elections*, 442.
5 Kenneth C. Martis, *The Atlas of Political Parties in the United States Congress, 1789–1989* (New York: Macmillan, 1989), 140–143; JGB to BH, November 9, 1888, in *The Correspondence between Benjamin Harrison and James G. Blaine*, ed. Albert T. Volwiler (Philadelphia: American Philosophical Society, 1940), 41.
6 David Wells to TFB, November 26, 1888, TFB to James Bayard, November 9, 1888, TFB to E. J. Phelps, November 19, 1888, TFB-LC; Richard Croker to GC, November 16, 1888, W. L. Scott to GC, November 9, 1888, GC-LC.
7 James Welling to GC, November 8, 1888, James Carter to GC, November 7, 1888, Fred Flower to GC, November 8, 1888, C. Augustus Haviland to GC, November 11, 1888, William Boggs to GC, November 22, 1888, Robert McLane to GC, November 27, 1888, CSB to GC, January 3, 1889, GC-LC; D. I. Murphy to SJR, November 13, 1888, SJR-HSP; Joseph Pulitzer to MM, November 23, 1888, MM-LC; *NYS*, November 14, 1888; S. S. Cox to LPM, November 10, 1888, with unidentified clipping, LPM-NYPL.
8 *NYH*, November 8, 15, 1888; DSL to DBH, November 7, 1888, DBH-NYSL.
9 *IS*, November 8, 1888; James G. Fair to TFB, November 13, 1888, TFB-LC; Smith Weed to DSL, November 7, 1888, GC-LC; Weed to SJR, November 8, 1888, W. H. Barnum to SJR, December 5, 1888, SJR-HSP.
10 James Carter to GC, November 7, 1888, John Bigelow to GC, November 8, 1888, GC-LC; *NYH*, November 15, 1888; Frances Cleveland to TFB, November 10, 1888, TFB-LC.
11 JCS to BH, November 7, 1888, Fred Stone to BH, November 7, 1888, Joseph Medill to BH, November 8, 1888, BH-LC; BH to MSQ, November 22, 1888, MSQ-LC; Chas. H. Weston to WBA, November 12, 1888, WBA-SHSI; *NYTr*, November 11, 1888.
12 William Lyon to BH, November 7, 1888, James Patterson to BH, November 8, 1888, BH-LC; Asher Barnett to SJR, November 9, 1888, SJR-HSP; TFB to E. J. Phelps, November 19, 1888, TFB-LC; Murat Halstead to LPM, November 15, 1888, LPM-NYPL.

13 BH to Albion Tourgée, December 12, 1888, BH-IHSL; James D. Richardson, *A Compilation of the Messages and Papers of the Presidents, 1789–1902* (Washington, D.C.: Bureau of National Literature and Art, 1903), 9:5–14.

14 Charles W. Calhoun, *Benjamin Harrison* (New York: Times Books–Henry Holt, 2005), 83–112, 114–118.

15 P. C. Cheney to LTM, March 23, 1893 [1896], LTM-LC; *Speeches of Benjamin Harrison,* comp. Charles Hedges (New York: United States Book Company, 1892); Calhoun, *Benjamin Harrison,* 77–82, 120–133; Robert L. Beisner, *From the Old Diplomacy to the New, 1865–1900* (Arlington Heights, Ill.: Harland Davidson, 1986), 96–106.

16 Charles W. Calhoun, *Conceiving a New Republic: The Republican Party and the Southern Question, 1869–1900* (Lawrence: University Press of Kansas, 2006), 232–288.

17 Richardson, *Messages,* 9:390.

18 Calhoun, *Conceiving a New Republic,* 279–280; Lewis L. Gould, *The Presidency of William McKinley* (Lawrence: Regents Press of Kansas, 1980).

19 Richardson, *Messages,* 8:776, 778; Harrison, *Speeches,* 68, 324–325.

BIBLIOGRAPHIC ESSAY

The election of 1888 occurred at a time when letter writing, supplemented by the telegraph, remained the main form of communication for Americans in all walks of life. Even within cities, written messages still held sway over the telephone in many circumstances. The happy result for the historian is that not only the election of 1888 but also much of the political history of the period generally lies recorded in the papers of many of the principal actors.

The Library of Congress is the chief repository for such papers from the late nineteenth century. The Manuscript Division houses collections of Benjamin Harrison's papers (approximately 70,000 items) and Grover Cleveland's papers (more than 100,000 items). Microfilm editions of both these collections, with comprehensive printed indexes, are available in many other libraries. Together they constitute the most important primary sources for the election of 1888. In 1933 Allan Nevins published a selection of *Letters of Grover Cleveland* (Boston: Houghton Mifflin). No such broad-ranging compilation of Harrison's letters exists, but highly valuable is *The Correspondence between Benjamin Harrison and James G. Blaine*, ed. Albert T. Volwiler (Philadelphia: American Philosophical Society, 1940). Additional important collections of Harrison's papers include those at the Benjamin Harrison Home in Indianapolis, the Indiana Historical Society, and the Indiana State Library. The Library of Congress also houses collections of the papers of several prominent Republicans who played important roles in 1888: Nelson W. Aldrich, Wharton Barker, James G. Blaine, James S. Clarkson, John W. Foster, Walter Q. Gresham, Joseph R. Hawley, Eugene Gano Hay, William McKinley, Louis T. Michener, Matthew S. Quay, Whitelaw Reid, John Sherman, and John C. Spooner. Among the Democrats represented in the Library of Congress's Manuscript Division are Thomas F. Bayard, Donald M. Dickinson, Daniel S. Lamont, Manton Marble, and William C. Whitney. Other useful collections include the papers of William B. Allison (State Historical Society of Iowa), Noble C. Butler (Indiana Historical Society), Chauncey Depew (Yale University Library), Stephen B. Elkins (West Virginia University Library), Charles W. Fairbanks (Lilly Library, Indiana University), David B. Hill (New York State Library), George F. Hoar (Massachusetts Historical Society), Henry C. Lea (Historical Society of Pennsylvania), Levi P. Morton (New York Public Library), Thomas Collier Platt (Yale University Library), Samuel J. Randall (Historical Society of Pennsylvania), William G. Rice (New York State Library), William Henry Smith (Indiana Historical Society), Lucius B. Swift (Indiana State Library), and John Wanamaker (Historical Society of Pennsylvania).

Newspapers and other periodicals made little effort to hide their leanings in politics, so one must read them with a skeptic's eye. Still, they are valuable sources for campaign speeches and other partisan material, and some covered behind-the-scenes machinations, rallies, and other events in great detail. Among the most valuable is the reporting in the ostensibly independent but pro-Cleveland *New York Herald*. The list of other useful papers is extensive, but worthy of mention are the *Chicago Tribune, Indianapolis Journal, Indianapolis Sentinel, New York Times, New York Tribune, New York Sun, New York World,* and *Washington Post*. Mugwump opinion appears in *Harper's Weekly*, the *Nation*, and the *Springfield Republican*. Valuable contemporary compendia of political and other information are *Appletons' Annual Cyclopaedia and Register of Important Events of the Year* and Edward McPherson's *A Hand-Book of Politics*, published biennially from the 1860s to the 1890s.

Over the years, several general studies have explored the politics of the late nineteenth century. The most important contemporaneous work came from the pen of British observer James Bryce, *The American Commonwealth* (London: Macmillan, 1888). Finding little to admire in American political life, Bryce concluded that no genuine policy differences distinguished Republicans from Democrats and that politicians from each major party put the quest for office above all else. Historians and others writing during the twentieth century followed Bryce's lead in generally condemning Gilded Age politics. These include Charles Beard and Mary Beard, *The Rise of American Civilization* (New York: Macmillan, 1930); Matthew Josephson, *The Politicos, 1865–1896* (New York: Harcourt, Brace, 1938); and Richard Hofstadter, *The American Political Tradition and the Men Who Made It* (New York: Alfred A. Knopf, 1948), chap. 7.

The 1960s and after witnessed the appearance of several revisionist works that paid less attention to the seamier side of politics and focused on the substantive questions and policies that informed partisan debate. The most impressive of these works is H. Wayne Morgan, *From Hayes to McKinley: National Party Politics, 1877–1896* (Syracuse, N.Y.: Syracuse University Press, 1969). Besides explicating contentious issues, Morgan offers engaging depictions of personalities and colorful incidents that move his analysis forward with inclusiveness and dramatic flair. Works in a similar revisionist vein include R. Hal Williams, *Years of Decision: American Politics in the 1890s* (New York: John Wiley & Sons, 1978), and Robert W. Cherny, *American Politics in the Gilded Age, 1868–1900* (Wheeling, Ill.: Harlan Davidson, 1997). A recent study, Mark Wahlgren Summers, *Party Games: Getting, Keeping, and Using Power in Gilded Age Politics* (Chapel Hill: University of North Carolina Press, 2004), tends to echo the condemnatory spirit of earlier works. Other works that pay attention to the structure as well as the substance of American political culture include Robert D. Marcus, *Grand Old Party: Political Structure in the Gilded Age, 1880–1896* (New York: Oxford University Press, 1971); Morton Keller, *Affairs of State: Public Life in the Late Nineteenth Century* (Cambridge, Mass.: Harvard University Press, 1977); Michael E. McGerr, *The Decline of Popular Politics: The American North, 1865–1928* (New York: Oxford University Press, 1986); Joel Silbey, *The American Political Nation, 1838–1893* (Stanford, Calif.: Stanford University Press, 1991); and Alan Ware, *The Democratic Party Heads North, 1877–1962* (Cambridge: Cambridge University Press, 2006).

The so-called new political history that became fashionable in the 1960s and 1970s shifted attention to the electorate and, employing quantitative methods, posited that voters' partisan affiliations tended to reflect their ethnic and religious backgrounds. Examples of this genre include Paul Kleppner, *The Cross of Culture: A Social Analysis of Midwestern Politics, 1850–1900* (New York: Free Press, 1970), and *The Third Electoral System, 1853–1892: Parties, Voters, and Political Cultures* (Chapel Hill: University of North Carolina Press, 1979); Richard J. Jensen, *The Winning of the Midwest: Social and Political Conflict, 1888–1896* (Chicago: University of Chicago Press, 1971); and Samuel T. McSeveney, *The Politics of Depression: Political Behavior in the Northeast, 1893–1896* (New York: Oxford University Press, 1972).

Heretofore, no published book-length study has focused on the presidential election of 1888. C. Joseph Bernardo, "The Presidential Election of 1888" (Ph.D. diss., Georgetown University, 1949), relied on limited sources. More valuable are Edward Arthur White, "The Republican Party in National Politics, 1888–1891" (Ph.D. diss., University of Wisconsin, 1941), and John Edgar McDaniel Jr., "The Presidential Election of 1888" (Ph.D. diss., University of Texas, 1970). Two studies of the presidencies of Cleveland and Harrison include discussion of the election of 1888: Richard E. Welch Jr., *The Presidencies of Grover Cleveland* (Lawrence: University Press of Kansas, 1988), and Homer E. Socolofsky and Allan B. Spetter, *The Presidency of Benjamin Harrison* (Lawrence: University Press of Kansas, 1987).

Neither Harrison nor Cleveland wrote an autobiography. After his presidency, Harrison published a work on American governance, *This Country of Ours* (New York: Charles Scribner's Sons, 1897). Cleveland's *Presidential Problems* (New York: Century, 1904), is a compilation of four lectures and articles, one of which deals with his battle with the Senate over appointments during his first term. Both presidents' messages to Congress appear in James D. Richardson, *A Compilation of the Messages and Papers of the Presidents, 1789–1902* (Washington, D.C.: Bureau of National Literature and Art, 1903). Additional documents may be found in *Public Papers of Grover Cleveland, Twenty-second President of the United States, 1885–1889* (Washington, D.C.: Government Printing Office, 1889) and *Public Papers and Addresses of Benjamin Harrison, Twenty-third President of the United States, 1889–1893* (Washington, D.C.: Government Printing Office, 1893). Other Cleveland writings were published in *The Writings and Speeches of Grover Cleveland*, ed. George F. Parker (New York: Cassell, 1892). Charles Hedges compiled virtually all of Harrison's speeches during his 1888 campaign and the first three years of his presidency in *Speeches of Benjamin Harrison* (New York: United States Book Company, 1892).

More biographies have been written about Cleveland than about Harrison, but the standard work on the twenty-second president is still the hagiographic Allan Nevins, *Grover Cleveland: A Study in Courage* (New York: Dodd, Mead, 1932). The authorized biography is Robert McElroy, *Grover Cleveland: The Man and the Statesman* (New York: Harper & Brothers, 1923). Though shorter, the best study of Cleveland's performance in the White House is Welch, *Presidencies of Cleveland.* Horace Samuel Merrill offers a critical account in *Bourbon Leader: Grover Cleveland and the Democratic Party* (Boston: Little, Brown, 1957). Henry Graff, *Grover Cleveland* (New York: Times Books–Henry Holt, 2002), places Cleveland in the context of his times. Two recent works—Alyn Brodsky, *Grover Cleveland: A Study in Character* (New York: St. Martin's, 2002), and H. Paul Jeffers, *An Honest President: The Life and Presidencies of Grover Cleveland* (New York: William Morrow, 2002)—are in the Nevins mold but are not as detailed. Robert Kelley offers insights into Cleveland's public philosophy in *The Transatlantic Persuasion: The Liberal-Democratic Mind in the Age of Gladstone* (New York: Alfred A. Knopf, 1969). For Cleveland's first election, see Mark Wahlgren Summers, *Rum, Romanism, & Rebellion: The Making of a President, 1884* (Chapel Hill: University of North Carolina Press, 2000). The character of Cleveland's leadership forms the subject of two important articles by Geoffrey Blodgett: "The Political Leadership of Grover Cleveland," *South Atlantic Quarterly* 82 (Summer 1983): 288–299, and "The Emergence of Grover Cleveland: A Fresh Appraisal," *New York History* 73 (April 1992), 133–168.

A half century ago, Harry J. Sievers published a three-volume biography of Harrison: *Benjamin Harrison: Hoosier Warrior* (New York: University Publishers, 1952), *Benjamin Harrison: Hoosier Statesman* (New York: University Publishers, 1959), and *Benjamin Harrison: Hoosier President* (Indianapolis: Bobbs-Merrill, 1968). The second volume has a detailed account of the campaign of 1888. The third volume is at best a perfunctory treatment of Harrison's presidency and should be supplemented by Socolofsky and Spetter, *Presidency of Benjamin Harrison.* A relatively brief but comprehensive interpretive biography is Charles W. Calhoun, *Benjamin Harrison* (New York: Times Books–Henry Holt, 2005). For Harrison's public philosophy, see Charles W. Calhoun, "Civil Religion and the Gilded Age Presidency: The Case of Benjamin Harrison," *Presidential Studies Quarterly* 23 (Fall 1993): 651–667.

Professor R. Hal Williams is preparing a full biography of James G. Blaine. A recent brief biography by Edward Crapol, *James G. Blaine: Architect of Empire* (Wilmington, Del.: SR Books, 2000), emphasizes Blaine's imperial designs. Older, unsatisfactory works include David Saville Muzzey, *James G. Blaine: A Political Idol of Other Days* (New York: Dodd, Mead, 1934), and *Biography of James G. Blaine* (Norwich, Conn.: Henry Bill, 1895), by Mrs. Blaine's cousin, Mary Abigail Dodge, and published under the pseudonym "Gail Hamilton." In the absence of a comprehensive biography of John Sherman, his own *Recollections of Forty Years in the House, Senate and Cabinet* (Chicago: Werner, 1895) remains the indispensable published work on his career. Biographies of other participants in the election of 1888 include Leland L. Sage, *William Boyd Allison: A Study in Practical Politics* (Iowa City: State Historical Society of Iowa, 1956); James A. Barnes, *John G. Carlisle: Financial Statesman* (New York: Dodd, Mead, 1931); Oscar Doane Lambert, *Stephen Benton Elkins: American Foursquare* (Pittsburgh: University of Pittsburgh Press, 1955); John R. Lambert Jr., *Arthur Pue Gorman* (Baton Rouge: Louisiana State University Press, 1953); Charles W. Calhoun, *Gilded Age Cato: The Life of Walter Q. Gresham* (Lexington: University Press of Kentucky,

1988); Herbert J. Bass, *"I Am a Democrat": The Political Career of David Bennett Hill* (Syracuse, N.Y.: Syracuse University Press, 1961); Richard E. Welch Jr., *George Frisbie Hoar and the Half-Breed Republicans* (Cambridge, Mass.: Harvard University Press, 1971); H. Wayne Morgan, *William McKinley and His America* (Kent, Ohio: Kent State University Press, 2003); Robert M. McElroy, *Levi Parsons Morton: Banker, Diplomat and Statesman* (New York: G. P. Putnam's Sons, 1930); James A. Kehl, *Boss Rule in the Gilded Age: Matt Quay of Pennsylvania* (Pittsburgh: University of Pittsburgh Press, 1981); William A. Robinson, *Thomas B. Reed: Parliamentarian* (New York: Dodd, Mead, 1930); Bingham Duncan, *Whitelaw Reid: Journalist, Politician, Diplomat* (Athens: University of Georgia Press, 1975); Dorothy Ganfield Fowler, *John Coit Spooner: Defender of Presidents* (New York: University Publishers, 1961); Herbert Adams Gibbons, *John Wanamaker* (New York: Harper & Brothers, 1926); Daniel S. Margolies, *Henry Watterson and the New South* (Lexington: University Press of Kentucky, 2006); Mark D. Hirsch, *William C. Whitney: Modern Warwick* (New York: Dodd, Mead, 1948); and Festus P. Summers, *William L. Wilson and Tariff Reform* (New Brunswick, N.J.: Rutgers University Press, 1953). The age of many of these works and the absence of any works at all on important figures point to the need for historians and biographers to revisit the political history of the late nineteenth century as represented in the lives of its leading players.

Several studies have examined the Mugwumps and other reformers. The leading critical work is John G. Sproat, *"The Best Men": Liberal Reformers in the Gilded Age* (New York: Oxford University Press, 1968). More sympathetic treatments include Geoffrey Blodgett, *The Gentle Reformers: Massachusetts Democrats in the Cleveland Era* (Cambridge, Mass.: Harvard University Press, 1966), and David M. Tucker, *Mugwumps: Public Moralists of the Gilded Age* (Columbia: University of Missouri Press, 1998). See also Nancy Cohen, *The Reconstruction of American Liberalism, 1865–1914* (Chapel Hill: University of North Carolina Press, 2002). The standard work on civil service reform is Ari Hoogenboom, *Outlawing the Spoils: A History of the Civil Service Reform Movement, 1865–1883* (Urbana: University of Illinois Press, 1961), which includes a brief discussion of the issue after passage of the Pendleton Act in 1883. On Cleveland and the civil service issue, see Justus Doenecke, "Grover Cleveland and the Enforcement of the Civil Service Act," *Hayes Historical Journal* 4 (Spring 1984): 45–58, and Geoffrey Blodgett, "Ethno-Cultural Realities in Presidential Patronage: Grover Cleveland's Choices," *New York History* 81 (April 2000), 189–210.

The persistent political impact of questions related to race, sectionalism, and civil rights continues to draw the attention of historians. See Charles W. Calhoun, *Conceiving a New Republic: The Republican Party and the Southern Question, 1869–1900* (Lawrence: University Press of Kansas, 2006); Vincent P. De Santis, *Republicans Face the Southern Question—The New Departure Years, 1877–1897* (Baltimore: Johns Hopkins University Press, 1959); Lawrence Grossman, *The Democratic Party and the Negro: Northern and National Politics, 1868–92* (Urbana: University of Illinois Press, 1976); Stanley P. Hirshson, *Farewell to the Bloody Shirt: Northern Republicans and the Southern Negro, 1877–1893* (Bloomington:

Indiana University Press, 1962); Heather Cox Richardson, *The Death of Reconstruction: Race, Labor, and Politics in the Post–Civil War North, 1865–1901* (Cambridge, Mass.: Harvard University Press, 2001); Thomas Adams Upchurch, *Legislating Racism: The Billion Dollar Congress and the Birth of Jim Crow* (Lexington: University Press of Kentucky, 2004); and Xi Wang, *The Trial of Democracy: Black Suffrage and Northern Republicans, 1860–1910* (Athens: University of Georgia Press, 1997). For treatments that posit sectional reconciliation, see Nina Silber, *The Romance of Reunion: Northerners and the South, 1865–1900* (Chapel Hill: University of North Carolina Press, 1993), and David W. Blight, *Race and Reunion: The Civil War in American Memory* (Cambridge, Mass.: Harvard University Press, 2001).

A study that sees Civil War veterans' pensions as foreshadowing modern welfare policies is Theda Skocpol, *Protecting Soldiers and Mothers: The Political Origins of Social Policy in the United States* (Cambridge, Mass.: Harvard University Press, 1992). Other works dealing with the issue include William H. Glasson, *Federal Military Pensions in the United States* (New York: Oxford University Press, 1918), and Mary R. Dearing, *Veterans in Politics: The Story of the G.A.R.* (Baton Rouge: Louisiana State University Press, 1952).

The primacy of the tariff issue in the election of 1888 is clear from Joanne Reitano, *The Tariff Question in the Gilded Age: The Great Debate of 1888* (University Park: Pennsylvania State University Press, 1994). On the issue, see also Charles W. Calhoun, "Political Economy in the Gilded Age: The Republican Party's Industrial Policy," *Journal of Policy History* 8 (1996): 291–309; Tom E. Terrill, *The Tariff, Politics, and American Foreign Policy* (Westport, Conn.: Greenwood, 1973); and Alfred E. Eckles Jr., *Opening America's Market: U.S. Foreign Trade Policy since 1776* (Chapel Hill: University of North Carolina Press, 1995). Useful older works include Edward Stanwood, *American Tariff Controversies in the Nineteenth Century* (Boston: Houghton Mifflin, 1903), and Frank W. Taussig, *The Tariff History of the United States* (New York: G. P. Putnam's Sons, 1913).

The tariff, as well as the currency question, figures largely in Richard Franklin Bensel, *The Political Economy of American Industrialization, 1877–1900* (Cambridge: Cambridge University Press, 2000). On the money question, Irwin Unger, *The Greenback Era: A Social and Political History of American Finance, 1865–1879* (Princeton, N.J.: Princeton University Press, 1964); Walter T. K. Nugent, *Money and American Society, 1865–1880* (New York: Free Press, 1968); and Allen Weinstein, *Prelude to Populism: Origins of the Silver Issue, 1867–1978* (New Haven, Conn.: Yale University Press, 1970) discuss the roots of the issue. A more recent work, Gretchen Ritter, *Goldbugs and Greenbacks: The Antimonopoly Tradition and the Politics of Finance in America* (Cambridge: Cambridge University Press, 1997), carries the analysis forward through the 1880s to the election of 1896, but it does so from the antimonopoly perspective outside the two-party contention.

For the background of foreign policy issues, see Charles S. Campbell, *The Transformation of American Foreign Relations* (New York: Harper & Row, 1976); John A. S. Grenville and George Berkeley Young, *Politics, Strategy, and American*

Diplomacy: Studies in Foreign Policy, 1873–1917 (New Haven, Conn.: Yale University Press, 1966); and Charles Callan Tansill, *The Foreign Policy of Thomas F. Bayard* (New York: Fordham University Press, 1940). On issues in 1888, see Charles S. Campbell, "The Dismissal of Lord Sackville," *Mississippi Valley Historical Review* 44 (March 1958): 635–648, and T. C. Hinckley, "George Osgoodby and the Murchison Letter," *Pacific Historical Review* 27 (November 1958): 359–370.

On women and politics in the Gilded Age, see Paula Baker, "The Domestication of Politics: Women and American Political Society, 1780–1920," *American Historical Review* 89 (June 1984): 620–647, and *The Moral Frameworks of Public Life: Gender, Politics, and the State in Rural New York, 1870–1930* (New York: Oxford University Press, 1991); Rebecca Edwards, *Angels in the Machinery: Gender in American Party Politics from the Civil War to the Progressive Era* (New York: Oxford University Press, 1997); and Melanie Susan Gustafson, *Women and the Republican Party, 1854–1924* (Urbana: University of Illinois Press, 2001).

Many of the works cited above touch on the matter of political corruption, but see also Peter Argersinger, "New Perspectives on Election Fraud in the Gilded Age," *Political Science Quarterly* 100 (Winter 1985–1986): 669–687; James L. Baumgardner, "The 1888 Presidential Election: How Corrupt?" *Presidential Studies Quarterly* 14 (Summer 1984): 416–427; and John F. Reynolds and Richard L. McCormick, "Outlawing 'Treachery': Split Tickets and Ballot Laws in New York and New Jersey, 1880–1910," *Journal of American History* 72 (March 1986): 835–858.

INDEX

patronage, 19–20
Cleveland and, 27, 33, 36, 58
Harrison and, 108, 114, 117, 128, 187, 218n82
Pendleton, George H., 42
Pendleton Civil Service Act, 11, 14, 19, 33, 34, 84, 131, 163
pensions, veterans', 20, 36–39, 65, 89–91, 153, 154, 185
People's Party, 136, 149
Phelps, William Walter, 79, 86–87, 93, 107, 113, 119–120
Philadelphia Civil Service Reform Association, 163
Platt, Thomas C., 54, 82, 85, 104, 106, 107, 218n82
and Republican campaign, 126
and Republican national convention, 109, 113–114, 117–120, 168
Plumb, Preston, 91, 93
political parties, 6–15. *See also names of individual parties*
population, 5
Populists, 136, 149
Prohibition Party, 13–14, 31, 53, 170, 171, 178
protectionism. *See* Republican Party; tariff issue
Puck, 17
Pulitzer, Joseph, 181
Putnam, William, 144

Quay, Matthew S., 82, 127
as Republican national chairman, 126, 128–129, 174, 176, 183, 219n4
and Republican national convention, 108, 119

race, 1. *See also* African Americans; civil rights
Randall, Samuel J., 71
and Democratic campaign, 146
and election of 1884, 28

and Mills bill, 139
and opposition to Cleveland, 57
and tariff issue, 28, 45–48, 50, 55, 57, 60–61
Raum, Green B., 95
Reagan, John H., 131
Reagan, Ronald, 188
Reed, Thomas B., 160, 180, 185
Reid, Whitelaw, 95
and Blaine candidacy, 76–79, 84, 98, 103–104, 106, 107, 116
and Republican campaign, 148–149, 167, 174
Republican Clubs, National League of, 126
Republican National Committee, 125–126, 128–129, 152, 172
Republican National Convention of 1884, 98
Republican National Convention of 1888, 108–120, 122, 124
Republican Party
activism of, 14, 18, 20, 185, 187, 189
campaign organization of, 125–126, 128–129, 174–175, 182
and Canadian fisheries, 111, 142–143
on Chinese immigration, 111
and civil rights, 15, 40–41, 73, 82, 109, 152–153, 172, 187
and civil service issue, 35, 111
and Cleveland's Confederate flag order, 40
and currency question, 111
and defense spending, 111, 185
finances of, 126, 128, 174, 219n4
and labor, 154–156
and polygamy in Utah, 111
and Sackville-West, 161
southern strategy of, 41, 109, 151–153, 172, 180, 187–189
state voting bloc, 12–13, 151–152
and tariff issue, 2, 15–18, 20, 47, 53–55, 61–62, 72–74, 84, 100–102, 109–111, 124, 147–155, 180
and temperance, 53–54, 147, 168, 170

temperance issue, 21, 53–54, 147, 168, 170, *171*

Tennessee, 180

Thurman, Allen G., 70, *138*, *173*
   and Democratic campaign, 136–140, 155, 176
   and election of 1884, 28
   nominated for vice president, 67, 69, 71

Thurman, Allen W., 137, 172

Thurston, John M., 109

Tilden, Samuel J., 28–29, 34, 59

Townsend, John P., 49

trade issues, 15–16, 20–21, 44, 51, 145, 146, 189

trusts, 51, 65, 111, 135, 185

turnout, 2, 11–12, 179

Turpie, David, 151

Tweed, William M., 27

Twenty Years of Congress (Blaine), 76

Twining, Kinsley, 30

Union Labor Party, 168, *169*, 178

United Labor Party, 168, 178

Vilas, William F., 33

Virginia, 180

Voorhees, Daniel, 79, 154

vote results, 178–185

Wallace, Lew, 155

Wanamaker, John, 128

Warner, A. J., 66, 146

Washington Post, 66

Watterson, Henry, 49, 51, 64–66

Weed, Smith, 60, 62, 144, 183

Wells, David A., 60, 62, 181

West Virginia, 180

White, Horace, 38

Whitney, William C., 40, 48, 53, 69
   and Canadian fisheries, 142, 143
   and Democratic campaign, 129, 167
   and election of 1884, 34

Williams, James D., 88

Woman's National Republican Association, 170

women in campaign, 170, 172